G.D.H. Cole and British Sociology

"Matt Dawson has done a brilliant job of recovering the virtually forgotten sociological work of G. D. H. Cole. A pioneer of guild socialism, member of the Fabian society, historian of the Labour Party, and writer of detective fiction, Cole was also a sophisticated social theorist and researcher into issues of class and power who introduced sociology at Oxford University in the 1940s. This book examines the origins of Cole's ideas, placing them in the context of the early development of British sociology, and outlines his key ideas and his contribution as a public sociologist. Dawson's book is essential reading not only for its historical interest but also for demonstrating the contemporary relevance of Cole's ideas. Dawson makes a strong case for us all to rediscover Cole's work."

—John Scott, *author of British Sociology. A History (Palgrave, 2020)*

Matt Dawson

G.D.H. Cole and British Sociology

A Study in Semi-Alienation

palgrave
macmillan

Matt Dawson
University of Glasgow
Glasgow, UK

ISBN 978-3-031-75483-8 ISBN 978-3-031-75484-5 (eBook)
https://doi.org/10.1007/978-3-031-75484-5

This Palgrave Macmillan imprint is published by the registered company Springer Nature Switzerland AG.
The registered company address is: Gewerbestrasse 11, 6330 Cham, Switzerland

Preface: G.D.H. Cole and the History of British Sociology: Recovering Footnotes

The history of sociology in Britain has not, traditionally, been seen as a particularly exciting field of study with one scholar suggesting it 'has always been a footnote to sociological research and literature; a footnote written and read by a tiny minority of historically minded sociologists' (Panayotova, 2019a, p. 1). Indeed, for much of the twentieth century, to speak of a 'history' of British sociology was seen as anathema, with the national discipline defined as a failure, whether due to the security of the English bourgeoisie (Anderson, 1968), pressure from established social survey movements (Harley, 2012), the lack of a 'great' figure to push forward the discipline (Barnes, 1948) or the amateur nature of early British sociologists (Bulmer, 1985). These factors led Becker and Barnes (1952, p. 794) to claim that sociology in Britain was 'almost as rare as gold in sea-water'. Therefore, despite the presence of a few important studies which attempted to question these claims (e.g. Abrams, 1968; Collini, 1979), not only was this history a footnote, but it was a footnote only the most devoted reader read; most assumed it was safe to skip.

However, this misconception is the process of being corrected as the first years of the twenty-first century saw a flood of rich reassessments of the history of British sociology. This included discussions of the movements which helped shape sociology (Renwick, 2012), outlines of early forms of British social theory (Scott, 2018), the development of the quantitative (Panayotova, 2020) and qualitative (Savage, 2010) traditions and mappings of sociology's institutional forms (Scott, 2020; Husbands,

2019; Kaspersen & Mulvad, 2017). This expansion in interest is also indicated by the two prestigious volumes of essays published on the topic in the 2010s (Holmwood & Scott, 2014; Panayotova, 2019b). We are, in many ways, in a golden age for the study of the history of British sociology. This has moved from a footnote to the main text and become a field of study in its own right.

G.D.H. Cole, however, remains in the footnotes. His name appears now and then, perhaps with a sentence saying who he was in relation to a group of a topic, before the author(s) moves on to seemingly more important things (e.g. Savage, 2010, p. 121; Scott & Bromley, 2013, p. 225; Mills, 2019, p. 187). This perhaps reflects Cole's broader position in intellectual life today. It was once remarked that 'obscurity has never been a threat to G.D.H. Cole' (Houseman, 1979, p. 7) and it seemed for a long time that this would be the case. Given the broad nature of his contributions—from socialist theory to labour history, to social and political theory, to biography and more—Cole's position as a major intellectual figure seemed secure. Furthermore, given his development of a theory of socialism focused on small groups and worker control it seemed the regular 'rediscovery' of less statist forms of socialism would aid Cole's continued renown. Nevertheless, it appears that if not obscurity then perhaps ignorance has become a threat to G.D.H Cole. He still appears as a figure in the history of libertarian socialism (Goodway, 2021) and remains a touchstone in the intellectual history of pluralism (see Holthaus, 2014). Despite this, references to, and knowledge about, Cole have become increasingly less common. This forgetting is especially marked in sociology where he is now restricted entirely to the footnotes.

This book uses the opportunity of this golden age to bring Cole out of the footnotes and reassess his significance to the history of British sociology, a significance which has long been overlooked. By doing this, I also aim to help fill a gap in this emerging historical literature. As significant as the writings of the new golden age have been, they have quickly claimed a 'forgotten era', or its own footnote. With some notable exceptions (most significantly Rocquin (2019)), the period between 1920 and 1960 has attracted less attention than the period before and after. It was these years in which Cole was active and this book seeks to use the work of Cole as a way to illuminate British sociology during this era. I will suggest Cole's 'semi-alienation' from the discipline reflects how during this period of establishing itself British sociology had a form it took neither before nor after. This was uniquely unreceptive to Cole's normative goals, despite his deep knowledge of, and investment in, sociology.

In this sense this book is a study of two connected issues, the sociological work and activity of G.D.H. Cole along with the history of the British discipline from 1920–1960. Both of these are too readily neglected to the footnotes but which, I suggest, deserve their own main texts.[1]

Glasgow, UK Matt Dawson

[1] The lesson here is to always read the footnotes.

Acknowledgements

In the Preface to this book I discuss how Cole is often a 'footnote'; this prompts the question of how exactly I became acquainted with him. This occurred during my PhD where, exploring traditions of democratic socialism through reading and conversations, the name of G.D.H. Cole kept coming up. I am forever grateful to my supervisor Luke Martell and fellow PhD student, and friend, Charlie Masquelier, who helped introduce me to Cole's work more broadly. In this regard, a thanks to all the writers who kept the flame of Cole alive for future generations to discover. A further thanks to Charlie for taking the time to read the whole of this manuscript and offer some valuable suggestions.

This book was first drafted during a period of study leave from my post at the University of Glasgow following a year as Head of Sociology. My thanks to the University for providing this period of study leave and to the Sociology department for the funding to make two trips to Oxford to visit the Cole archives. A note of thanks also to my colleagues in sociology at Glasgow, not just for the general collegiality they continually demonstrate, but also for putting up with my many invocations of Cole with a patient smile.

Unpublished material from the G.D.H. Cole archives is reproduced with the kind permission of the Warden and Fellows of Nuffield College, Oxford. I owe a huge thanks to all the librarians at Nuffield College Library who hosted me for those two visits and were immensely helpful and patient in locating material and responding to messages. It was an absolute joy to be in pleasant surroundings of the college and hold papers marked by Cole's handwriting (though, given how untidy his handwriting was, I was even more grateful for the typed pages!) and I am thankful for the work of the many archivists and librarians who made it possible.

The portrait of Cole found on the cover of this book is reproduced with kind permission of the National Portrait Gallery. My thanks to their rights team with their help in securing this wonderful photo of Cole.

Thank you to Palgrave Macmillan for their eagerness to publish this text, along with their willingness to publish texts on the history of sociology more generally. In this regard, a special thanks to Sarah Hills and Karthika Devi at Palgrave who have been a huge help throughout the drafting process especially when the inevitable happened and an academic missed their initial deadline. My thanks also to Palgrave's reviewer for their detailed comments on the manuscript, which have improved it greatly.

Of course, those who deserve the most significant thanks are my friends and family for their constant support. As always, my biggest thanks are for Catherine not only for her love but since, among other things, she has had to bear living in a flat with more William Morris-designed items than she (or any rational person) may consider reasonable. Sorry honey, an admiration of Morris is just one of the many things I took from Cole, I hope this book might help justify it.

Contents

CHAPTER 1

G.D.H. Cole: 'Enlightenment on the Surface, the Romantic Movement Underneath'

George Douglas Howard Cole (Douglas to friends, G.D.H. to history) was born in Cambridge on 25 September 1889. His father was an estate agent (the family moved to Ealing, London, for this purpose when Cole was very young) and his mother came from a wealthy farming family. Douglas was their third child, with two sisters who were 10 and 12 years older. His upbringing was quite conventional for a male child of his class and Cole excelled as a student at the private St. Paul's School, then in Hammersmith.[1]

It was fitting that Cole was schooled at St. Paul's since it is here that perhaps the most significant event for his future life occurs: he reads William Morris' *News from Nowhere*, a utopian tale set in a future, communist, Hammersmith. Recounting the experience later when he was invited to give a lecture to the William Morris Society, he said:

> I became a Socialist[2] more than fifty years ago when I read *News from Nowhere* as a schoolboy and realised quite suddenly that William Morris had shown me the vision of society in which it would be a fine and fortunate experience to live. Needless to say, I have not lived in such a society, or in

[1] I draw heavily in this section on Margaret Cole's biography of her husband which is, unsurprisingly, the best resource for details of Cole's life (Cole, 1971).

[2] Cole tended to put 'Socialism' and 'Socialist' in capital letters. This reflects the almost mystical nature Cole gave socialism, as something divine in its transformation of life and therefore requiring a capital S.

M. Dawson, *G.D.H. Cole and British Sociology*,
https://doi.org/10.1007/978-3-031-75484-5_1

> any even remotely like it; but I count myself not the less fortunate to have been shown that vision; and I can truthfully say that from the day when I first read *News from Nowhere* my socialist convictions have remained firmly fixed. (Cole, 1960, p. 1)

Reflecting on what appealed from Morris' vision, Cole turns to another one of his works, *A Dream of John Ball* to say:

> This quality is, I think, best summed up in the words Morris put into the mouth of the hedge-priest, John Ball, when he said that 'Fellowship is heaven, and lack of fellowship is hell' – a deep, pervading sense that all men[3] should live together as brothers, not contending one against another for sordid advantages but uniting their strength to make the best of the world as their common living-place, conserving and developing its beauty and sharing its fruits and not needing to be troubled with politics or to be badgered about by persons set in authority over them. (Cole, 1960, pp. 1–2)

Morris would remain a significant figure throughout Cole's life. He would write on him on multiple occasions (Cole, 1931a), including editing a collection of his writings (Cole, 1934a). Indeed, Cole starts one lecture on Morris with the claim that:

> William Morris is to me a hero who makes me want to go all goosey. When I think of him, I am like a flapper contemplating her favourite film-star. I want to say 'oh my dear, isn't he too positively marvellous'. I want to simply say 'oo-er' and leave it at that gurgle of delight and veneration. (Cole, 1934b, p. 2)

The significance of Cole's veneration of Morris was that, as others have noted (e.g. Wright, 1979) he was initially drawn to socialism not on an economic basis, through Marxist analysis or a concern with poverty; as we shall see, these came to concern Cole later. Instead the appeal of socialism was at this point aesthetic and moral. Indeed, these touchstones of Cole's socialism would never fully leave him. He was always concerned with the good life, the freedom of the individual and fellowship which socialism could achieve. Cole acknowledged this late in life saying:

[3] Cole's writing problematically uses the masculine as a universal noun. I will be discussing Cole's relation to gender in Chap. 3 and would ask the reader to take the note of 'sic' as read in these instances.

> I can still feel the glow of that conversion; and I find no difficulty in giving an account of it. I became a Socialist because, as soon as the case for a society of equals, set free from the twin evils or riches and poverty, mastership and subjection, was put to me, I knew that to be the only kind of society that could be consistent with human decency and fellowship and that in no other society could I have the right to be content. The society William Morris imagined seemed to me to embody the right sort of human relations, and to be altogether beautiful and admirable; and I decided to work for something as nearly resembling it as appeared possible, without at that stage of my conversion inquiring at all deeply into the ways and means. That is to say, my initial conversion was essentially idealistic; and my Socialist convictions have always kept this foundation of idealism. (Cole, 1956a, p. 3)

As we shall see in this book, he linked these concerns into economic and political ideas, but it was a libertarian vision of freedom which drove him.[4]

Fired by these new socialist convictions, Cole attended Baliol College, Oxford, to read Greats. While here, he took his hand to writing socialist romantic poetry; some of these were published but even his wife could only manage the defence that it was 'bad, though not abysmal' (Cole, 1971, p. 46). He founded a socialist newspaper in 1909, causing some stir at a university which until this point had been largely free of leftist politics. Also, beginning another long relationship in his life—though in this case one of love-hate—he joined the Fabian Society. Upon graduation, Cole spends an unhappy year as lecturer in Philosophy at Armstrong College in Newcastle upon Tyne before becoming a prize fellow of Magdalen College and returning to Oxford in 1912 where he would spend most of the rest his career.

The period between 1913 and 1920 was hugely significant for Cole and one in which he made his most original contributions to socialist theory. Cole's first book, *The World of Labour* (1913) was an overview, and defence, of the trade union movement. While drawing on other countries (most notably France and America), Cole focused, as he did in most of his work, on the UK. Here Cole began to add some political theory to his

[4] It is worth noting at this point that Cole was not alone in British sociology for seeing Morris as a key inspiration. Ruth Levitas' work on the utopian potential of sociology is deeply influenced by Morris and she followed in Cole's footsteps by giving a lecture to the William Morris Society, which in her case focused on Hammersmith and Morris' utopianism (Levitas, 2005a).

vision of socialism claiming that 'the class-war is real, and that no solution which ignores or denies it can be accepted by those who are trodden beneath the cloven hoof of Capital' and asserting the trade union movement was 'the great force by which almost alone, for the present, progress can be truly furthered' (Cole, 1913a, p. 424). *The World of Labour*, the first of 77 non-fiction books Cole would single or co-author in his life,[5] set the trajectory for his career in its normative focus; Cole would be an author always concerned with furthering the socialist cause. During World War I (WWI) Cole, who opposed the war, worked as research officer for the Amalgamated Society of Engineers (ASE). It seems he was already on the radar of the secret service in the UK, with official discussion of whether Cole's exemption due to prima facie working for the munitions industry should be overturned. Indeed, his MI5 record from this period states that 'the only war he approves of is the war against capitalists', which was a statement he would have happily agreed with (Caute, 2022, p. 29). With the end of WWI, Cole became the key intellectual figure in the movement for guild socialism, reaching its apotheosis in *Guild Socialism Restated* (Cole, 1920b).

I will discuss guild socialism in Chap. 3. It is sufficient to say for now that this advocated the forming of democratic associations of producers and consumers as a form of non-statist democratic empowerment of individuals in a socialised economy. Based strongly within a libertarian tradition of socialism which had produced Morris, this reflected a common position throughout Cole's career, as he became detached from dominant intellectual traditions, in this case from the emerging hegemonic statist conception of socialism in Britain. He resigned from the Fabian Society in 1915, writing of them (while still a member!) as 'beneath contempt' full of 'the middle-class in search of a hobby…reactionaries and old fogies' (Cole, 1913b). Instead, he aligned himself to the much more marginal National Guilds League (NGL, Taylor, 2002) and the Labour Party research committee, both of which were more receptive to his politics. He also, in 1918, married Margaret Postgate (thereafter Margaret Cole) who,

[5] Cole's output was, frankly, superhuman. If one adds to these 77 sole or co-authored non-fiction volumes the 8 edited texts, 13 literary books (collections of poems, songs and short stories, by Cole and others) and 38 detective novels co-written with his wife Margaret it equals 136 books produced by Cole, either solo or as co-producer. This is in addition to an unquantifiable number of articles and pamphlets. Wright's (1979, pp. 285–296) selection of Cole's most significant articles and pamphlets lists 389 items.

in addition to being his life partner, would be a frequent collaborator on intellectual work and detective stories.

As we move into the 1920s, the guild socialist movement begins to collapse due to a variety of factors including the pull of communism, internal strife in the NGL and the increased dominance of the Labour Party. With this collapse begins Cole's perpetual movement between different roles and fields. He spends an ill-fitting period as Labour Correspondent for the *Manchester Guardian* before in 1921 becoming Director of Tutorial Classes for the University of London. Cole had been involved with adult working-class education, most notably via the Workers Education Association (WEA), since his year in Newcastle and this new role solidified that relationship. The WEA was central in providing something resembling a university education to workers in the early years of the twentieth century, when such a thing was otherwise unavailable to them. Importantly, the WEA not only provided education and knowledge, but gave an opportunity of a different experience to the working class. Indeed, one student of Cole's who attended a WEA summer school reported that 'all of us students, miners, clerks or mill-workers...felt it was a holiday to be able to work in seminars in the morning and spend the rest of the day in the country, walking, swimming, playing cricket or just loafing in the ground of Easton Lodge...as undergraduates do' (see Rose, 2021, p. 441). In this new role Cole played a significant role in the colleges of the University of London's increased enrolment of working-class students, who often combined studying with work. As we shall see later in the book, in addition to aligning with Cole's political goals, it was also via that WEA that he became increasingly more interested in the teaching of sociology and Marxism. He also in 1920 began another lifelong link, this time to *The New Statesman*, often producing an article a week for the rest of his life, mostly covering political matters, but sometimes offering sociological discussions (see Chaps. 3 and 5 for examples).

In 1925, drawn by the master of the college and a return to academia, Cole became Reader in Economics at University College, Oxford. Cole was never really an economist, even by the standards of the discipline in his day, to say nothing of the current day. As Wright (1979, p. 189) puts it, he was 'an amateur who refused to employ an idiosyncratic vocabulary and who...turned to economics only as part of a much wider social concern'. Partly this was due to an almost pathological dislike of arithmetic and quantification—which would be shared by much of a later generation of British sociologists (Williams et al., 2013)—but also by his desire to treat economics as an applied discipline, more akin to political economy. Reflecting this, it is during this period that he becomes closest to the Labour Party as a party intellectual. He rejoins the Fabian Society in 1928, helping to establish the New Fabian Research Bureau in 1931. Cole, somewhat amazingly given his earlier comments, is later twice elected Fabian Society Chairman. He also becomes a member of the 1929–1931 Labour Government's National Economic Council. Consequently, his writings during this period become more focused on providing Labour with a policy programme, perhaps most notably in *The Next Ten Years in British Social and Economic Planning* (Cole, 1929a). As I will discuss in Chap. 5, these activities have become a matter of much debate. Some argue that during this Cole becomes, albeit briefly, a more conventional statist Fabian socialist. Others, however, argue he maintained his libertarian beliefs. As I will demonstrate, this is perhaps better framed as a question of Cole's role as a public intellectual where circumstances—the election of an always precarious Labour government, the legacy of the financial crisis and the rise of fascism—led Cole to believe the greatest service he could provide to the public, especially the working class, at that moment was to help support Labour.

However, not limiting his activity to short-term political concerns, it is also during this period that Cole, as later writers would put it, 'invented' the field of labour history (Owen, 1966). He produced a number of biographies of labour and working-class heroes; he was especially proud, it is said, of his biography of William Cobbett which his wife considered his best written book (Cole, 1924a, 1971, p. 133) as well as texts such as his *Short History of the British Working Class Movement, 1789–1927* (Cole, 1932a). This latter text perhaps reflects Cole's encyclopaedic approach to history given one could quibble over whether a 653-page book counts as 'short'.

Another significant event in Cole's life occurred in 1931 when he was diagnosed with a serious form of diabetes which, in his wife's words, meant he changed 'from a normal person who was not very robust to a man who was never for long out of doctors' hands' (Cole, 1971, p. 183). She rejects the claim, offered by others, that Cole was at this point given a 'death sentence' (Cole, 1971, p. 186) but the diagnosis did perhaps make him wonder how much time he had left and undoubtedly changed his activity. In the short term, he picked up the pace of his writing, moving from a superhuman to Herculean pace and became slightly more impatient and humourless. This is perhaps unsurprising given the intensive regime of insulin treatment which now became his life. It also meant that for the rest of his years Cole had to limit his public activities and while, especially in the early 1950s as treatment improved, he was able to travel more, he remained largely a scholar whose focus was on England. Some argued this exacerbated his tendency to be somewhat of a Little Englander (see Wright, 1979) though, as I will discuss in Chap. 3, the matter is more complex than that.

Cole, despite his earlier pacifism, developed an early concern with the dangers of fascism and accepted that war may be needed to stop its progress (Cole, 1971, p. 210). Consequently, he was a supporter of World War II (WWII). Reflecting a common position on the British Left, he was a somewhat reluctant supporter, seeing the war as stopping fascism, but also as an opportunity to justify a new world after. During the war Cole was appointed to the Ministry of Labour to work with William Beveridge on a manpower survey. Cole's MI5 watchers, who had kept an eye on him since WWI, suggested he was unsuitable for appointment since he was a 'communist and pacifist'; it seems his published statements in favour of this war overruled this (Caute, 2022, p. 180). Following this work, his post as Reader of Economics having expired, Cole was appointed director of the Nuffield Reconstruction Survey at Oxford, part of the broader, Labour supported, efforts at imagining 'reconstruction' after the war. I will discuss these activities in Chap. 3.

Having resigned from the survey in 1944 Cole entered the last phase of his life with his appointment to the first Chichele Professor of Social and Political Theory at All Souls College, Oxford. Following an unsuccessful candidature as a Labour MP for the University of Oxford seat, Cole settled into the life of the Oxford don. Reflecting the remit of this post, it was during this period that he became most directly involved in question of sociology, notably in its relations to other social sciences and to social theory. I will discuss this work, and Cole's attempts to help establish sociology at Oxford, in Chap. 4. He also developed an increasingly international focus in this period, working with UNESCO, the Workers Education Conference in Oslo and The International Association for Political Sciences. Cole was also the only English person invited to sit on the Committee of Indian Universities post-independence (though he declines due to increasing problems with his diabetes) and formed the International Socialist Society as its first president. This final activity led to a call back to his earliest work, with the publication of *World Socialism Restated* (Cole,

1956a). Finally, during this period, Cole produced his magnum opus, the five-volume (seven parts) *History of Socialist Thought*.

There are then, in effect, three periods to Cole's intellectual work. The first runs from 1913 to the early 1920s, when he is involved in developing both the intellectual and practical basis of guild socialism. The second then runs from the mid-1920s to 1940, when he develops his historical interests and becomes a kind of public and, perhaps, party intellectual. Then, the final period, running from 1940 until his death sees him most involved in the teaching and research of political theory and social science (though, as we shall see, he hated that term) via the Nuffield survey and then his professorship. The first and third periods are most significant to Cole's sociology and views on the discipline contained in Chaps. 3 and 4. Here we will see how Cole created a form of voluntarist structuration theory which was linked into guild socialism as a normative goal. This desire to see sociology as a normative endeavour, which was the key issue in his 'semi-alienation' from the discipline, can be seen in his inaugural lecture as Chichele Professor, where he argues:

> 'Social Theory', then, I regard as an essentially normative study, of which the purpose is to tell people how to be socially good, and to aim at social goods and avoid social evils. It is not, however, for that reason a branch of Ethics; for its concern is necessarily with the means to be employed in seeking social goods through social institutions. It has, therefore, a large technical field of its own to explore; for it has to find out what sorts of social institutions will be most helpful towards the pursuit of social goods in the general environment and climate of values appertaining to the broad civilization of which the theorist belongs, and for which he formulates his doctrine. (Cole, 1945a, p. 10)

The second period will then be most important for the arguments I wish to make about Cole's public sociology considered in Chap. 5. It is not his work as a party intellectual which is most significant here, but rather the immense journalistic and creative (poems, songs, films, etc.) output Cole produces between 1920 and 1940. However, we can only appreciate the sociological significance of this work by linking it to Cole's broader sociological framework.

G.D.H. Cole died on 14 January 1959, aged 69, finally succumbing to the diabetes which had hampered the last 28 years of his life. Increasingly dependent on his wife in his final days, his final words, spoken to her, were

'I'm sorry to be a nuisance' (Cole, 1971, p. 288). It is clear reading the tributes how much he meant to his contemporaries. I have quoted Asa Briggs' (1960) categorisation of Cole as enlightenment on the surface, romantic underneath in the title to this chapter. In the same piece he speaks of how 'there was a contrast between the cool cogency and apparently effortless fluency of his arguments – he seldom retreated into metaphor – and the volcanic power of his convictions' (Briggs, 1960, p. 672). Kingsley Martin (1959), Cole's close collaborator on *The New Statesman* begins his obituary therein with the claim that 'Douglas Cole was a secular saint' who was 'full of invention, biting wit and a passion – which never left him – to abolish capitalism'. A collection of essays in his honour speak universally of his kindness and commitment, even if they were combined with a classic intellectual aloofness and some humourlessness, exacerbated by the discomfort of his diabetes, during his later years (Briggs & Saville, 1960). Within 20 years of his death, he could claim four major intellectual biographies devoted to his work (Cole, 1971; Carpenter, 1973; Houseman, 1979; Wright, 1979). Reviewing one of these the historian A.J.P. Taylor claims that 'Douglas Cole came as close to complete integrity as any man of his time. I venerated him' (Taylor, 1979, p. 442). Stuart Hall later paid tribute to Cole as the 'austere and courageous veteran of the independent left' whose seminar (the 'Cole Group', see Chap. 4) was the place in which many of the protagonists of the New Left first met (Hall, 2010, p. 178, 180).

The above has been an inevitably 'whistlestop' and brief recounting of Cole's life. The chapters to come will delve further into his work. What is significant already are three things. Firstly, Cole's deeply felt, and William Morris-inspired libertarian instincts. Secondly, the sheer breadth of his commitments and duties which led to him being known, and valued, across a huge number of fields and by colleagues. Finally, somewhat linked to this, the way in which Cole never truly had a clear home and/or identity, moving between different jobs and academic fields as the circumstances dictated. In this final element, we can already see some overlap with the history of British sociology to be discussed in the next chapter. It is the relationship between these two which I will define as one of 'semi-alienation'.

Cole's Semi-Alienation from British Sociology as a Sociologist

In this book I discuss Cole's relation to British sociology as one of 'semi-alienation'. In doing so, I am following Cole himself who, as we shall see in Chap. 4, reinterpreted Marxist thought towards his own ends. In his discussion of alienation Marx discusses how the product of labour appears as 'something alien' to the worker (Marx, 1988, p. 71) and that, consequently, the more the worker produces the more the products of the labour become alienated to him. It is this, almost literal, sense of alienation as 'something alien' that I am using here. In many ways, as we shall see in this book, due to the particular time in which Cole confronted British sociology it was 'something alien' to him as a discipline with its emphasis on value-freedom, unempirical evolutionism, hostility to class along with Marxism and unwillingness to confront the political.

Yet, this was only 'semi' alienation since while the practices of British sociology appeared alien to Cole, the ideals of sociology of a discipline were not. As we shall see throughout this book, not only was Cole engaging in sociological thinking but he openly advocated, and supported, sociology both in his writings and his professional activities. Therefore, to reuse more Marxist terminology, one might say Cole was alienated from actually existing sociology in Britain, but supported what sociology could and, in his view, should be. This was not just a passive, but active, support, with Cole seeking to create that vision of the discipline as a scholar and professional academic.

This also means this it is not my claim in this book to say that Cole was 'really' a sociologist. As the above has indicated, Cole was a prime example of what we now call—in a phrase he would despise—an 'interdisciplinary' thinker. He was a sociologist, but he was also a historian, political theorist, philosopher, occasional economist and socialist theorist. Granted, as I will show in this book, often these things occur together, with Cole's Rousseauian sociology underpinning his guild socialist theorising, but I would not want to reduce the scope of Cole's intellectual contribution to just sociology. That being said, I *do* want to make clear that Cole was a sociologist, among other things, and this book offers the first account of Cole as a sociologist. Furthermore, while it is not my goal to claim that Cole should now be inserted into the canon of sociology, British or otherwise, I do think that any history of British sociology is incomplete without accounting for the contributions he made.

In this sense, my contribution here is twofold. Firstly, by providing a new reading of G.D.H. Cole's work as a sociological project. Secondly, by providing a new history of the discipline in its forgotten period told through the work of Cole and his feeling of semi-alienation. I would also suggest this conception of semi-alienation could have a broader use beyond the case of Cole, particularly helping to enrich the applicability of 'positioning theory' to intellectuals. I will explore this further in the Conclusion. I think we can learn much about the past, and potential future, of British sociology by putting these two arguments into conversation, as I do in this book.

Conclusion

This chapter has provided a plotted biography of Cole's life. As we saw, Cole was always driven by an aesthetic, libertarian vision of socialism which shaped his work across a variety of areas. He was also somewhat intellectually homeless, moving across disciplines and jobs as circumstances required. The chapters which follow in this book will bring these two stories together and explore Cole's semi-alienation from British sociology.

Chapter 2 summarises the history of British sociology prior to 1960 and splits it into three periods. The first period covers the eighteenth and nineteenth centuries and how early intellectual traditions, most notably the Scottish Enlightenment, political economy and statistics can be seen as 'implicit' sociology in the UK (Kumar, 2015). I will emphasise how many of these perspectives, sharing what has been called a 'gentlemanly' approach to social science (despite Harriet Martineau and Florence Nightingale being two of key figures), held a positive relationship to the desire for reform and, while being seen as atheoretical, had some general acceptance of a form of positivism. The second section, covering 1900–1920 discusses the appointment of the first Professor of Sociology at the London School of Economics (LSE). This discussion is focused on four figures: Patrick Geddes, Francis Galton, L.T. Hobhouse and H.G. Wells. I will explore the reasons for Hobhouse's appointment and what this meant for the emerging sociology discipline in the UK. The final section, covering 1920–1960 will explore how, between sociology finding a home at the LSE and the broader expansion beginning in the late 1950s/ early 1960s the discipline had three forms: what was happening at the LSE (both within, and outwith, the Sociology Department); LePlay House and the Geddesian tradition; and some other scattered developments, such as extramural teaching. I will conclude by highlighting the differences between this later period and earlier periods which were more comfortable with the notion of sociology as reformist/utopian/normative.

Chapter 3 explores Cole's sociological writings. I begin by discussing Cole's structuration theory. Developed via an engagement with Rousseau, I highlight how this shares similarities with other attempts at structuration theory while also, reflecting Archer's claim that agency is a collective force, providing a political outcome often seen as lacking in structuration theory. I will then highlight how this is the sociological basis for Cole's vision of guild socialism. From here I will explore Cole's other sociological contributions. These include his publication of one of the first sociology textbooks, *Social Theory* (1920) and one of the first monographs of the sociology of class in the UK, *Studies in Class Structure* (1955). I will also explore Cole's contribution to the 'social survey' movement with a discussion of his leadership of the Nuffield Social Reconstruction Survey. This chapter will then explore other elements of Cole's sociological work and subject them to interrogation from feminist and decolonial perspectives; here I pay particular attention to Cole's significant writings on imperialism. I then conclude by discussing the distinctiveness of Cole's perspective from the British sociology of his day, most notably in comparison to the LSE and Geddesian traditions.

Whereas Chap. 3 outlined Cole's writings which could be classified as sociological, Chap. 4 is more inward looking, by exploring what Cole had to say about sociology. Having established the normative basis of Cole's work in the preceding chapter, here I will explore how Cole explicitly sought to defend a normative vision of the discipline, including in a (poorly received) keynote address to the British Sociological Association (BSA). I will discuss Cole's writings on how sociology should be taught, highlighting the ways he imagines the discipline to be innately interdisciplinary in its attempt to grasp, and transform, human social life. From here I will highlight Cole's writings on the canon of sociology, especially Marx and Durkheim, each of whom he wrote on extensively. These writings will then be compared with the British sociology Cole confronted which not only rejected his normative vision of sociological practice and teaching but had little space for either Marx or Durkheim at this point. This chapter will also highlight the work Cole pursued at Oxford to try to give sociology a home, including advocating for its first lectureship and his formation of the 'Cole Group' as a forum for sociology.

Chapter 5 begins by highlighting the claim (from some) that British sociology has long had an uncommented upon public face and suggests that Cole is one of the prime examples of this. This will start with a discussion of Cole's changing political commitments. There is a broad debate concerning this in the literature, with my view being that Cole's core political commitments were unchanging. However, the changing way he presents these, and seeks their implementation, reflects a continual desire for public relevancy in order to have his work speak to the contemporary political ideas. Having discussed this, I then turn to the different ways in which Cole expressed himself to a public audience. This will cover: (1) his 'public' books which sought to make agency possible by giving individuals the knowledge of their history and possible futures with suggestions on how society could be changed; (2) his magazine and newspaper articles, which linked critical sociological lessons into everyday sociological concerns such as enjoying the countryside or his children asking for money to go to the cinema; (3) Cole's creative endeavours through poems, songs and films to spread his sociological message. I will then put these themes into discussion with contemporary writings on public sociology and public intellectuals more broadly. Here I will discuss Cole's refusal to separate out what Burawoy terms 'public' and 'policy' sociology, instead seeing both as intimately tied together in a public attempt to produce social change on the part of the sociologist. I will also suggest the importance of the means Cole used to produce his public sociology as suggesting new ways for sociologists to be 'public'.

The Conclusion will then argue three things. The first of these is that we need to pay more attention to the history of British sociology in the interwar period, given this was when sociology increasingly gained a secure home in Britain. Secondly, that we can read Cole as a sociologist and, in so doing, locate a thinker who had something important to tell us about the connection of sociology and politics. And thirdly, that we can look at Cole and the history of sociology together and, in so doing, highlight how the elements which may make Cole such a vital figure now for sociology produced his semi-alienation from the discipline of his day. Here I will discuss further the value of conceptualising this relationship as one of semi-alienation. I will then finish by drawing out Cole's contemporary relevance. I will focus particularly on how, although British sociology has become increasingly comfortable with normativity in critique, it has become unwilling to engage in ideas for what the good society should look like. I will argue Cole reminds us of the need to link these two elements together.

In many ways Cole was born both too late *and* too early for the vision of sociology he favoured to be available to him in Britain. There is great value in returning to this life and seeing how it can show us more about the history of sociology in Britain and where we may go in the years to come.

CHAPTER 2

A (Brief) History of British Sociology Prior to 1960

What follows is a brief overview of the history of sociology prior to 1960. I have chosen this date not only since it is the year after Cole's death but also since the 1960s is a fateful decade for British sociology with the significant expansion of university education and sociology departments as a result of the Robbins Report.[1] Acknowledgement of this in the literature has also produced an unfortunate tendency to see the period before this as lacking anything like 'sociology' as we understand it today (Savage (2010) is a good example). Thankfully, as mentioned in the Preface, we now have a significant body of historiography to overcome this shortcoming. However, as also mentioned earlier, while this history has expanded it has paid much less attention to the period from roughly 1920–1960, the years in which Cole was active. Therefore, in what follows, I will map the nature of British sociology in three periods: the eighteenth century; /nineteenth century, 1900–1920; and 1920–1960. Since I will be returning to these periods, especially the latter two, in the chapters that follow, my discussion

[1] The 'Robbins Report' was a report for the Committee on Higher Education led by Lord (Charles) Robbins, published in 1963. Among its recommendations were that university places should be available to all with the ability, an expansion of universities was recommended to facilitate this. This led to the establishment of so-called glass plate universities which developed significant sociology departments and drew in working-class students. Speaking personally, I am a result of this legacy, given my sociology training at two such universities: the Universities of Essex and Sussex.

M. Dawson, *G.D.H. Cole and British Sociology*,
https://doi.org/10.1007/978-3-031-75484-5_2

here will not be exhaustive, but rather will provide the reader with the broad overview of the key events and debates of each era. I will also, bar some comments at the end, largely leave Cole out of the discussion in this chapter, picking this up in the chapters to come.

The Eighteenth and Nineteenth Centuries: Political Economy, Statistics, Reform and the Lack(?) of Theory

This period saw little work that would openly have been called 'sociology' in the UK. However, we should not see this as unique. France (Lepenies, 1992) and the US (Morris, 2015) were somewhat alone globally in having something defined as 'sociology' prior to the twentieth century and therefore in the British case we are, like most other national sociologies, looking for the forerunners or predecessors.

There has been no shortage of claims for such predecessors in the UK. Firstly, reflecting a trend we will see in the next era, it has been argued that Scotland was much further advanced than the rest of the UK in this era due to the Scottish Enlightenment (Swingewood, 1970). These thinkers asked questions concerning social institutions, the division of labour and social stratification, among other topics which we now identify as sociological. For example, echoing later considerations from Durkheim, both Smith and Ferguson took the division of labour as not simply an economic matter, but one with social consequences in terms of stages of social evolution, specialisation of knowledge, alienation and individualisation (Swingewood, 1970, p. 176). While it has also been suggested that these Scottish forerunners were not systematically sociological, instead containing snippets of sociological insight which were neither fully developed nor integral to their thought (MacDonald, 2019) it can at the very least be said they indicate the beginning of *thinking sociologically* in Britain, in this case in the philosophical tradition. This mode of thinking is then continued in the nineteenth century with thinkers such as Herbert Spencer and John Stuart Mill (Ziff, 1978) and in literary writers, such as the future Tory Prime Minister Benjamin Disraeli (Kumar, 2015) and Matthew Arnold (Lepenies, 1992).

Somewhat distinct from this trend, we get the most significant figure of this era who could be identified as the first British sociologist: Harriet Martineau (1802–1876). Driven by a positivist outlook—she was an early translator of Comte—Martineau was concerned with the development of social laws in evolution (see Hoecker-Drysdale, 1992). She developed a sociological method in her *How to Observe: Morals and Manners* (1838/2009) which was applied to America in her three-part *Society in America* (1837/2009) which suggested that:

> moral values shape social structures/social institutions; that the attendant tensions between theory and practice generate the conditions for reforming social and political institutions and that a society should be judged by its treatment of weaker groups in society. (Alatas & Sinha, 2017, p. 103)

Her work was sociologically sophisticated and indicated a combination of theoretical insight with empirical analysis which was rare for this period. Indeed, some have argued that Martineau was significantly ahead of the curve, with her theory discussing what Durkheim would later call 'social facts' (Lengermann & Niebrugge, 2002). While more sociologically sophisticated than her peers, what Martineau shared with other writers from this period was a concern with 'reform': the desire to understand, in order to change, society. This was linked to a form of social liberalism which would continue to be significant for sociology into the twentieth century (Collini, 1979).

This urge for reform made itself felt in what were, at least in terms of institutions and ambitions, the two most significant disciplinary forerunners of sociology during this period: political economy and statistics. Chris Renwick in his outstanding *British Sociology's Lost Biological Roots* (2012) argues that political economy is the earliest institutionalised forerunner of sociology in the UK. This discipline was immensely popular in the 1820s and as a 'gentlemanly science' occupied politicians, scholars and industrialists. As Renwick highlights, given its basis in the economics of Smith and Ricardo, this work 'was rooted in a conception of political economy as an enterprise dedicated to the study of human behaviour and how the interactions between people could give rise to rules according to which public lie should be governed' (Renwick, 2012, p. 22). For example, much of the discussion concerned class and its role in the capitalist system (Renwick, 2012, pp. 24–25). The exclusion of political economy from the British Association for the Advancement of Science (BAAS) led to the formation of a Section F in the 1830s which bought together political economists and statisticians. What united the political economists who made up Section F was not just their topic, but a heavy normative focus manifested in the desire to see political economy as not just government practice but as a way to understand the social. As Abrams (1968) noted, many political economists were part of the governmental elite, often on the liberal side, and wished to improve government legislation. These normative concerns meant that the 'scientific' status of political economy, and therefore section F, in the BAAS was questioned. Indeed, as Renwick notes, in 1878, the statistician J.K. Ingram suggested that the activities of the section should be subsumed under a new discipline: sociology. Ingram, arguing on Comteian grounds, saw a positivist sociology as a way of uniting the social sciences. His address was quickly countered by Robert Lowe, a man who had previously been Gladstone's Chancellor of the Exchequer who, in a common British refrain, questioned to what extent sociology could be identified as a science with clear methods and doctrine. Even more fatally, its name was unappealing to the classically educated British intellectuals being, as it is, half Greek and half Latin (Renwick, 2012, pp. 38–42). For Renwick, this event is the first in a long-running process of British scholars seeking, and often failing, to define sociology. Importantly, such acts of definition started from a normative position: how would something called 'sociology' be useful for the normative ends they were pursuing? Beyond some indulging of positivism, there was little consideration of theory in such work, it was mostly a practical question.

The other side of Section F, statistics, also has a strong claim to being a forerunner of British sociology. For Goldman (2019) we can identify a broad statistics movement from roughly the 1830s–1860s, in which the Belgian statistician Adolphe Quetelet and the mathematician Charles Babbage are central. These writers turned to statistics in order to discern sociological matters, most notably concerning social stratification, and their work was centred on the Social Science Association (SSA). The role of this organisation in the formation or frustration of sociology is conflicted. For Abrams (1968) statistics retarded the development of sociology in Britain by putting energies that would have been directed into developing the discipline into statistics (see also Scott & Bromley, 2013). In turn, the SSA was simply a body for reporting facts and reproducing liberal political assumptions. Instead it was socialists, who were excluded from this statistical milieu due to its liberal politics, who took up the effort of developing sociology more formally. For Goldman (1987) and Panayotova (2020) however the SSA was instead the earliest form of sociology and it is only when the reformist efforts which drove the SSA met with frustration at a governmental level that these energies were driven into sociology. This is unfortunate for these scholars, given these more formal efforts favoured an idealist and evolutionary unempiricism over the more sophisticated work of the early statisticians.

Whichever side one takes in this debate—like most accounts, each is partially true—one thing that unites them is the claim that statistics was, much like political economy, taken up for the cause of political reform. It is in this cause that British sociology finds its earliest disciples. This can be seen in the names of those who sought most explicitly to unite statistical analysis and reform, researchers such as Joseph Rowntree and Charles Booth who both conducted large scale surveys into the lives of the poor. Booth was greatly assisted in these efforts by Beatrice Webb, a figure who will appear again in this book and who made important developments in the field of research methods (McDonald, 1994, pp. 129–133). But, perhaps the most significant figure seeking to unite statistics and reform was Florence Nightingale.

Indeed, Nightingale is a good example of the key themes we have seen in this section (see McDonald, 1994; Alatas & Sinha, 2017, pp. 269–301). Reflecting the position of a 'gentlemanly', or 'gentlewomanly', science (to paraphrase Savage, 2010) she came from a wealthy background and combined her sociological work with other pursuits. This befitted an era where, with the exception of Martineau, it is hard to identify a figure who was primarily a sociologist in Britain before 1900.[2] In doing so, she drew upon a positivist understanding, to understand social 'laws' of development. We should be careful not to overvalue the extent to which positivism was universally accepted in this period, but certainly it was the one identifiable sociological perspective in a field largely lacking theory. Nightingale then used these sociological insights as part of a programme for reform following a broad social liberalism, in her case linked to nursing, but in other cases, such as in the work of Booth and Rowntree, a concern with poverty and the development of the social survey (Platt, L., 2014). The method for achieving this for Nightingale, was statistical analysis. She kept up to date with developments in the SSA and BAAS and, indeed, sought Francis Galton's (see next section) advice and support in an ultimately doomed

[2] The other possible figure here is Spencer. I would argue however that Spencer was a philosopher doing sociology; a similar position to John Stuart Mill, albeit with very different politics (which were, it must be said, discordant with most of the early sociological work identified here). Though, see Offer (2010) for a different perspective.

attempt at establishing a chair in statistics and their social use, or what we might now term a quantitative sociologist, at Oxford University (Goldman, 2019, p. 85).

In these elements, the 'gentlemanly', amateur status of its practitioner, its commitment to positivism (to the extent it committed to any theoretical perspective), its concern with social reform, the centrality of statistics and/or political economy and the fact it was absent from any university and actively shunned by Oxbridge, Nightingale reflects the type of sociology we have seen in this section. Kumar (2015) refers to this as a type of 'implicit sociology', it was not fully formed as a discipline but had the key elements of what a distinctively national, British, sociology could look like. In many ways, as I will suggest in this book, while Cole would not fit perfectly in this period, the concern with reform, on making sociology linked to a programme of social change, fits him very well. What is significant then is how sociology in the early twentieth century begins to diverge from this path.

1900–1920: The Battle for Institutionalisation

This 'implicit' sociology of the nineteenth century remained largely intact at the start of the twentieth. However, it would be inaccurate to say there had been no advances. For example, as Husbands (2019) notes, by 1900 sociology was being taught across a few institutions, though largely in a 'disparate and anarchic nature' (Husbands, 2019, p. 271). Conducted primarily by religious non-conformists, this teaching drew across anthropology and sociology with a reading list heavy on philosophical texts. Also, the social survey work of Booth and Rowntree had inspired several social reformers to use similar methods, including Webb who, guided by a positivist approach, continued her work after the Booth study (Lepenies, 1992). However, 'sociology' as a discipline, as opposed to a way of thinking that others may draw upon, lacked any clear presence at the start of the twentieth century. This was all to change in 1907. In that year Martin White, a Scottish businessman who was also a short-lived Liberal MP, agreed to fund a Professorship of Sociology at the LSE. White had both a financial and intellectual history in sociology, having previously helped establish and fund the Sociological Society (see below) in 1903 (see Husbands, 2019, pp. 24–30 for the best biography of White who was a colourful character). This professorship stoked the interest of four men[3] who I will use to explore the contours of the emerging institutionalised British sociology.

The favourite for the post was Patrick Geddes. Geddes was born in Ballater, Aberdeenshire, and in addition to periods studying in London and France had lived in Perth, Dundee and Edinburgh. Before 1907 Geddes had combined holding a Martin White-funded (and very favourably designed) Professorship of Botany, the subject he had been trained in at Dundee, with sociological activity in Edinburgh. Here, building upon Scotland's earlier sociological advances, he was the key figure in what has been called 'The Edinburgh School of Sociology' (Scott, 2007; Rocquin, 2019), where he had begun teaching co-ed summer schools as early as 1887 and in which he fine-tuned his sociological perspective. Influenced by LePlay, whom he had encountered in France, Geddes' sociology had a strong focus on the environment reflecting his position as perhaps the founder of environment sociology (Studholme, 2007). He developed a triad of 'place > work > folk' which explained how the physical environment would produce particular forms of activity and customs which, in turn, would be adjusted when that environment was changed (see Scott (2016a) for a summary of Geddes' theory). Such concerns led him to a focus on city planning and he used his time in Edinburgh to develop improvement measures for the slums of the Old Town; visitors can now take the Patrick Geddes Heritage Trail to see the impact of these changes. To facilitate these efforts he had purchased the Outlook Tower, a camera obscura close to Edinburgh Castle which he used as a base for his

[3] It is somewhat of an irony of history that we can identify key female British sociologists of the early 'gentlemanly' era in Martineau, Nightingale and, later, Webb. However, in the period of institutionalisation, it is a solely masculine field. This can be explained by the fact these earlier female writers had a class position which allowed them to do their sociological work in a 'gentlemanly' way, as a vocation, when institutional positions were closed off to them. Nevertheless, we can identify some female sociologists in this period. Scott and Bromley (2013) highlight the work of Syblia Branford (née Gurney) as part of a trio with her husband Victor and Patrick Geddes. She was one of the first sociology students at the LSE but followed her female predecessors in having to do her work outside the academy, in her case often in housing reform and in collaboration with the co-operative movement. Gurney does however own an accolade which, I believe, no other English sociologist has in having a road named after her, Gurney Drive, in Hampstead, London (Wilson, 2018). Goldthorpe (2019, pp. 345–348) also draws our attention to Emily Perrin who, working as Karl Pearson's research assistant was probably the author of the first intergenerational social mobility table (Perrin, 1904).

developing team of what we would now call urban sociologists. Charles Zueblin, visiting from the Chicago School of Sociology, christened it 'The World's First Sociological Laboratory' and argued it should be duplicated back home (Zueblin, 1899).

The circle around Geddes, most notably Victor Branford, a businessman and amateur sociologist who admired Geddes, became invested in securing him an institutional home as a sociologist, ideally in London. Their initial attempt at this was the formation of the Sociological Society, the first professional association for sociologists in the UK, founded in 1903. Given that, as we have seen, sociology at this point was not just a broad church but also one lacking a clear theology, membership of The Society was diverse and included, in addition to academics from different disciplines, businessmen, civic actors, clergymen and politicians, including two future Prime Ministers in Asquith and MacDonald (Scott & Bromley, 2013, pp. 55–57). While The Society would not fulfil its initial goal of establishing sociology as a significant presence in the UK, partly due to splits within the group which would play out in the 1907 professorship battle (see Halliday, 1968; Panayotova, 2019c) it did publish *The Sociological Papers*, the forerunner of *The Sociological Review* journal, a records of papers read at its meetings. Here Geddes developed his notion of 'sociology as civics':

> This department of sociological studies should evidently be, as far as possible, concrete in treatment. If it is to appeal to practical men and civic workers, it is important that the methods advocated for the systematic study of cities, and as underlying fruitful action, be not merely the product of study, but rather be those which may be acquired in course of local observation and practical effort. (Geddes, 1904, p. 103)

Reflecting the normative focus of such work Geddes would go on to develop, in collaboration with Branford, a 'The Third Alternative', one of many attempts for sociology to develop a 'Third Way' (Eldridge, 2000; Dawson, 2015). Geddes saw his Third Alternative as reflecting his Sociology as Civics since it was concerned with practical outcomes, such as the remaking of cities through what he termed 'conservative surgery' (Geddes & Slater, 1917). Central to such a project was the use of the 'regional survey', which effectively was a mapping of an area which could then be used to design the 'experimental solutions' which Geddes believed sociology should focus upon (Branford & Geddes, 1919, p. 20).

The second candidate for the professorship, and certainly at this point the biggest 'name', was Francis Galton. A cousin of Charles Darwin, Galton was at this point already in his eighties and had had a distinguished career across a number of fields, with his contributions to statistics being most notable to sociology today (see Goldthorpe, 2021). He had also been a vocal presence in the previous debates on Section F of the BAAS where he was critical of political economy and, inter alia, sociology for its lack of scientific grounding. Galton instead emphasised the need for identifying scientific 'laws' on which we can all agree. His public standing as a serious scientific figure and previous position as a critic of sociology made him a strategically important person for Branford and the Sociological Society to secure. As Renwick (2012, pp. 123–146) details, Branford was desperate to secure Galton's contribution to the society and agrees to him giving the key paper of the society's first meeting, with his protégé, and fellow statistician, Karl Pearson chairing.

The topic of this paper, and Galton's vision for sociology, was eugenics, which was influential in sociology circles at the time. While of course much of eugenics teaching is rightly condemned now, there was also at the time a branch of 'reform' eugenics which, in rejecting the racism of 'mainline' eugenics focused on how a negative social environment could produce negative outcomes, such as health, for individuals. This branch of eugenics was often implicit, and sometimes explicit, in the social mobility studies which would leave a legacy in British sociology's focus on inequality and the founding of the British welfare state (Renwick, 2017, 2019). Galton himself, unfortunately, leaned more towards the 'mainline' rather than 'reform' branch of eugenics and used his paper to advocate eugenics as 'the science which deals with all influences that improve the inborn quality of a race' along with 'the improvement of the inborn qualities' of humans (Galton, 1904, p. 45) and argued that 'Eugenics co-operate with the workings of Nature by securing that humanity shall be represented by the fittest races. What Nature does blindly, slowly, and ruthlessly, man may do providently, quickly, kindly' (Galton, 1904, p. 50). In a follow-up paper considering questions of marriage, Galton advocated that an authority should issue marriage certificates to those consider suitable (Galton, 1905). While eugenics was undoubtedly popular in this stage of sociology's development and even Geddes in his second paper on civics encouraged their combination (Geddes, 1905, p. 109), Galton's paper did not go down well. This was partly since many of the audience were receptive to reform eugenics, but hostile to its mainline form. Nevertheless, it is notable here that while we find the ends Galton advocates abhorrent (as did indeed some at the time) his focus is also on a practical, normative agenda for sociology.

The third candidate for the professorship was Leonard Hobhouse. Hobhouse had been working as a journalist, including for Cole's future brief employer, *The Manchester Guardian*, and had become strongly connected to the social liberal circles which figured so heavily in sociology's earlier history (Renwick, 2012, pp. 98–110; Collini, 1979). Hobhouse, who shared with Geddes a background in biological science, had developed a sociological view based on evolution. He held that whereas human evolution had previously been a process that happened to humans blindly, we now had the ability to direct it. His *Morals in Evolution* (1906) had argued that ethics and sociology should now be combined in seeking the correct form of moral development for society (see Scott, 2016b for a summary of Hobhouse's thought).

While Hobhouse had stronger political connections than the other candidates and, as indicated above, saw a future goal for sociology in helping guide moral development, he was the most eager of the three candidates to make sociology a science withdrawn from normative ends. While not giving a paper at the society himself, Hobhouse offered a response to Galton which encouraged separating the 'biological' concerns of 'stock and environment' from sociology arguing that 'I fear we cannot, as sociologists, expect to do much for society on these lines' (Hobhouse, 1904, p. 63). At a later meeting, while chairing a paper on sociology and ethics, he made a distinction between sociology as a science which 'has to do with what is and has been' and ethical philosophy, which confronts questions of morality and what could be (Hobhouse, 1905, p. 187). Therefore, despite being seemingly the most 'political' figure, Hobhouse was also the candidate most clearly advocating for sociology as an autonomous science rather than tying it to existing 'sciences' such as civics or eugenics.

The final candidate was H.G. Wells. In reality, my calling Wells a 'candidate' for the first Professorship of Sociology in the UK is factually untrue. There is no evidence anyone truly considered Wells a candidate for the post at the time, except Wells himself. In 1904 and 1905 he wrote numerous times to Beatrice Webb, and once to the prime minister of the time, Arthur Balfour, demanding such a chair be established for him at the LSE. However, a year later, he was rejecting any notion he thought of himself as a sociologist or ever desired a chair (Levitas, 2010, p. 534). The reason for including him in this discussion is, as Levitas (2010) has shown, his vision of sociology was a legitimate source of competition at the time.

Wells was on the Executive Committee of the Sociological Society from its formation and delivered his most significant discussion of sociology: 'The So-Called Science of Sociology' at the society the year before the Martin White Chair would be decided. Here Wells dismisses what he terms the 'scientific pretensions' (Wells, 1906, p. 360) which all the other candidates, in different ways, wished to claim for sociology. Instead, he argued sociology should be a fundamentally utopian endeavour, concerned with developing what he terms the 'Social Idea', or the best model of society. To achieve this:

> sociology must be neither art simply, nor science in the narrow meaning of the word at all, but knowledge rendered imaginatively, and with an element of personality; that is to say, in the highest sense of the term, literature. (Wells, 1906, p. 365)

This literary work should look at how societies have been and how they could be, with Wells mapping what he imagines to be the ultimate end goal of sociology:

> There used to be in my student days, and probably still flourishes, a most valuable summary of fact and theory in comparative anatomy, called Rolleston's 'Forms of Animal Life'. I figure to myself a similar book, a sort of dream book of huge dimensions, in reality perhaps dispersed in many volumes by many hands, upon the Ideal Society. This book, this picture of the perfect state, would be the backbone of sociology. It would have great sections devoted to such questions as the extent of the Ideal Society, its relation to racial differences, the relations of the sexes in it, its economic organisations, its organisation for thought and education, its 'Bible', its housing and social atmosphere, and so forth. Almost all the divaricating work at present roughly classed together as sociological could be brought into relation in the simplest manner, either as new suggestions, as new discussion or criticism, as newly ascertained facts bearing upon such discussions and sustaining or eliminating suggestions. (Wells, 1906, p. 368)

Therefore, Wells was creating a very different vision of sociology, one concerned with utopian vision which involved studying what is, critiquing it *and* providing alternatives. Indeed, Wells was very clear on the link of these elements, arguing: 'There is no such thing in sociology as dispassionately considering what *is*, without considering what is *intended to be*' (Wells, 1906, pp. 366–367).

Whether due to his rejection of a scientific approach or not, captured in Lepenies' (1992, p. 152) suggestion that Wells' ideal sociologist was a utopian novel reading 'boy scout' rather than a 'bookworm', Wells was never a serious contender for the chair. Renwick (2012, pp. 123–169) is our best guide for how the post was decided in a series of Sociological Society meetings which heard the competing visions for the discipline. As Baert and Morgan (2018) argue, such performances are key intellectual interventions with both the staging and performance, if convincing, giving the intellectual projects and advocates behind them significant power, or, in the case of a poor performance, not achieving such a status. This was the case for the Society meetings. Geddes was undoubtedly the frontrunner but hurt his chances by initially being absent while working on a report for Dunfermline council which was late, overly long and ultimately useless for the council. Then, when he arrived in London, his first talk on sociology as civics was poorly received, with Geddes mixing up the practical and the visionary in a paper that seemed to want to cover everything. As Scott and Bromley (2013, pp. 26–28) note, Geddes was always 'chaotic and disorganised' and 'had neither the inclination nor the discipline' to systematise his ideas. All of this, on top of the fact he was not a great speaker, hurt his chances at gaining support in what was, in effect, the extended job interview of attending the Sociological Society. When Geddes returned to the Society to deliver his second paper on sociology as civics, it was again considered too broad (it covers 57 pages in *The Sociological Papers*) and unclear in how to take forward its suggestions for sociology as civics. When in the next year, Geddes, always coming up with new schemes, suggested sociology focus on a 'civic museum' (Geddes, 1906), his support ebbed away.[4] Ultimately, given these issues, it seemed unclear to the Society how Geddes' vision of sociology had either practical *or* scientific use.

Meanwhile, Galton's initial address to the Society had also been poorly received and members of the audience (including Wells and Hobhouse) had raised objections to Galton's eugenics project and defended the

[4] Scott and Bromley (2013, p. 28) suggest that on top of this Geddes fluffed his actual interview for the post. However, Renwick (2012, pp. 165–167) indicates there was not a formal interview process at all. Renwick's account seems to have a stronger base in the evidence.

variety of humanity. This included some feminist critiques. In addition, Galton's chosen chair for his talk, Karl Pearson, used the occasion to trash the Society and sociology as an endeavour. Branford, ever eager to gain the institutional position of sociology, managed to smooth Galton's anger to the extent he kept coming to the Society and delivering talks. Nevertheless, when Galton declared his desire to leave money for eugenics projects in his will for University College London, despite Branford's failed attempt to align the Society to this, Galton's candidacy for the chair, and his association with sociology, was over.[5]

All of this meant that Hobhouse appeared as the clear, if not quite compromised then at least not objectionable to any one group, candidate. As Renwick (2012, pp. 165–166) details, Branford throws the weight of the Society, and patronage of Martin White, behind Hobhouse precisely because he is seen as able to unite the differing views of sociology around a vision of it as an autonomous science. Consequently, Hobhouse was appointed to the Martin White Professorship of Sociology at the LSE, a chair which still exists today. As Husbands (2019, p. 18) has demonstrated, Hobhouse was not technically the first Professor of Sociology appointed in the UK, or even at LSE. White endowed two professorships, one permanent (this went to Hobhouse) and the other for five years in the first instance which, with Branford's backing, went to the Finnish anthropologist Edward Westermarck. Westermarck accepted his offer first and since Hobhouse took a number of months to accept (apparently not entirely sure he wanted to tie himself to sociology), the 1907–1908 LSE Calendar listed only Westermarck as Professor of Sociology. Nevertheless, it is clear that while Westermarck was held in great regard by members of the Society, it was Hobhouse who was seen as the key appointment at the time, in Renwick's (2012, p. 169) terms the '*de facto* leader' of British sociology. He was therefore gifted editorship of *The Sociological Review* (the relaunched *The Sociological Papers*).

[5] The fact Branford was unsuccessful in aligning sociology to what would become the Galton Eugenics Laboratory is a fascinating sliding doors moment for British sociology. Given that UCL has, in face of student protests, since closed the Galton laboratory and undergone a process of removing his name, along with other eugenicists from its buildings, it could be suggested British sociology got off lucky from not having the shame of association. On the other hand, it could be argued this lack of formalised connection to eugenics in its birth has meant that most of British sociology remains ignorant of how central eugenics, both of the mainline and reform variety, were to the early formation of their discipline (Renwick, 2012).

Hobhouse used his early years in post to further this mission of the institutionalisation of sociology as a science. As Abrams (1968) notes despite the fact Hobhouse and his students were all united in their desire for political reform, the need to establish sociology as a science was too strong to allow space for this. Hobhouse, in Renwick's (2012, p. 175) terms 'froze Geddes out of sociology in the UK' and rarely acknowledged the possibility of different conceptions of sociology in his role. A broadly theoretical evolutionary and historical focus, detached from practical application, became the dominant form of British institutionalised sociological practice via the LSE. Even when Hobhouse resigned from *The Sociological Review* in 1910 due to a disagreement in editorial practice and Branford took over, this did not help Geddes' cause, since it now was cut off from the LSE. Geddes, perhaps sensing the mission lost, left for Professorship of Sociology and Civics at Bombay University in 1919.

As we have seen, the battle for institutionalisation in this period saw differing conceptions of sociology battle for recognition. Significantly, none picked up the baton of the earlier statistical work from the implicit sociology of the nineteenth century. Galton was of course a key figure in the development of statistics, but by this point he was advocating eugenics as his focus. Instead, this work would remain the activity of the 'gentlemanly' reformers and the break between sociology and statistics, the latter a field in which Britain had developed some of the most significant techniques, would be set in motion (Panayotova, 2020). In turn political economy was also silently dropped in these approaches, with economics beginning its shift to an increasingly mathematised science in the UK. Instead, during this period there were four potential paths for sociology in Britain. One, represented by Wells, involved the rejection of a scientific basis and instead a normative, literary focus and had little chance of success at the time. Two other approaches, Geddes' environmental sociology and Galton's eugenics each had a chance and tried to combine the practical and normative focus of an earlier era with a theoretical perspective. But each failed due to lack of problems with its main advocates, an unappealing synthesis and a lack of a clear vision for sociology. Not only had their performances been unconvincing but, in doing so, they failed to establish the 'legitimacy and respectability' which intellectuals seeking to advance their position need (Camic & Gross, 2004, p. 248). It would be inaccurate to say that the successful approach, that represented by Hobhouse, won by default; this would be to overlook the appeal of Hobhouse's claim of sociology as an autonomous science with a clear theoretical framing (the key elements seen as lacking in the nineteenth century), but there is some truth to this. Consequently, Hobhouse's vision of sociology would define the following period of sociology. This is a vision which Cole had to confront and which, as I will demonstrate in this book, was so alienating to him.

1920–1960: 'The Floating Discipline'

Therefore, by the time Cole was becoming intellectually active sociology had an institutional home, a learned society and a journal. This institutional activity was, at this point, largely limited to the LSE but, nevertheless, sociology had a presence in the UK. In the chapters that come I will be exploring how Cole related to the form of sociology practised from 1920–1960 and therefore here will simply provide a broad overview of key events, trends and figures in this period.

As noted in Chap. 1, this period of British sociology's history has been somewhat ignored. Perhaps one explanation for this is the suggestion, offered in one of the most notable histories of the British discipline, that the history of sociology prior to 1950 is simply the history of sociology at the LSE (Halsey, 2004, p. 47). The work of Baudry Rocquin has done much to correct this misconception. Rocquin focuses on the broader practices of sociology in this period when, for him, it is a 'floating discipline' (Rocquin, 2006). This is due to its being split between three camps: the LSE, the LePlay House/Geddesian tradition and scattered developments elsewhere. I will discuss each in turn.

To start with the LSE, Hobhouse's appointment was soon followed by the appointment of his protégé Morris Ginsberg[6] who succeeded him as Martin White Professor after Hobhouse's death in 1929 and remained in the post until 1954. Given the length of their professorships, Hobhouse and Ginsberg had a central role in defining what formal sociology would be in the UK; it is hard to find many now who see that as a success. For

[6]While Ginsberg himself was not in exile—his family moved from his native Lithuania when he was a teenager for his father's work—he is the first in a long line of key British sociologists born elsewhere and often exiled from their home. Frequently, like Ginsberg, Jewish and fleeing the Nazis and/or other anti-semitic attacks, such scholars have hugely enriched British sociology and given it an openness to European ideas and historical sociology it would otherwise have lacked (Turner, 2014). A partial list of such scholars would include such significant names as Norbert Elias, Karl Mannheim, Viola Klein, Ruth Glass, Ilya Neustadt, John Rex and Zygmunt Bauman (see Turner (2014) for a further discussion).

Rocquin (2019, pp. 67–101) despite Hobhouse's claims of establishing sociology on a scientific basis, his aversion to empirical data and a reluctance to engage with contemporary sociological theory from abroad left it unsure. Ginsberg, while happiest producing exegesis of Hobhouse's thought and its evolutionary focus, did make some moves towards empirical data and the work of scholars such as Durkheim. Nevertheless, the overall effect of their position, despite Hobhouse's open liberalism 'ensured the reputation of sociology at the time as being, if not conservative, then at least only quietly progressive on the basis of the gentle meliorism of Hobhouse and then Ginsberg' (Husbands, 2019, p. 54). It was also the case that the sociology 'department', such as it was at this point, was largely disorganised, with a rotating cast of teachers coming in on a temporary basis and riven with internal politics (Husbands, 2019, pp. 41–83). The latter of these factors were so strong that when Karl Mannheim arrived at the LSE, undoubtedly the most significant scholar to move through the sociology departments in this period, he could never advance beyond a lectureship and the animosity between him and Ginsberg was so strong that Mannheim's widow blamed it for his early death (Dahrendorf, 1995, p. 295, Shils, 1997, p. 217).

Consequently, those who look to the LSE in this period for inspiration turn to events beyond the Sociology Department. Here we see scholars such as R.H. Tawney and T.H. Marshall (who later moves from Social Work to Sociology) developing a tradition of sociology focused on questions of equality, citizenship and mobility which, in Raymond Aron's words was 'an attempt to make intellectual sense of the political problems of the Labour Party' (Aron, quoted in Halsey, 2004, p. 70). Marshall's *Citizenship and Social Class* (1992) is perhaps a paradigmatic example of this form of sociology with its questions of how the Labour Party could respond to, and advance, the new relation between citizenship and class after WWII. This tradition later took hold outside of the LSE (Rocquin, 2019; Butler, 2020) and, as we shall see, is one that via the connection of Michael Young, an LSE student, Cole had some relation to.

In addition to this, the short-lived Department of Social Biology at the LSE, a vanity project from then director William Beveridge which was doomed to fail (Dahrendorf, 1995), facilitated the work of David Glass. Glass, sometimes in collaboration with his wife Ruth Glass, helped establish a British sociological tradition by conducting the first large scale social mobility study (Mills, 2019), albeit one which even Glass' admirers note was theoretically poor and not well developed statistically (Goldthorpe,

2019). Finally, anthropology at the LSE, led by Bronislaw Malinoswki, was central in developing Durkheimian theory in the UK and was international in scope (Kuper, 2015; Rocquin, 2019, pp. 173–213; Smith, 2020, pp. 115–129). Therefore, despite the hopes of Hobhouse's appointment, sociology at LSE in this period did not develop the clear unity of empirical and theoretical consideration in an autonomous science. Instead, it was more piecemeal with some worthy work going on (largely outside the formal Sociology Department) but not brought together as part of a distinctively 'British' sociology. Nevertheless, while later histories have on occasion overplayed the supposed lack of competitors to the LSE in this period (e.g. Halsey, 2004), it is correct to say it was dominant during this period. This can be seen in how in the initial years after its 1951 formation the BSA largely reflected the interests and concerns of both staff and students from the school (Banks, 1967). This dominance continued for some years to come: between 1950 and 1970 academics from the LSE made up 15.6% of the BSA Committee and 12% of authors for all major British sociology journals—including 19% of authors in *The British Journal of Sociology*—far exceeding all other universities (Collison & Webber, 1971, p. 528).

The second body of work came from the remnants of the Geddesian movement. Following Hobhouse's resignation as editor, Branford regained control of *The Sociological Review* which then became the publication seeking to defend Geddes' approach, especially the regional survey. Despite seemingly heartfelt attempts by Branford to reconcile with the LSE, Hobhouse, and later Ginsberg, refused, with the latter saying he would only countenance this if both Geddes and Branford stepped down from the board (Scott & Bromley, 2013, p. 61; Rocquin, 2019, p. 38). The Sociological Society also increasingly lost steam following the battles of institutionalisation and would eventually be subsumed into its successor organisations which continued the Geddesian project: LePlay House and the Institute of Sociology.

LePlay House, named after the French theorist who had so inspired Geddes, was the organisational promotor of the regional survey movement. As Evans (1986) demonstrates in his history of the House, it had varying levels of success. It undertook surveys under commission from councils/organisations or under its own steam. Some of these were published in *The Sociological Review* while others appeared elsewhere or not at all. In many ways, LePlay House continued the 'gentlemanly' nature of sociology, including the focus on reform, found in the earlier period.

Indeed, when we expand the definition of the social survey to take in the earlier poverty-focused work of Booth, Rowntree and their successors then, for Rocquin (2019) it is perhaps British sociology's greatest contribution during this period. While LePlay House continued an earlier penchant for a lack of theory, it was a fundamentally public sociology which not only raised society's collective knowledge of itself, but also had a political impact. Its success can be seen in the work it inspired, such as the Mass Observation group (e.g. Mass-Observation, 1939) and documentary writing, such as Orwell's *Road to Wigan Pier* (Orwell, 1937). Indeed, it was British sociology's only successful export in this period. The French were eager to copy the methods of LePlay House with the *Centre de Documentation Sociale* established at the *Ecole Normale Supérieure* for this purpose (Rocquin, 2019, p. 159).

The Institute of Sociology was established as a mechanism to defend sociology more generally, beyond the regional survey. With Branford and Geddes' deaths it was another Scot, Alexander Farquharson, who took the Institute through the 1930s–1950s. Despite Farquharson's efforts to secure intellectual prestige and a home for the Institute, it was able to achieve little, primarily due to a cast of disinterested presidents who either ignored the Institute and/or used it solely to further their own interests (Rocquin, 2019, pp. 43–53). It's one success, and this is no small achievement, was to keep *The Sociological Review* alive and even to eventually welcome Ginsberg back into the fold. The *Review* continues today thanks in no small part to the efforts of Farquharson and the Institute, which would eventually collapse by the 1940s, though only formally disbanding in 1955. In this, British sociology owes Alexander Farquharson a debt he has only rarely been credited for. Despite this, the Geddesian project largely disappeared by the 1940s in Britain,[7] only to be revived in the twenty-first century as part of the rise of environmental sociology (Studholme, 2007).

The final stream of sociological activity in this period was more dispersed, most notably in the increased teaching of sociology. As noted previously, there had been some sociology courses prior to Hobhouse's

[7] Geddes' project was however kept alive in America via the work of Lewis Mumford, who at one point Branford almost secured as editor of *The Sociological Review*. During this period Mumford wrote a summary of the work of Geddes and Branford in which he commented that the papers of Geddes 'are comparable to the notebooks Leonardo da Vinci left behind' (Mumford, 1948, p. 677).

appointment and this 'anarchic' tradition (Husbands, 2019) continued. Substantial developments occurred at a number of institutions, including: (1) Bedford College, a progressive all-women's college which included an oft-overlooked early female sociologist in Barbara Wootton (later Baroness Wootton and the first female member of the House of Lords, Oakley, 2011) among its staff; (2) Aberdeen, where Robert Morrison McIver convinced the university to add 'Sociology' to his title as Lecturer in Politics and Sociology in 1911 (Brewer, 2007); (3) Liverpool University, where a School of Social Work founded in 1905 quickly became a broader department focused on sociological problems which built upon the tradition of Rowntree and Booth (their professorship was named after the latter (Scott, 2020, pp. 9–10)). (4) a number of settlements and small-scale sociology teaching at Leeds, Glasgow, Manchester and Birmingham and (5) the growth in degrees with, by the end of the 1950s, ten universities offering sociology degrees, either of their own, or by extension of the LSE (Scott, 2020, p. 26). In addition to this, the development of sociological research centres was also significant in this period. The most prominent of these is probably The Institute for Community Studies founded by Michael Young, himself one of the most consequential sociologists to begin working during this period and very much of a product of the 'sociology as answering the questions of the Labour Party' formed outwith the Sociology Department at the LSE (Butler, 2020). It could be argued, by expanding the teachers and students of sociology (which, despite notions of British 'failure', were similar in number at the time to those in France, Rocquin, 2019, p. 136), these developments were most significant to the establishment of the discipline during this period. Perhaps most importantly, it produced a market for textbooks in sociology (Scott, 2014), which in turn helped define a tradition of British Social Theory (Scott, 2018), as well as series of texts on sociological issues, most notably the Mannheim-edited *International Library of Sociology and Social Reconstruction* (Platt, J., 2014). As we shall see, Cole contributed to both of these.

As a result of these efforts, by the end of the 1950s sociology was ready to enter its golden age of expansion. As Rocquin (2014, p. 206) puts it, 'Inter-war British sociology was [not] just "an invisible discipline" and was a foundation for the post-war era'. Come 1951 the BSA, a more successful attempt at what had been tried with the Sociological Society was founded and developed an alliance with a new journal, *The British Journal of Sociology*, which had begun publishing two years previously (Platt, 2003).

Therefore, over the course of Cole's working life as an intellectual, sociology in the UK had experienced an initial flourish of enthusiasm following its institutionalisation battles; the split which came from this; the failure of both the Hobhouseian and Geddesian projects; and then finally some revival as the teaching and studying of sociology expanded. As we shall see, Cole was involved in these activities in real time as both a commentator and participant. In 1948 he suggested that the development of sociology, meant like, unlike previously when it was a 'gentlemanly' activity undertaken alongside other activities it now had its own, independent existence:

> we should once and for all give up the bad habit of calling by the name 'Sociology' all the odds and ends of Social Studies that we cannot conveniently bring under any main head. Sociology is not a residue, after Economic and Politics and Demography and Law and Geography and Social Psychology have been taken away. (Cole, 1948a, pp. 266–267)

This positive view of sociology as a discipline worthy of study was one that Cole held not just due to his knowledge of sociologists from other countries, but also due to his awareness of, and distance from, the British sociology he experienced which he felt did not live up to these standards. Yet, as I will explore in this book, Cole fits very well into a tradition of British sociology, with its normative, political and public focus, it just was not the tradition of sociology he confronted during his lifetime.

Conclusion

This chapter has provided an overview of the history of British sociology prior to 1960. Here I identified three key periods: (1) the eighteenth and nineteenth centuries where, bar positivism, we see a somewhat theory-absent discussion of sociological thinking shaped heavily by statistics and political economy which had a strong focus on reform and a 'gentlemanly' nature; (2) the period from 1900–1920 where we see the battle for institutionalisation with different attempts to provide (or in one case reject) a vision of sociology as a science which is then tied to Hobhouse's appointment as the intended first Professor of Sociology in the UK; (3) a period between 1920 and 1960 where, despite claims to the contrary we can see a tradition of British sociology which, despite a disperse nature, laid the groundwork for further institutionalisation and expansion in the 1960s following the Robbins Report.

One key element of this history has been the role of normativity and the connection of sociology to reform. As we saw, this was dominant in the first, 'gentlemanly' period, but then loses out in the institutionalisation battles to a notion of sociology as objective science. In our third period this normative tradition finds some continued expression, but this is outside formal sociology, whether in other departments at the LSE, or in the extramural tradition. Formalised sociology remains opposed to it, significantly since the sociology degree at the LSE was the main form of training available to sociologists in this period (Halsey, 2004). This will figure in what follows.

The second key element here is the somewhat 'disorganised' nature of sociology during this period. Despite the efforts of many key figures, sociology during this period is somewhat poorly defined, as Cole himself would comment upon. Indeed, to use the terms of Collini (1988), it is not enough to study 'disciplinary history', those activities distinctively labelled 'sociology', instead one has to take a broader 'intellectual history' approach to this topic to understand where what we now call 'sociology' in Britain came from. This limited disciplinary identity and space meant that inevitably people would come in and out of sociology and to speak of 'insiders' and 'outsiders' is much more difficult during this period than in later years where clear markers such as having a sociology degree or having 'sociology' in one's job title made this much clearer. For example, Rocquin's analysis of student numbers suggests that from 1920–1940, 900 students in Britain gained sociology degrees, or an average of 45 per year across the country (Rocquin, 2019, p. 136). Inevitably, this meant that a figure like Cole could be more easily both in and out of sociology than he could in later years. While this is true, as we shall see, Cole also highlighted, and contributed towards, an emerging view of what sociology actually *is* and, while in retrospect we can identify only a confused subject unclear what it is actually is, as we shall see in Chap. 4, Cole saw a subject which was clear on what it was and it was one he shared some concerns with, but was fundamentally alienated from its desire for value-freedom. Therefore, in placing Cole into the third period of the history traced in this chapter, it is not my goal to claim that he is actually an 'insider' to sociology during this period. Instead, following the 'floating' nature of the discipline in this period, Cole is a contributor, and on occasion a very notable one, but one who remains both on the inside *and* outside of the discipline. In my terms, he is semi-alienated.

CHAPTER 3

Cole's Sociological Works

Margaret Cole reports that immediately after her husband's death 'students engaged in studying the work of G.D.H. Cole were much concerned to show either that his was not a "normative" philosophy or that, if it was, there was an ample excuse for him'. She then notes, just over ten years having passed, 'I do not think that this line would be pursued with such vigour today' (Cole, 1971, p. 267). Reflected here are the changing responses in intellectual life, both within and outwith sociology, to a perspective like Cole's. Cole's intellectual project, including his sociology, was unquestionably, and unapologetically, normative. Unfortunately, he happened to encounter the British sociological field during the one period in which this was considered problematic, something which needed an 'excuse' in his wife's words. This chapter outlines this sociology and its normative project of guild socialism. This element of normativity will also be central to the discussion of Chap. 4, which focuses on what Cole said about sociology.

This chapter has five sections. The first outlines Cole's sociology, here I will highlight how Cole's Rousseauian influenced sociological perspective carried an embryonic version of structuration theory focused on notions of the general will. This sociology then underpins Cole's normative vision of guild socialism, which will be discussed in the second section. Here we will see the ways in which Cole's guild socialism is built upon his concern with equalising the possibility of expressing individual wills in an equitable

M. Dawson, *G.D.H. Cole and British Sociology*,
https://doi.org/10.1007/978-3-031-75484-5_3

democratic system. The third section then turns to the other sociological contributions Cole made; here I will focus heavily on Cole's sociology of class, culminating in his *Studies in Class Structure* (1955c), though I will also discuss Cole's authorship of one of the first sociology textbooks. The fourth section, by drawing across the preceding material while also bringing in Cole's work on the Nuffield Social Reconstruction Survey, discusses Cole's connection to British sociology in his day. Here I will more explicitly begin to highlight the nature of Cole's semi-alienation from the discipline. What we see across these elements is how, in varying ways, Cole developed a clear sociological perspective which shaped his intellectual project and in which he made several contributions to the field. Yet, this remained a somewhat strained connection with Cole maintaining a semi-alienation from the discipline he confronted. The final section then will interrogate Cole's sociology around its treatment of gender and empire, inspired by the feminist and decolonial critiques which have encouraged us to look anew at the assumptions of sociology.

The material concerning guild socialism discussed in this chapter is certainly the most well-discussed section of Cole's output. Therefore, my goal here is to frame Cole's political commitments slightly differently to how most commentators have done, namely, seeing them as grounded in a sociological perspective. For Wright (1979, p. 236) Cole sought to 'equip democratic socialism with a distinctive sociology'; as we shall see, there is truth in this. However, I would question the ordering, rather than Cole beginning with socialism and then seeking to add sociology on it, I would argue they are mutually occurring. Cole's socialism had a sociological base and, in turn, his sociology cannot be fully understood outside of its democratic socialist commitments.

Cole's Sociology: Rousseau, The General Will and Structuration

In speaking of Cole's 'sociology' in this section I am being significantly restrictive and focusing solely on the intellectual underpinnings of his project, most notably around the relations of the individual and society, a key focus of sociology then and now. Needless to say, as I will go on to demonstrate, this perspective then informs much of Cole's broader work which we could identify as 'sociological' including his guild socialism and his discussion of class. I would also suggest it influences his work on non-sociological issues beyond the scope of my discussion in this book.[1] In this section however my focus is on these underlying principles of the relation of the individual and society.

Cole's sociology starts with the individual. This is befitting for a scholar whose guild, or libertarian, socialism, aimed at individual emancipation and who once suggested that 'my Zeus is man' (Cole, 1945a, p. 16). However, it poses some challenges for categorising his sociological approach. An obvious home is in the school of methodological individualism and, like many from this school, Cole shares a focus on understanding how the individual exists in a web of interconnects which both produce and are constituted by social institutions. Take, for example, Cole's claim that sociological investigation must start:

> from man in all his complex groupings and relations, partially embodied in social institutions of many sorts and kinds, never in balanced equilibrium, but always changing, so that the pattern of loyalties and of social behaviour changes with them. (Cole, 1945a, p. 15)

However, contrary to what is said in this quote and most classic methodological individualist approaches in sociology, such as the Weberian school, Cole does not focus overly on how forms of social action are shaped by socially sanctioned codes. There is no equivalent of a 'Protestant Ethic' for Cole. Instead, I would argue that Cole's methodological individualism starts from the assumption that individuals are fundamentally political, meant both in the sense that they are immersed within a political context *and* seek to create particular political outcomes in their daily activity. Cole's sociology is a kind of methodological political individualism. It was partly this concern with how individual actions seek to produce political outcomes which led him to Rousseau.

Cole wrote broadly on Rousseau; he both translated and wrote a lengthy introduction to the Everyman's Library publication of *The Social Contract and Discourses* (1955a),[2] taught a lecture course on him at

[1] For example, Cole's history of the Labour Party (Cole, 1948b) has a focus on individuals and their intentions which perhaps mirrors the form of structuration theory outlined here.

[2] Everyman's Library was established in 1906 to make classics of literature, both fiction and non-fiction, available to working-class readers. They were affordable, facilitated by a change in copyright law which meant many texts were in the public domain, and often contained explanatory introductions. They were a huge success, selling more than 60 million copies of 1239 titles by 1975, with a significant working-class readership (see Rose, 2021,

Oxford (Cole, n.d.-a) and discussed him extensively across his key sociological writing (Cole, 1914a, 1926) including in his sociology textbook, *Social Theory* (Cole, 1920a) as well as a chapter in his later *Essays in Social Theory* (Cole, 1950a). Lamb (2005) argues that Cole's engagement with Rousseau was partly his attempt to solve the fundamental sociological question of the 'problem of agency'. Reflecting what I have said already, this was based in a fundamentally political conception of individuals since 'in his belief that citizens could identify the general will Cole assumed the human capacity to become fundamentally egalitarian' (Lamb, 2005, p. 286).

Cole starts his sociology with a claim about the nature of the pre or non-social individual, claiming that:

> Primitive, non-social man would be neither an egoist nor an altruist in any moral sense: he would be pre-moral. But he would have in him already, as essential parts of his nature, the qualities which under the influence of society would subsequently take on a moral character. (Cole, 1955a, p. ix)

As noted by Bauman, the notion of a 'non-social man' is such a clear fiction that it is only sociologists and philosophers, concerned with understanding how society works, who can conceive of it (Bauman, 1990). Here, making use of this common sociological hermeneutic device, Cole posits certain qualities as innate to the individual, which only take on their moral form in the social situation. These are what he would term the 'obligations' (Cole, 1914a) or 'loyalties' (Cole, 1926) that shape our social action. We are, for Cole, innately associative; we have, a 'living impulse' to 'live and work together' which forms the building blocks of society (Cole, 1926, p. 155). Indeed, for Cole, 'the subject-matter of social theory is the action of men in association' (Cole, 1920a, p. 17).

Here we need to carefully define what Cole sees as an association; it is not what later would be defined as assemblage, a short-term grouping to satisfy a particular end, but something more long-lasting and with a moral element. This can include work associations, such as companies and collaborators, political formations from the small-scale parish council up to the state and civil associations such as churches and our families (Cole,

pp. 131–136). Therefore, Cole's involvement with them—he also wrote the introduction to their publication of Marx's *Capital* (Cole, 1933a)—was an inevitable outcome of his commitment to what we now call public sociology. I will discuss this further in Chap. 5.

1920a). All these associations exist 'for the purpose of satisfying common wants' (Cole, 1920a, p. 49) and therefore generate loyalties from the individuals who are members of them. Such loyalties for Cole (1926, p. 165) emerge from these pre-social impulses but also are the realisation of our social action since they reflect 'a mass of instincts, prejudices, customary ideas and assumptions caught up at second hand, selfish and unselfish purposes, ethical strivings and corporate egoisms, all mixed up together'. These loyalties also, in their associative form, take on a moral form by producing allegiances and commitment to ideals; as Cole puts it: 'nothing is done without loyalty. Loyalty is the root of the tree of good and evil conduct' (Cole, 1926, p. 156). In this sense, Cole shares an unexpected link with the sociology of W.E.B. Du Bois who in his 'Sociology Hesitant' is critical of the 'metaphysical wanderings' of structuralist sociology and instead advocated the study of 'the natural unit of associated men' (Du Bois, 2000, p. 39, 40). Like Du Bois, Cole believes that to understand the nature of social life we need to understand how people come to form associations with each other and the impact these associational loyalties have on social action rather than positing atomised actors subsumed by structure.

These associations are expressions of what Cole, reflecting Rousseau, sees as the 'associative will' (Cole, 1914a, p. 145). This is the 'will, based on a sense of loyalty or obligation, to act for the collective benefit of any group to which he belonged' (Cole, 1950b, p. 116). Here we begin to see the development of the question of agency in Cole's work. Reflecting the later work of Archer (2000) Cole sees agency, the ability to act upon the world and shape it, to be collective, in his case based in the associations and their respective wills. Here, by developing an associative will and expressing desires, most notably around ideal social forms, the individual helps shape the nature of social institutions since: 'Society is a wider complex of institutions which resemble one another throughout only as being one and all expressions of man's associative will' (Cole, 1914a, p. 145). It is our acting together in associations which helps give shape to the body politic, including particular state formations (Cole, 1914a).

Importantly, Cole sees a connection between the associations of which we are part and individuality. For him, each individual has two elements to their 'personality', one is the private, backstage part, which remains beyond the reach of our associative activity. The other is the public part, which finds expression in associative action (Cole, 1914a), not dissimilar to Durkheim's (1973) dualism of human nature. Here, Cole's concept of 'function' is central. Cole (1920a) sees all individuals as involved in different functions. These often reflect the aforementioned associations, since they include our associative actions such as the workplace and civic groupings but can extend beyond this. For example, as consumers, we are engaged in a 'function' as a consumer since we have particular interests and concerns while acting in this manner. This function as a consumer then, of course, interacts with the various other functions individuals are part of (e.g. we act as a consumer in one instance and then as a producer in the next). It is in our functional activity for Cole that individuality is made 'particular' (Cole, 1914a, p. 154) in the sense of being grounded in sociality and having both sanction and the promise of recognition from society. Therefore, associational activity not only produces an associative will which shapes the social but also, at an individual level, gives expression to individuality and recognises our 'function' within the whole. It gives us a purpose and a place.

While the above comments reflect Cole's comments concerning agency, his Rousseauian sociology is also an attempt to understand the role of structure. These associative wills are then the basis for the general will, which reflects the collected associative wills (Cole, 1914a). Therefore, the forms of social institutions such as the state and economy should mirror these associative wills—I will discuss later why they may not—since as he puts it, '*There is no General Will unless the people will the good*' (Cole, 1955a, p. xxxvii). Social order then, suggested by Rousseau's notion of the social contract is, for Cole, not something that happens once and is settled but rather is subject to renegotiation and constant change in light of the expression of the associative will (Cole, n.d.-b, p. 8).

However, this general will is not simply a passive expression of the associative will but rather has its own, coercive, function. By existing as above, and reflecting, the associative wills, the general will develops a set of fundamental laws and principles that will 'induce the citizens' to act in particular ways, most notably in their public political activity (Cole, 1955a, p. xxx). The general will therefore gives society a sense of 'collective personality' (Cole, 1914a, p. 150) which shapes individual action and provides moral norms and customs. However, in turn, these general precepts of morality which hold good for all of society are only accepted *because* they have the legitimacy of reflecting individual expression via the associative wills.

Therefore, for Cole, society and its institutions exist as a result of the associative will; this will not only drives individuals to associate, but also gives them the means of agency as collective expression in their functionally specific activity. In turn, these associative wills give shape to social institutions by collectively generating the general will, which determines the shape of macro social institutions. Once the general will is produced, it also has a coercive power, since it produces sets of moral rules which hold good for the collective—expressed in laws—and which shape individual action within associations. Therefore, Cole is in effect producing an early form of structuration theory (Giddens, 1984). While taking the name from Giddens' perspective, here I use the term 'structuration' more generally to refer a theory which presents structure and agency as mutually occurring and dependent factors. In addition to Giddens, we can identify structuration writers such as Bourdieu, Bauman and Mouzelis, as well as, perhaps, Elias (Stones, 2005). Structuration theorists then wish to reject both the 'oversocialised conception of man' (Wrong, 1961), where individuals are seen simply as carriers of structural demands and any notion of the individual as making the world. Rather, they wish to see both structure *and* agency as constitutive of the social. In Cole's case, this duality is grounded in the loyalties of individuals:

> Loyalties, then, can find free and rational expression only within a harmony which is two-fold – a harmony of men and institutions one with another, on a basis of sufficient agreement about fundamental ideas; and a harmony of institutions with the underlying conditions of life, so that the institutions of society are consistent with, and help forward, the best use of men's material resources in accordance with their power over nature. (Cole, 1926, p. 169)

Much as Giddens' structuration theory discussed the duality of structure as providing both the medium for *and* the outcome of action (Giddens, 1984, p. 374) we can say that Cole's notion of the general will has its own duality as both the outcome of associative action *and* the institutionalised forum which allows for it.

There are three outcomes from Cole's structuration theory which are significant for his broader approach. The first is that, at this point, it paints a somewhat benign, positive image of social life. Indeed, I would suggest Cole reflects a broader sociological trend, noted by Levitas (2010), of creating a utopian vision of how society should work and then using that to condemn our failure to live up to that image. As I will discuss below, Cole's sociology is fundamentally critical and he criticises the failure for society to live up to this Rousseauian ideal. Cole highlights that the value of Rousseau's approach is his desire to find a 'legitimate' basis for social order (Cole, 1955a, p. xvii) and Cole takes the normative desire behind this as a key part of his sociology.

The second element is that, in drawing upon Rousseau as the basis for his sociology, Cole reflects a broader trend in the discipline. Abraham (1973) from an approving position and Carroll (1980) from a critical position each highlights the importance of Rousseau to contemporary sociology, including on topics such as the relation between community and society, the development of structuralism and the idealist desire to remake the world. It is perhaps unsurprising therefore that Rousseau was a point of reference for Durkheim, who shared a sociological reading of the social contract with Cole (Durkheim, 1970; Dawson, 2023, pp. 37–38). As we shall see in the next chapter, Durkheim was also a key point of reference for Cole.

Finally, a potential criticism that can be made of Cole's formative structuration theory is its limited application. In contrast to a Giddensian approach to structuration theory—to say nothing of Bourdieusian approaches—Cole has little focus on what Giddens calls the *durée*, the day-to-day customs and norms in which agency (in the singular) is expressed. Instead, Cole's focus is largely one of politics. Agency is expressed through the involvement in associations with a political desire. Structure in turn is manifested largely, though not wholly, through the translation of the general will into laws. In this sense, it is true to say Cole's structuration theory is narrower than Giddens' and also would not capture the 'continuous sense of self' Archer (2000, p. 3) seeks to account for in agency via her 'methodological dualism' approach. However, there are two caveats to this. Firstly, structuration theory has been criticised for its lack of political focus, instead being seen as 'ambivalent' when it comes to how actors produce political outcomes (Stones, 2005, pp. 195–197). Therefore, Cole's sociology does account for something often seen as lacking in similar approaches. For example, in his discussion of how social change occurs in the mediation of politics and power, Giddens emphasises the role of 'intersocietal systems' which specify the relations between, and within, societal totalities. Let us take the example of the nation state as such a totality (Giddens, 1984, p. 244). Here, Giddens largely sees the governing instruments of the nation-state, once it reaches a modern form, as given (Giddens, 1984, pp. 244–255). His concern is then with the dominance of the educative systems which allows states to reproduce themselves (Giddens, 1984, pp. 286–287). While, of course, we must account for the reproduction of political orders, this perspective allows little space for the use of the political sphere for *change*, reflecting how Giddens' structuration theory cleaves so heavily to the notion of an individual free for self-recreation rather than political critique (Bauman, 1989a; Dawson, 2010). Cole, on the other hand, places this element front and centre in his structuration theory.

Secondly, Cole's notion of function is significant here since it extends the reach of the associative will beyond the formal political sphere and accounts for consumerism as well as civic activities, such as religious practice. While maintaining a claim, correctly I would assert, that these activities are 'political', it seeks to account for social action beyond the formal political sphere. For Cole, we should have the opportunity to practice our agency in varied ways, as he puts it:

> The associative act has two relations: it is, as Rousseau says, general in relation to the association which performs it; but it is particular in relation to the Society of which the association forms a part. It may be general in the second case, in the sense that it may be directed to the good of the community as a whole; but it is still the act of an individual in relation to the Society. (Cole, 1914a, p. 154)

Cole's sociology therefore starts with the premise that individuals act to shape social institutions, which in turn influence their behaviour, across multiple functions they occupy. While this is undoubtedly political it includes an expanded conception of what the 'political' is to take in topics often seen as the sociology of work, consumption or even community. Again, here we have an advance on the narrow political focus of Giddens.

Having outlined the basis for Cole's sociology, let us now turn to the normative ends to which he put it, his vision of guild socialism.

The Sociology of Guild Socialism

Cole developed his model of guild socialism at the same time as his Rousseauian structuration theory. It is therefore unsurprising that we see overlaps in the two. In particular, I would suggest, this is where Cole's sociology becomes 'critical' and where he begins to outline how and why the benign ideal of the Rousseauian sociology traced above has not been realised.

As we have seen, Cole's sociology rests upon a conception of will, with individuals able to contribute, as collective agents, to the whole through the expression of associational wills. The starting point of guild socialism is that this was not allowed to happen under the conditions of capitalist liberal democracy. As Cole puts it:

> Guildsmen assume that the essential social values are human values, and that Society is to be regarded as a complex of associations held together by the wills of their members, whose well-being is its purpose. They assume further that it is not enough that the forms of government should have the passive or 'implied' consent of the governed, but that the Society will be in health only if it in the full sense democratic and self-governing, which implies not only that all the citizens should have the 'right' to influence its policy if they so desire, but that the greatest possible opportunity should be afforded for every citizen actually to exercise this right...Moreover, and this is perhaps the most vital and significant assumption of all, it regards this democratic principle as applying, not only or mainly to some special sphere of social action known as 'politics', but to any and every form of social action, and, in especial, to industrial and economic fully as much as to political affairs. (Cole, 1920b, p. 12)

Here we see how Cole posits the expression of will as required across all areas of social life; such expression also had to be effective. Therefore, implied consent as well as the claim that one has the 'right' to influence without being given the resources to do so were both insufficient. Freedom for Cole was always defined positively with the need to be able to exercise agency ***and*** being given the means to do so central to his socialism. As he puts it, guild socialism was a 'theory of institutions' and 'a policy directed to the transformation of the social structure' because these institutions are 'the means either of furthering, or of thwarting, the expression of human personality' (Cole, 1920b, p. 25).

The two key social institutions in need of transformation for Cole were liberal democracy and capitalism. For the former, the reduction of democracy to simply an irregular vote for a representative makes a travesty of the possibility of expressing will:

> States to-day, flagrantly violate the fundamental principles of democracy. The first is that the elector retains practically no control over his representative, has only the power to change him at very infrequent intervals, and has in fact only a very limited range of choice. The second is that the elector is

> called upon to choose one man to represent him in relation to every conceivable question that may come before Parliament, whereas, if he is a rational being, he always certainly agrees with one man about one thing and with another about another, or at any rate would do so as soon as the economic basis of present class divisions was removed. (Cole, 1920b, pp. 31–32)

There are then two key lessons to take from this for Cole, one is that the nature of the relationship between the elector and elected has to be an ongoing relationship in which the elector has the opportunity to influence their representative. The second returns us to Cole's concept of 'function', which, as we saw above, Cole uses to indicate that we can express our agency across multiple fields, including in our role as workers, as consumers, and in what he terms our 'civic' activity, such as religion and community organisation (Cole, 1920b). It therefore stands to reason for Cole that democracy should be 'functional democracy', in which we have a mechanism to express our democratic desires across multiple areas. This means a new notion of democracy:

> The essentials of democratic representation, positively stated, are, first, that the represented shall have free choice of, constant contact with, and considerable control over, his representative. The second is that he should be called upon, not to choose someone to represent him as a man or as a citizen in all the aspects of citizenship, but only to choose someone to represent his point of view in relation to some particular purpose or group of purposes, in other words, some particular *function*. All true and democratic representation is therefore *functional* representation...Brown, Jones and Robinson must therefore have, not one vote each, but as many different functional votes as there are different questions calling for associative action in which they are interested. (Cole, 1920b, pp. 32–33)

This is where Cole turns to the guilds. Initially developed as self-governing organisations for skilled workers in pre-modern times (see Black, 1984), Cole argues they should be revived, with each function having its own guild which would organise, legislate and co-ordinate the activity within that function. It would be democratically run and established at a sufficiently devolved level to allow for direct democratic control. These guilds are therefore Cole's attempt to socialise the means of production; private capital is removed from the economy and instead each area of production is a self-governing collective, with devolution down to the lowest possible level. For example, not only would car manufacturers have a guild, but it is likely guilds would be organised down to a factory level, with representatives then being sent 'upwards' to a national guild.

Significantly however, Cole's model did not limit this functional democracy to production, but also advocated the establishing of guilds for consumers, with co-operatives forming for domestic consumption and collective guilds for industrial consumption. These bodies would then express consumer desires to producer guilds. Here we have, in effect, a form of what has been termed 'negotiated coordination' (Devine, 1988) as production and consumption are managed by the democratic expression of will. This then replaces the market as the means for allocating goods. Meanwhile, guilds would be formed in our civic activity to organise, and allow for democratic expression, across these parts of our activity. For Cole, given that many of these services are often run by 'free communal devotion', it should be relatively easy to establish them (Cole, 1920b, p. 96).

This expansion of democracy via the guilds is, as we have seen, a way to shift the economy away from a capitalist approach. Cole stuck to the broader guild socialist creed that 'economic power precedes political power' (Cole, 1917, p. 19). This inequitable economic situation had two outcomes for Cole. Firstly, 'those who control the means of production are able, by means of that control, to dominate the State' (Cole, 1917, p. 5); reflecting a classic Marxist understanding, the class domination of the bourgeoisie is continued in the political sphere, with the state as their organisation of domination. For Cole (1914a, 1920a) political theory has often been complicit in this by assigning total sovereignty to the state without interrogating the social forces which it represents, a job for which sociology is much better suited. Secondly, class inequality comes to be seen purely as a question of economic distribution. While Cole was, as we shall see in the next section, intimately aware of, and concerned with, the uneven economic rewards that class produced, he argued class is significant beyond this, since it produced a further degradation of everyday life for the workers. As he put it: 'poverty is the symptom: slavery the disease…socialists have all too often fixed their eyes upon the material misery of the poor without realising that it rests upon the spiritual degradation of the slave' (Cole, 1917, p. 41). This notion of wage-labour as degrading was a significant part of Cole's guild socialist advocacy and reflects, as discussed in Chap. 1, a broader romantic notion of the individual whereby labour should be undertaken freely, with Morris' (1993) *News from*

Nowhere as the ultimate model. This can only be achieved by the ending of capitalism and its replacement with the democratic guild socialist system detailed here.

This system would then require a fundamental change in the form of the state, as it loses its claim to a position of ultimate authority and sovereignty. Instead, for Cole (1920b), the state assumes the form of a national 'commune', whose functions are reduced to co-ordination, demarcating boundaries, being a court of appeal and foreign affairs. While national parliaments would still exist these would be made up of representatives of different functions who have been democratically chosen to represent that function's interests in the limited discussion of national parliaments.

Therefore, Cole's model of guild socialism, which reflected broader ideas within the guild socialist movement of which Cole was the pre-eminent, though not only, theoretician (Taylor, 2002) included a drastic transformation of democratic control based around a conception of function which not only socialised the economy but ensured the further extension of functional democratic control. It was also a model for ensuring a decentralised socialised economy based on negotiated co-ordination at the lowest possible level. There was a political need for this for Cole; capitalism had created such significant class differences that alienation at work and stark differences in life had made any form of fellowship impossible which, for Cole, all socialist intellectuals must reckon with:

> Differences of wealth are always marring fellowship, and, within what we call a single 'community', differences of social class interfere with it even more...all these differences are formidable obstacles in the way of fellowship. Personally, I am most conscious of the obstacles that arise from social and economic inequality, because I am most often brought up against them. Though I may say, and really believe, that 'a man's a man for a' that', I cannot, in fact, get away from the obstacle that Society has made one a pundit and another a hewer of wood and a drawer of water, and has given to them different upbringing supposed to accord with their different stations in life. With some men I have community of culture, education, ways of speech and social behaviour; and with others I have not. Whatever my social views and ideals may be, that is a present fact from which there is no escape, and of which I cannot help taking account. (Cole, 1932b, p. 324)

Such divisions had to be overcome for Cole. This could only be achieved by removing capitalism and instigating the kind of democratic polity Cole imagined.

While guild socialism was undoubtedly driven by political commitment and, as Cole would note later in his *History of Socialist Thought* (Cole, 1958), a political context which included emerging trade union power and the influence of syndicalism, it was also shaped by an implicit engagement with sociology. For Cole 'every social system in part throws up, and is in part thrown up by, an equivalent social theory. Guildsmen, therefore, cannot afford to neglect social theories' (Cole, 1917, p. 13). Cole's Rousseauian-influenced sociology is the basis for the guild socialist system, where the focus becomes ensuring that people have the opportunity to become 'agents' and to collectively influence the structural forms of society, through the guilds and their extension of associative wills. Here we see the fulfilment of Cole's political individualism by connecting it to a critique of capitalism and liberal democracy which ensured a greater harmony between the associative and general wills or, in the language of sociology, ensured the harmony between the expression of agency and the collective precepts of structure.

A frequent criticism against any form of normative sociology is that sociology has no clear 'values' and therefore sociologists have to engage in a form of 'moral gerrymandering' to present their own personally political views as the views of 'sociology' (Hammersley, 1999). While there is truth in this claim, in Cole's case we can see a normative perspective which flows clearly from a sociological position. Of course, a potential response here is either (a) that is a *particular* sociological perspective and not one all sociologists would share and/or (b) even if we do accept this position the notion that the role of sociologists is to help agency is a further political choice. Both of these claims are undoubtedly true, however, it is also true to say that in the sense that Cole's perspective is an attempt to understand the relation of the individual and society, it reflects a question that most sociological perspectives will confront at some point, even if their answer is different. If the political commitment flowing from this is to make agency as effective for as many citizens as possible, it is quite a low political commitment, even if one which may be taken in different directions.

As we have seen in these two sections, Cole made a significant sociological contribution in developing an early attempt at a form of structuration theory and then linking this to a normative political project. The next section considers Cole's sociological contributions beyond this.

Other Sociological Contributions: A Textbook and the Sociology of Class

As discussed earlier, when Cole entered the academic world in the late 1910s, the teaching of sociology was expanding, both at the LSE and in its extramural form. As Scott (2014) noted, the growth in the teaching of sociology in the early twentieth century produced a need for textbooks, particularly ones which achieved some level of 'systematisation' of the discipline by presenting a clear image of what sociology stood for. As the century moved on, systematic statements which would be familiar to the modern reader began to appear in books entitled 'Sociology'. One of these texts, W.P.H. Sprott's (1949) contribution, was actually published in a book series for which Cole was the editor, Hutchinson's University Library, and made reference to his work (Sprott, 1949, p. 24). Before then, however, those teaching sociology drew on four textbooks, only two of which had 'sociology' in the title; Scott refers to these as the 'pioneers' of sociology textbooks in the UK. One of these four was Cole's *Social Theory* (1920a). This, initially, did not seem an obvious candidate for a sociology textbook. It was published in the same year as Cole's definitive political statement, *Guild Socialism Re-Stated* and shares much of that book's goal of seeking to justify Cole's political programme. However, it has the presentation of a textbook given its chapters with themes such as 'the principle of function', 'the state', 'the economic structure of society' and so on. It also referenced the work of the key figures considered 'sociologists' in Britain in the time, with discussion of Hobhouse (Cole, 1920a, p. 93), Geddes (Cole 1920a, p. 160) and Spencer (Cole 1920a, p. 180), though, unsurprisingly given the above, the most referenced writer was Rousseau (e.g. Cole, 1920a, pp. 19–21). The topics listed in the index would not also look a million miles away from what one would expect to see in a sociology textbook, with entries for themes such as 'capitalism', 'classes, economic', 'environment', 'family', 'individual', 'nation-state' and 'social content of action'.

Social Theory was therefore somewhat of a liminal text in the British conception of sociology. Its notion of sociology is fundamentally normative, of studying society in order to change it. In the conclusion, Cole often makes the claim that social theory is not simply an attempt to explain or even just critique society, but rather a theory of how society should be organised, in his case a theory based within the principles of his guild socialist sociology (Cole, 1920a, pp. 201–209). While the political angle of guild socialism was distinct here, the claim that one theorises about the world in order to then reorganise it reflects much of the nineteenth-century conception found in the 'gentlemanly' sociology discussed in Chap. 2, explaining the allure of positivism which, especially in the work of the late Comte, tried to do precisely this, as Cole notes elsewhere (Cole, 1948c). Completely lacking in this volume is any 'scientific' conception of sociology. Indeed, early in the text, mirroring a trend we shall see in the next chapter, Cole explicitly rejects any link of sociology and science (Cole, 1920a, p. 18) and uses the conclusion to make clear his work is based on political assumptions he personally sees as desirable. Therefore, while it would quickly be eclipsed in the textbook market by books which cleaved more closely to the notion of sociology as science, most notably from MacIver and Ginsberg, it was for a period an early reference point for the teaching of sociology (Scott, 2014). Indeed, Cole's WEA course on Social Theory used it as the key text alongside others such as MacIver's *Community*, Michels' *Political Parties* and, interestingly, Lenin's *State and Revolution*. Across the course Sidney Webb, Ginsberg, Hobhouse, Mary Follett[3] and Tawney also appear on the reading list (Cole, 1923).[4]

Here we can also identify a rare case of Cole's international standing as a sociologist, since Albion Small reviewed *Social Theory* in the *American Journal of Sociology*. It is a cutting, albeit witty, review, since Small reviews the text less for what it says, but more for tying Cole into the institutional politics of sociology at the time. This is how it opens:

> This is truly an exceptional book. It goes far toward vindicating the rash hope of a few super-sanguine American scholars that eventually Oxford, yea possibly Harvard, may discover what has been going on since the middle eighteen-seventies in the minds of American sociologists. The publishers inform us that false doctrine need no longer delude, for a prophet with a new truth has arisen at Oxford, and his book has already been adopted as a text at Harvard. We open the volume with reverence and fear. We wish to be devout in the presence of new truth, yet we tremble at the prospect of blinding revelation. What the effect may be upon Oxford or Harvard vision we

[3] Now largely forgotten in sociology, Mary Follett was an American graduate of Cambridge (and one-time invited lecturer at the LSE) who wrote largely on what would now be called organisational and management theory (see Tonn (2008) for a discussion of Follett's work).

[4] Cole's later collection *Essays in Social Theory* (1950a) is termed an 'auxiliary' text in Scott's argument, namely one meant to supplement the emerging 'mainstream' textbooks through more specialist conceptions of the discipline (Scott, 2014).

> are unable to state, but after the experiment of facing the demonstration we are in a position to assure normal readers that we have issued from the ordeal without insufferable enlightenment. (Small, 1920, p. 247)

The more substantial claims Small offers against the text are (1) that individuals are more than their relation to the state, only a small part of Cole's claim; (2) that many of its topics, such as community, have been discussed before and (3) that it makes too little use of the American literature. Whatever truth lies in these claims—as noted above, Cole's use of sources reflected *his* vision of sociology much more than a vision of sociology internationally—it is hard not to see Small's review as not at least, in part, a desire to assert the Chicago School of Sociology as pre-eminent in the US at a time when Harvard was beginning to develop its own sociological work. More of his review is devoted to this than to *Social Theory*. Retrospectively, we can see Small's review as an exercise in 'predecessor selection' (Camic, 1992) seeking to assert the prominence of American pragmatism against any European imports.

Thirty years later, Cole would produce another book which became a significant 'first' in British sociology. His *Studies in Class Structure* (Cole, 1955c) was published as part of Routledge's 'The International Library of Sociology and Social Reconstruction' series. Initially edited by Karl Mannheim this produced key sociological texts with a post-war focus on social reconstruction, reflecting Mannheim's own work (see Platt, J. (2014) for the series, Dawson (2016, pp. 89–97) for Mannheim and reconstruction). By the time Cole contributed to the series it was edited by W.P.H. Sprott who, as noted above, published his own sociology textbook in a series edited by Cole. Here, according to Abraham (1973, p. 626), is where Cole published one of the first sociological monographs on class in the UK.

As intimated above, class was a key concept in Cole's sociology but it would be fair to say that in his earliest writings it was largely untheorised, with a somewhat simplified Marxist approach in which workers are the working class and employers the bourgeoisie. This was then reflected in a politics, not uncommon to the Left at the time (see Sassoon, 2010) in which the working class will naturally vote for Socialist/Labour parties. Initially in his sociology, therefore, this dialectical notion of class was theorised as limiting the ability for the workers' will to be organised and recognised, whereas the bourgeoisie had socially sanctioned outlets for their will. Consequently, social institutions furthered the bourgeoisie's dominance while the working class did not have such functional outlets since, in their daily, economic functions, they were the subordinated group (Cole, 1913a). As Wright (1979) notes however, the 1930s led Cole to reconsider his conceptualisation of class. There were three factors driving this, one was the emergence of fascism with its own particular class base, the second was the failure of socialist movements in the UK while the third was a more empirical factor, the changing nature of the British middle class with an expansion in technical and managerial roles. As highlighted in the introduction to this chapter, Wright believed one of Cole's goals was to equip democratic socialism with a distinctive sociology. While I questioned the ordering Wright gave to this formulation I agree with him that Cole's sociology of class is one indication of how 'in academic terms, it was as a sociologist (rather than as economist or social philosopher) that Cole promised most' (Wright, 1979, p. 236, 232).

Studies in Class Structure, as the name indicates, is made up of a series of essays in which Cole assesses the changing class structure from the 1850s. Unsurprisingly, given its topic and context, its main interlocutor are Marxists and, in this discussion, Cole argues that Marxism too readily sees the national class structure as one, coherent system. Instead:

> I have described the present class structure of Great Britain as consisting of three separate systems, of which the second and third have been in turn superimposed on the first, in such a way as to leave all three still in existence, but with their relative importance greatly changed. These three are, first, an old structure based on relations to the land, and essentially aristocratic in character; secondly, a predominantly plutocratic structure based on the development of modern commerce and industry; and thirdly a much more diversified structure based on the growth of professional and administrative work, and closely affected by the wider diffusion and considerably differentiated development of the educational system. (Cole, 1955c, pp. 106–107)

In an echo of what Wright (1985) would later theorise as the contradictory class locations which emerge as remnants as feudalism, Cole sees multiple economic systems leaving the mark on the class structure. The first, aristocratic, system maintains some significance, most notably in the continued dominance of British public schools aimed at generating a 'cultured' elite seen as fit to rule. However, it is the changes in the second (plutocratic) and third (professional) systems which, both based more securely within capitalism, he sees as most significant. To fully understand

Cole's arguments here, he suggests we must engage with a question all later British sociology of class asked itself (see Savage, 2016): what do we mean by 'class'?

Cole is an advocate of what would later be termed the 'employer-aggregate' approach to class in the UK (Crompton, 2008), namely one of using occupation as a proxy for class. Cole suggests that there is no one perfect definition of class, but since in discussing it we are seeking to understand how individuals may be grouped around a certain distribution of resources (albeit while recognising those classes can themselves be internally differentiated) then occupation is the best option. However, Cole is different from later employer-aggregate approaches in the UK, perhaps most notably those advocated by John Goldthorpe and the Nuffield School (Goldthorpe, 1987), since (a) he does not seek to provide a 'map' of the class structure in the UK and/or measure rates of social mobility and (b) his notion of class is intersected by his own conception of function. While our class position may well match our 'function', in terms of the occupation of which we are part and therefore where we express our will, this is not ultimately a perfect fit, with the specificity of our function sometimes being twinned with a class position far from where we sit. For example, the function of medicine sits across different class positions depending on position, field, practice and so on. Therefore, Cole keeps a focus on the political ends of function alongside class (Cole, 1955c, pp. 1–3).

Cole then proceeds to map the changes for the three key classes in the UK over this period. For the elites, while public schools maintained a traditional aristocratic position, the rise of technical education and joint stock holding of companies helped redefine the elite as less aristocratic and instead dependent upon wealth and technological expertise. In turn, the growth of the labour movement produces its own elite as trade union leaders gain prestige and power, including via appointment to the House of Lords.[5] Much of this new elite came via a managerial position and perhaps held qualifications. This has led to a fundamental change in mainstream Labour politics where, as Cole laments:

[5] Cole was incredibly critical of any socialist who took a place in the Lords. For example: 'I used to have some respect for Mr. Attlee; but he forfeited it all when he became an Earl and a Knight of the Garter. How on earth could he wish to be degraded in these ways? I do not know the answer; but I am grieved and hurt, even more than I am angry, for he has brought discredit on the Socialist cause'. (Cole, 1956a, p. 29).

> the very advance of the Labour movement in power and prestige has gone a diminution of the evangelistic fervour which moved the pioneers. One hears frequent lamentations that the crusading spirit of the early Socialists and of the leaders of the 'New Unionism' of sixty years ago has been dying away since Socialism and Trade Unionism have become respectable. (Cole, 1955c, p. 128)

Therefore, the British elite has seemingly become more openly diverse, with different pathways to entrance beyond the aristocratic. Indeed, it seems even socialists can be part of the elite! However, Cole argues this can only be accommodated within the British political system since the Houses of Parliament are, in effect, made up of representatives of different elite groupings. This then produces a common 'governing class' who govern by consensus and with deference to the status quo. The elite may be more open than previously, but this does not, for Cole, change its political focus; it remains a 'respectable' governing class dedicated to continuing the status quo. A similar argument concerning the role of an elite class tying Labour to the status quo was later offered by Bauman (1972).

Somewhat differently from the elite, the middle class has undergone significant changes in both form and role for Cole. The expansion of managerial and technical jobs has expanded the number of workers in this group and, in turn, their political position. For Cole, whereas classical Marxist approaches had seen the middle class as a group in decline, for him they have been the key group in modifying capitalism as their support has enabled certain agendas to be put forwarded or frustrated. Most notable here is the welfare state:

> Certainly the development of the Welfare State in Great Britain has not, in raising the living standards of the worst-off, thrown down the professional and managerial groups into the ranks of the proletariat or ground down shopkeepers and farmers into the mass of the unprivileged. On the contrary, it has made large concessions to the claims of doctors, shopkeepers, farmers, and small business men, giving them both bigger incomes and greater security than they have ever before enjoyed. (Cole, 1955c, p. 98)

The middle class, likely if anything to grow for Cole, occupies an increasingly significant position not just numerically but also politically as it becomes the key group the warring elites seek to win over, as indicated by their significance where fascism has been successful (Cole, 1955c, p. 97).

When it comes to the working class, beyond the removal of the worse forms of poverty, Cole sees the labour movement as having had little impact. While the number of manual jobs are declining at the time Cole writes, they are still numerically large. Furthermore, the expansion of trade union membership, which for Cole emerges from the skilled workers in the guilds, beyond manual and to non-manual working-class jobs, maintains this group's coherence. This remains the case even if, as we have seen, it is likely the political elites from the labour movement will tend more and more towards the status quo.

Therefore, Cole sees a shifted class structure largely in its middle and top, with expanded middle class and elite groupings. While this expanded elite maintains a similar political positioning and significance, the middle class has become more significant politically and has swung behind both fascism and Labourism when they have suited their ends. The working class, bar the removal of the most extreme poverty and expanded union membership, remain largely in their subjected position in this structure. In many ways, Cole anticipates debates to come in the sociology of class most notably around the increase of the managerial class, how working-class identity may fall with the decline in manual production, the impact of post WWII social mobility and so on. Giddens' (1973) *The Class Structure of the Advanced Societies*, published 18 years later, touches on many similar themes for instance. Interestingly, Cole's book is not cited here. Indeed, sociology's ignorance of Cole's monograph began upon its publication. As Mills (2019) highlights, the first large scale survey of social class undertaken at the LSE, led by David Glass, ignored Cole's book, despite the fact Glass must have come across it.

In this section I have explored Cole's sociological contributions beyond his normative structuration-infused project for guild socialism. This included Cole's contribution of one of the first sociology textbooks in the UK and publication of one of the first monographs on the sociology of class in the country. As we have seen, both of these share common factors with his broader sociological project, around factors such as normativity, political individualism and the problems of capitalism. In the next chapter I will expand the discussion further to what Cole had to say about sociology as a discipline and sociologists, but before then, let us consider how the above impacted his conception of British sociology.

The Nuffield Social Reconstruction Survey and Cole's Conception of British Sociology

In the Cole archives there is a lecture entitled 'Politico-Economic Theories Part II' (Cole, 1952). At 172 pages long, this is effectively a small book which provides a history of social thought from the mid-nineteenth to the mid-twentieth centuries. This includes a whole section on sociology. Here Cole argues that from its formation sociology had been split into two currents, divided by a disagreement concerning method. One trend, which takes its lead from Comte and Saint-Simon, is grounded in a concept of social evolutionism which maps the transformation of societies over time. This tradition is 'semi-philosophical, dominated by the idea of evolutionary progress of mankind and at the same time strongly hostile to metaphysical rationalism' (Cole, 1952, p. 123). This perspective encompassed most Marxist approaches, Weber's work and the emerging British tradition represented by Hobhouse, Ginsberg and the LSE. The second tradition, which for Cole took inspiration from Durkheim, could be found more frequently in cultural anthropology, where the focus is on a 'direct study of "social facts" (Durkheim's phrase) of the character of social institutions and social behaviour'. This approach was united in seeking a 'scientific method' for cross-cultural analysis and was centred 'not on the State or government as such, and not on economic conditions as such, but the whole "pattern of culture"' (Cole, 1952, p. 123).

This depiction of sociology and social anthropology in the British context was largely correct at an institutional level, with the evolutionary focus of the Sociology Department at the LSE facing off with those scholars in the Anthropology Department who had provided a British home for Durkheimian approaches (Kuper, 2015; Smith, 2020). It was, however, not a split which provided a home for Cole. The lack of appeal of the anthropological approach, from a writer so focused on the state, politics and economic was clear, but this also indicated a broader ambivalence on Cole's part towards empirical work.

It would not be accurate to say that Cole was against empirical, or even what we might term 'applied' sociology. Indeed, the opposite can be seen in his headship of the Nuffield Reconstruction Survey. Established in 1941, this was one of many government sanctioned efforts aimed at 'reconstruction' after the war. Benignly tolerated, or in some cases ignored, by the Tories, they were central to securing Labour's participation in the wartime coalition. While, as Margaret Cole later detailed (Cole, 1971, pp. 235–252), the survey had a complex beginning reflecting its being funded by an endowment to establish Nuffield College which had then been delayed by the war, the content of the survey fit within this broader reconstruction trend. Indeed, early on it had a huge scope, running across industrial demands, the impacts of evacuation, voluntary organisations and ways of living, among others (see Cole, 1971, p. 240). Given the focus of the survey was, in Cole's own telling, the collection of 'social facts' (Cole, 1946), it had an undoubtedly sociological basis, seeking to understand how the impacts of war had changed customs and expectations of people across different social groups. A good example here was one particular part of the survey which sought the views of working-class people on their desires for any future welfare state and what form of social security best fit their lives (Harris, 1983).

Very quickly however, the survey demonstrated a clash between competing visions of sociology. Cole had decided that the survey should not be overly expensive since, in Margaret's words:

> Douglas maintained for many years – indeed, until the end of his life – that social-research projects tended to be run on extravagantly wasteful lines; for this he blamed German and American sociologists who demanded an immense quantity of apparatus (and of ancillary workers) to be used in their enquiries, and the foundations, particularly big American foundations, which having vast sums at their disposal could not believe that any enquiry was worthy of their support unless it presented a budget of costs comparable with their own. (Cole, 1971, p. 239)

Therefore, to achieve such large-scale work cheaply, Cole relied upon a collection of middle-class volunteers reflecting the 'Victorian tradition of volunteer service performed by enlightened members of the privileged classes' (Carpenter, 1973, p. 199) which, as discussed in Chap. 2, was a mark of the earliest social surveys of Booth and Rowntree. Whatever the virtues of this approach, it did not fit the circumstances of 1940s Britain or the more sophisticated methodological demands of sociology and, perhaps unsurprisingly, led to a number of methodological faults. For example, the aforementioned survey on workers' desires for the welfare state produced a huge disparity of research strategies. Some surveyors did what would now be seen as semi-structured interviews with workers, including analysed transcripts. Others interviewed workers but provided more impressionistic reports on their views. Meanwhile a third group did not talk to workers at all, but instead relied on middle-class intermediaries such as social workers to report on what they believed workers wanted or, perhaps more commonly, should want (Harris, 1983). Therefore, while the survey did produce some interesting data, for example on how workers were at this point not enthused by the notion of a welfare state, its methodological flaws reflected the earlier survey movement which, while Britain's most significant sociological import (Rocquin, 2019), was being usurped by new modes of investigation.

While these methodological flaws were notable, they were not the key reason for the Nuffield Reconstruction Survey closing earlier than expected; after all, forms of 'gentlemanly' social research continued well into the 1950s (Savage, 2010). Instead, it was brought down by political considerations, namely, concerns about Cole being such a vociferous socialist who was critical of government (including, perhaps fatally for Cole, Labour governments). Despite Cole's many attempts, including one published in the *American Journal of Sociology* (Cole, 1946), to defend the objectivity of the survey's findings, there was some truth to the critics' claims here. Cole did indeed see empirical research as subservient to the broader goal of his sociology as a normative endeavour focused on how to create the good society. As he put it in his paper delivered to the BSA which I will discuss further in the next chapter:

> This does not mean that I reject, or seek to minimize, the importance of studying as impartially as possible all the relevant 'social facts' on the presence of which any effective action for change must needs rest to a very great extent. I am well aware that one must know the actual in order to know how best to change that in it which needs changing. But I am quite unable to see how there can be any derivation of values from facts alone, or from actual values regarded simply as facts...In short, I am not a 'social scientist', but a social idealist who tries to make use of the factual verdicts of scientific investigators, but not to be ruled by them, except in excluding the impracticable from my field of aspiration. (Cole, 1957a, pp. 167–168)

Therefore, as I will explore further in the next chapter, Cole always sought a normative and political outcome for the use of empirical analysis. This certainly fits the earlier period of British sociology and is in chime with some debates which begin following the years of his death, but it left him outside of the Durkheim-influenced school of cultural anthropology.

It also, of course, meant that he was not in chime with the dominant form of sociology being practised at the LSE. While, as Cole notes, the largely philosophical nature of such sociology meant disagreements about research methods were less marked, this school maintained a scientific focus and thus the split around politics remains. Cole's antipathy to this approach was pronounced and suggested in a book review of Ginsberg's *The Idea of Progress: A Revaluation* (1953). Cole's (1953a) review of this text, published in what was at that point the house journal of the BSA, *The British Journal of Sociology*, is remarkable in what it does not do. Over the course of 19 pages, Ginsberg and his text are discussed on the first page, then barely mentioned thereafter. Instead, the 'review' is a discussion of the value of the concept of progress in social thought. Here, Cole sees some notion of 'progress' as a central element of much sociology but one he does not accept. The reason for this returns us to the question of moral versus knowledge judgements. For Cole, to say a society 'progresses' is to claim that it is becoming 'better', with some idea that the 'good society' sits at the end of the path of progress. This rests upon a somewhat unspoken assumption shaping the notion of sociology of scientific: much as in the natural science, an increase of knowledge brings an increase in human capability and therefore, much as the natural sciences progressing allows us to further control and adapt our environment, social scientific progress allows us to improve our social environment. But, while our knowledge of the world may progress, this knowledge does not, for Cole, equal moral improvement since 'factual knowledge about human nature may help those who believe in the goodness of justice, or of equality, or of both, to devise better methods of furthering their beliefs. It cannot furnish any ground for the beliefs themselves' (Cole, 1953a, p. 281). Indeed, such knowledge should make us wary of teleological claims since 'there is in human history as a whole no evidence at all of a continuous tendency towards greater fairness, or justice, or towards equality' (Cole, 1953a, p. 281). Therefore, a sociological approach which makes use of teleological claims will, for Cole, ultimately fail in its own attempt at progress since we cannot collapse their increased 'knowledge' to meaning increased 'good'.

This is not to say for Cole that sociology has no role in such discussions. During the review he cites T.H. Marshall's (1992) *Citizenship and Social Class*, which he had previously reviewed (Cole, 1951a) and taught on (Cole, n.d.-g). Here Cole argues that Marshall's discussion of the development of citizenship rights from civil to political to social clearly shows an example of 'progress'. However, we can also recognise, reflecting later commentators on Marshall (Giddens, 1982) that such progress was not benignly given as a result of increased knowledge, but won politically (Cole, 1953a). Therefore, Cole ends his review of Ginsberg's text with a claim very much befitting his sociology:

> We must base our hopes, not on a progress that is to be achieved for us by the inexorable movement of historical law, but on ourselves and our children and our children's children, who will make the world better or worse according to the goodwill, the courage, and the skill with which they face the tasks of the present and the future. In place of the belief in a progress guaranteed by the order of nature we need to put a faith in our collective power to make the good prevail, if we try hard enough-but not otherwise. (Cole, 1953a, pp. 284–285)

Therefore, Cole confronted two forms of sociology which either in their empiricist concern with culture against politics or in their idealist attachment to ideas of progress did not fit his notion of the discipline.

It would not be correct to say Cole was completely alienated from sociology; as the above indicates, he was an active participant to debates in the discipline and had a clear sociological perspective. But, it would be correct to say he found the particular form of sociology as practised in the UK to be alienating and contrary to his plans. As we have seen above, this led him in some problematic directions, for example embracing forms of 'gentlemanly' methodological practice which, while not unknown in the period, were coming to be questioned. But, it also led him down paths which would prove more fruitful, such as a questioning of emerging notions of progress and rethinking the connections of facts and values. This leads us however to one more area we need to consider, how Cole discussed the questions of gender, race and empire.

Interrogating Cole: Gender, Race and Empire

It is essential, given the contributions of both the feminist and decolonial critique that, when returning to a writer such as Cole, we engage in what Witz and Marshall (2004) term a 'politics of interrogation' wherein blindspots, biases and absences are highlighted. It could be suggested this is especially the case for Cole as a white, middle class, man who has been called a 'Little Englander' (Wright, 1979). Therefore, that is exactly what this section will do and, following the lessons of the feminist and decolonial critique, interrogate Cole on the three issues of gender, race and empire. As we shall see, it is a mixed bag.

Gender

Following the notion that the personal is political, there is no better place to start here than the account of Cole's wife, Margaret, who distinguished between a 'bark' and 'bite' when it came to Cole's attitude to women. The 'bark' was, as she put it, a general kind of sexism based in the idea that 'the mass of women were not good socialist material' and that 'no woman (except Jane Austen) had ever achieved first-class honours in arts and literature' (Cole, 1971, p. 92). While not, of course, suggesting any link between sexuality and misogyny, this reflects a broader trend about Cole, noted by others, that he always preferred the company of men (see Martin, 1959; Gaitskell, 1960) which, as Margaret details (Cole 1971, pp. 92–93), led to claims of homosexuality, closeted or not. Indeed, there have been attempts to place Cole in the history of queer politicians (Bloch, 2015) or writers (Evans, 2017). Despite this, his wife Margaret's view that Cole, despite his close friendships with men which could be described as loving, was largely asexual seems the most convincing claim on the matter (Cole, 1971, pp. 92–93, see also Cook, 2005, pp. 174–175).

This 'bark' of Cole's sexism was, for Margaret, largely insignificant; she dismisses it as 'undergraduate-like remarks' (Cole, 1971, p. 92) and suggests that his 'bite'—i.e. how he actually related to and treated women—was very different. She details the equality and respect with which he treated the women he worked with during his career and, indeed, women with whom he worked spoke positively of Cole, such as Beatrice Webb (despite their differences) and Barbara Wootton (Cole, 1971; Oakley, 2011). Indeed, while many intellectuals have historically relied on the uncredited labour of wives, beyond a note to thank them for the typing if they were lucky (Dresvina, 2021), Cole would always credit his wife in their co-publications. One could argue this reflects a particular type of 'gentlemanly' misogyny in which women who have 'proven themselves' are accepted as equals, but others are considered lower. This may be true, but Margaret's comments are worth noting.

How, then, did these personal views impact his intellectual work? Returning to Witz and Marshall (2004), they argue a feminist critique should pay attention to the 'strategic absences' in sociological thought. It is not the case for most male classical thinkers that women are absent, rather they only appear when they are considered exceptions to the male 'norm'. We can certainly find evidence of this in Cole's work. For example, in his discussion of the associative will discussed above, he makes a distinction that 'association' is strongest among men, but 'custom' is strongest among women (Cole, 1920a, p. 5). Here we can see a claim which reflects broader claims of women being closer to nature, with men part of the 'civilised' modern world (Sydie, 1987), a theorisation Cole shares with one of his main sociological interlocutors, Durkheim (Cristi, 2012). This in turn reflects a broader trend of Cole's sociology whereby his focus is excessively on the masculine world (the masculine pronoun is the only pronoun he uses, though he does at some points speak of 'men and women' collectively). His wife Margaret traces that to the fact that from guild socialism onwards Cole had a focus on the public and productive sphere, without any focus on the private sphere underpinning it, a key focus of the feminist critique developing as Cole wrote (Cole, 1971). Indeed, Cole is quite specific on this. In an essay entitled 'The Essentials of Democracy' he comments on the difficulties of 'bringing the ordinary housewife right into politics without interfering with her duties as housewife and mother' (Cole, 1950d, p. 109). There is a clear presumed sexist division of labour here.

Yet, you can also find some evidence of more enlightened views in Cole's writings. For example, in *The Meaning of Marxism*, published two years prior to the above essay, he makes the somewhat revolutionary claim that 'housewives' should be represented in trade unions since they are part of the proletariat and therefore should be part of the socialist movement (Cole, 1948d, pp. 178–179). This echoes later claims of the 'wages for housework' campaign that having housework paid highlights its status as 'work' and brings women previously excluded into the fight for socialism (Dalla Costa & James, 1971). Later, Cole also speaks of the significance of the increased entry of women into the labour market as a transformative factor in the class structure and speaks positively of the women's rights movements that brought this into being (Cole, 1955c, p. 60, 114). It is also worth noting that among his survey of the 'forerunners' of socialist theory, Cole gives a chapter to Flora Tristan and highlighted the significance of her argument for socialism as the combination of emancipation for women and the working class and credits her as the first person to develop a plan for an all-inclusive proletarian International (Cole, 1953b, pp. 183–188).

How do we reconcile these different relations to women and, via that, to gender in Cole's work? I would suggest, in many ways, Cole reflects the views of his great idol, William Morris and his form of 'Victorian Socialist Feminism' (Boos & Boos, 1990). This, reflecting the politics of socialism, was willing to accept the emancipation and political participation of women as long as it did not upset the fundamental division of labour, nor challenge the notion of separate spheres of activity in which men and women should be 'naturally' found. This can explain why Cole can both simultaneously welcome women into the trade union movement as housewives, but also—and here he would be fundamentally opposed to wages for housewives—not undercut their position *as housewives*. It would also explain why Cole, despite his careful attention to the ways women had entered the labour market, never considered, in the way later feminist writers would, how the labour market is a product of patriarchal expectations (Crompton, 1989).

Therefore, it is accurate to say that Cole had a sociology that did not fully account for or theorise gender. While he was open to including the experiences of women in his sociology and certainly politically agreed with campaigns for female political emancipation, this was always conditional on the notion that it not upset the fundamental order of modern patriarchy. In this sense women and gender remain a 'strategic' absence in Cole's sociology.

Race

Whereas, with gender, we are dealing with a 'strategic' absence in Cole's work, when it comes to race, it is largely just an absence. We can find scattered across Cole's work some passing references to race. For example, he cites lynching in the US as one exception to the notion that coercion tends to sit with the state in modernity (Cole, 1920a, p. 130). Also, he mentions, and dismisses, racial theory in one sentence in *The Meaning of Marxism* (Cole, 1948d, p. 78) and similarly briefly notes, though does not discuss the implications of, the divisions within race by class (Cole, 1955c, p. 21). Beyond this, however, it is difficult to find any discussion Cole offered of race distinct from empire.

Why this silence? A major reason concerns the next factor in our discussion. Cole did write extensively on empire and therefore largely considered questions of race to be confined to 'elsewhere'. However, it is worth noting that while Cole did not fully attempt to include race in his work, others have. Masquelier, in his advocacy of 'intersectional socialism' argues that Cole's libertarian socialism, most notably in its advocacy of functional democracy, can 'be regarded as a necessary (political) corollary of self-managed organizations and a principle of political life essential for giving political expression to the ontological relationality and plurality embodied in pluriversal intersectionality' (Masquelier, 2023, p. 34). With its emphasis on self-organisation and the realisation of 'radical interdependence' whereby each individual is dependent upon, and invested in, the freedom of others, Masquelier sees clear overlaps between theories developed from black radical social thought, along with decoloniality and queer theory, and the work of Cole. Therefore, this reminds us that the legacy of a writer can go beyond their remit and, indeed, we can fill in the silences they left hanging in the air.

Imperialism

Connell's statement that sociology was 'formed within the culture of imperialism' (Connell, 2007, p. 9) is undoubtedly true when referring to British sociology. However, there can at points too readily be an exercise in what Go (2016) has termed geographic essentialism, in short, assuming that since British sociologists were located within the imperial core, they supported, or at least benignly accepted, imperialism. This is not the case, with empire playing a significant, albeit contradictory role in British sociology during the first half of the twentieth century (Steinmetz, 2014). Indeed, both tendencies were played out in the LSE. When sociology was first taught at the school it was advertised as appealing, among others to 'Civil Servants destined for the more tropical portions of the Empire, and Missionaires' (Husbands, 2019, p. 13), reflecting the broader notion of the School as producing an 'enlightened', but not radical, mild mannered civil servant (see Dahrendorf, 1995). Such an orientation can be seen in the earliest teaching content at the LSE which, drawing in staff from anthropology, often had a focus on 'primitive' or 'simple' peoples and the ethnology thereof (Husbands, 2019, pp. 44–54). This, in turn, reflected some sociologists' activities and views around empire, with Geddes for example happily serving the imperial government in India (see Scott & Bromley, 2013, pp. 118–120). Indeed, Steinmetz identifies the British sociological field in 1949 of consisting of 38 people (identified primarily as working in sociology departments or undertaking funded PhD projects; therefore, Cole is excluded here). Of these 38 'a third of sociologists were doing colonial research, and more than half participated directly in the colonial Empire' (Steinmetz, 2014, p. 313). These figures are comparable with another case study of Steinmetz's, France (Steinmetz, 2023).

Yet, as Steinmetz also notes in both the UK and France, not all of those scholars should be considered imperial sociologists, since many were critical of the endeavour. A prominent earlier example is Hobhouse, who had critiqued imperialism going back to his times as a journalist (Collini, 1979, pp. 81–90, 176–179). Significantly, this included a critique of notions of biological racial superiority which, while meaning he was open to notions of a commonwealth of nations, meant he could not support imperialism and developed his own form of liberalism in argument against it (Tan, 2024). Indeed, reflecting the language of his interlocutor W.E.B. Du Bois, Hobhouse engaged in a critique of the 'colour-line', condemning it as the 'last ditch of group humanity' (Hobhouse, 1906, p. 316; Tan, 2024). Therefore, as with Hobhouse, the 'colonial sociology' of Britain in this period could just as easily be critical rather than celebratory.

Cole belonged to this critical tradition and his critique had four elements. The first, a form of imperialism sometimes occluded in contemporary discussions on decoloniality, concerned Ireland. Cole notes that the development of guild socialism occurred 'side by side' with Irish republicanism and 'in part association' with it (Cole, 1956c, pp. 242–243). This then fed into his theorisation of guild socialism where he cites Ireland as an example where domination by an external power limits the forms of associative activity (Cole, 1920a, p. 28) and his political work where, at the height of the Dublin lockout of 1916, he invited James Larkin to come to Oxford and address a mass meeting (Cole, 1971, p. 71). Cole even addressed one of his poems (see Chap. 5 for more on these) entitled St. Patrick's Day (1921) to the cause of Irish republicanism (Cole & Cole, 1921, pp. 21–23). Cole goes as far at one point as saying that the 'conservativism' which had set into British trade unionism had not yet befallen its Irish counterpart and therefore its radicalism should be easier to pursue (Cole, 1922). Here Cole shared some similarity with Marx who saw the situation of the Irish workers, as a struggle against capitalist imperialism, as a potential spur to further revolution in Britain (see Anderson, 2016, pp. 115–153; Cole, 1956a, p. 34). Cole however differed from much of the British labour movement which had either supported the movement only reluctantly or, in most cases, not at all (Bell, 2016). Indeed, I would suggest Ireland, and British imperialism therein, remains a blind spot in British sociology, including its decolonial forms.

The second element concerns Cole's writings on imperialism beyond Ireland. Writing in his late pamphlet *World Socialism Restated* Cole acknowledges that early in his career his focus had been too limited to what he, reflecting the language of his time, calls the 'more advanced' countries. However, movements for national liberation and decolonisation had forced him, as they had many other socialists, to confront these lacunae in his outlook and, consequently:

> today it has become the plain duty of Socialists in all countries to take their stand energetically on the side of popular nationalism in the colonial and semi-colonial countries and to give full support to the claims of the exploited peoples to self-determination and to the control of their own development, in sharp opposition to all attempts to maintain imperialist rule or to insist on the preferential claims of white settlers or capitalist investors. This involves recognising to the full the human equality of all peoples, to the exclusion of every form of racial discrimination. (Cole, 1956a, p. 9)

Here we see how, in line with the discussion above, while Cole did not fully capture the role of race 'at home', he linked the battle against imperialism to race. It is in this context that Cole explicitly rejects biological racism and, using the case of South Africa, notes that the strength of such biological racism is so strong that capitalist nations can implement policies contrary to the long-term interests of capital—as in apartheid which, leaving aside its moral reprehensible-ness, harmed the consumer base (Cole, 1955e). Given his political focus, Cole sees this as an especial duty on behalf of socialists in the West to not only actively oppose imperialism but to assist popular nationalist and socialist movements in the countries fighting for liberation (Cole, 1956a, p. 35). He argued that while many of the British Left were, in principle, willing to accept this claim, their support evaporated when those fighting for liberation made what they considered the 'wrong' choice, such as not wanting to join the Commonwealth or seeking to implement communism. For Cole, this simply sought to continue the colonial relationship and needed to be rejected (Cole, 1956a, p. 37).[6] Cole was particularly interested in India here and notes that under colonialism the Indian government has been forced to spend heavily on

[6] Cole held to this view in his candidacy for Labour MP for Oxford University in 1945, with his election address noting while personally he wished that after independence India would join the Commonwealth, this was for India to decide and that he would support independence either way (Cole, 1945b, pp. 70–71).

the (British) military and foreign (often British) 'debts'. He argues any socialist government should seek to forgive those debts and repay any military spending as a matter of urgency (Cole, 1932c).

It is one thing to politically support the end of imperialism but is another to theorise empire as part of one's sociology. This is the third element of Cole's critique of imperialism and occurs most notably across two of Cole's *New Statesman* articles published in 1935 entitled 'The Problem of Colonial Empire' parts I and II. Cole is unequivocal here in saying that 'imperialism itself is evil' (Cole, 1935e, p. 550) and sees its continuation as fundamentally a question of economics, with a veneer of claims from the colonising powers to being more 'advanced'. This economic drive for imperialism had three factors for Cole. Firstly, it becomes linked with prestige since, as Cole puts it, 'the colour on the map is the means used in every country to teach children the notion of national greatness' (Cole, 1935d, p. 472). To be a great economy, and country, is to have an empire which, for Cole, was a statement of fact. Secondly, linked to this, ownership of an empire gave the imperial power their own free trade area, where a wide variety of resources and goods could be traded, or simply taken, without any concern for tariffs and taxation. This gave such powers a huge economic advantage and indicated why after WWI the victors were so eager to claim former colonies from the vanquished; in Cole's words 'the other thieves went off with the spoil' (Cole, 1935d, p. 473). Thirdly, empires provided extensive resources, both in terms of goods and personnel to be used in times of war. This is an economic consideration for Cole since wars often occurred as a desire to gain these territories, as the outcome of WWI indicated. This economic justification for empire means that after WWII Cole identified the US as an imperial power since their lack of territorial annexation was irrelevant in light of their economic power (Cole, 1956a, p. 36).

To this point, Cole's theorisation of imperialism is unremarkable and could sit quite nicely within dominant Marxist notions. However, Cole rejects both the notion that imperialism generated no advantage for the working class of the colonising power *and* that the improvements in lifestyle in the West were the product of imperialism. To make this claim, Cole acknowledges that the increased wealth in an imperial power such as Britain is the result of the resources and labour of multiple countries, but the increased share of this that has gone to the working class is the result of the successes of the British labour movement (Cole, 1956a, p. 16). It could, of course, be fairly argued in response to this that perhaps the labour movement should have been more ready to condemn imperialism rather than fight for a greater share of its spoils, perhaps reflecting a historical willingness, at some points, to indulge racism and imperialism rather than class solidarity (Virdee, 2014). As indicated above, Cole does condemn the willingness of socialists to oppose imperialism only rhetorically though not through acts, most notably in relation to Ireland and India (Cole, 1956a, p. 34).

This brings us to the fourth element of Cole's engagement with imperialism. A key element of the decolonial critique has included raising awareness of what Meghji (2021) calls 'intellectual imperialism' and Go (2016) terms 'analytic bifurcation'; in short, the belief that 'theory' occurs in the West and can speak about the conditions elsewhere, while 'the rest' produces no theory of its own. Cole, despite his schooling in the European tradition, was a clear exception to this. Most notably, Cole advocated an awareness of not just the political activities of Mahatma Ghandi but discussed him as a social theorist. For example, Cole reviews Gandhi's *Hind Swaraj* ('Indian Home Rule') and treats it not just as a political manifesto but as a social theory of both India and the West, speaking of how 'Gandhi's case against the West looks infinitely stronger' than much of Western social theory (Cole, 1938, p. 3). He concludes by advocating it as a book which made one both think and feel (Cole, 1938, p. 8). Furthermore, Cole's *History of Socialist Thought* contains chapters on societies from the Global South. Among the writers discussed here are Victor Raoul Haya de la Torre, a Peruvian writer who developed a 'specifically Latin American conception of socialism' (Cole, 1961a, p. 761), Sun Yat-Sen, a Chinese writer who theorised a form of socialism 'to suit the Chinese conditions and to develop rather than destroy the traditional way of life' (Cole, 1961a, p. 776) prior to the rise of Mao and M.N. Roy, the 'outstanding leader of Indian communism' (Cole, 1961a, p. 811). Meanwhile his final volume of the history, which discussed the years prior to WWII was likely to expand this cast of characters but was left incomplete due to Cole's death (Cole, 1961b). The history is not perfect, and developments beyond the West are not considered prior to 1914, but given the volume's production in the twilight of empire and from a writer raised during its pinnacle and otherwise regarded as a 'Little Englander', this scope is noticeable.

What are we to take from this interrogation of Cole's thought along the lines that now become so important post the feminist and decolonial critique? I would argue, like most social theorists (given they are all human), Cole was imperfect. When it comes to imperialism (both political and intellectual) he was markedly advanced for his period. However, when it comes to race (detached from imperialism) and gender, the picture is a lot more mixed. Again, much like many other writers, Cole's omissions neither condemn his work outright, nor do his insights absolve these omissions. Instead, it is important to engage in this interrogation to place Cole's work and recognise its scope. In this sense, despite his semi-alienation from it he reflected much of British sociology at the time (Steinmetz, 2014).

Conclusion

This chapter has summarised Cole's sociology. I began here with the basis of his sociological project which, inspired by Rousseau, developed a form of political individualism which outlined an early form of structuration theory. Here Cole saw individuals an innately engaged in associations which, in developing agency by a collective expression of the associative will, fed into the construction of social institutions and collective moral ideals in the general will. In turn, this general will then had some coercive function, encouraging individuals to reproduce these common ideals. From here I outlined how this notion produces Cole's normative vision for guild socialism. Cole's critical sociology started from the premise that the proper functioning of the social system, outlined in his sociology, was not being achieved due to the perversion of liberal democracy and capitalism, which in turn produced the problems of class, and therefore a new system of functional democracy in a democratically socialised economy had to be achieved. I then discussed Cole's other sociological contributions, focusing on his writing of one of the first sociology textbooks and perhaps the first sociological monograph on class in the UK. Both of these texts reflected Cole's broader sociology with their focus on a normative conception of the discipline and the relation of class and function. We then saw how Cole related to what he saw as the two dominant forms of British sociology at the time. While undertaking empirical work via the Nuffield Social Reconstruction Survey, he rejected many of the key principles of what he saw as the Durkheimian-influenced school of cultural anthropology. Meanwhile, a benign view of progress made the emerging tradition of sociology at the LSE unappealing, despite Cole's increased engagement with it and recognition of its significance. Finally, reflecting the importance of the feminist and decolonial critiques to sociology, I engaged in an interrogation of Cole on the points of gender, race and empire. This was a somewhat mixed picture, with Cole's record on gender and race being largely defined by absence (either literal or 'strategic') but empire being a key concept in much of his work. In this ambivalence I suggested that Cole reflected much of British sociology at the time.

Taken together, this chapter has shown what I call Cole's semi-alienation from the sociology he confronted. Despite the value he saw in sociology, this was not being followed in the evolutionary attempt at 'scientific' laws, while also being unempirical, taking place at the LSE. This, with its theory divorced from empirical matters and desire for political neutrality was complete anathema to Cole's approach to the subject. Instead, Cole finds more ready contemporaries in an earlier period. His leading of the Nuffield Reconstruction Survey indicates a continuation, in his own view (Cole, 1946) with earlier attempts at large-scale surveys in Britain of the Booth and Rowntree type. Furthermore, his desire to see sociological endeavour as focused on visions of the good life and his desire to use sociological findings to further such visions finds chimes in earlier sociological visions. This is true not just of the debates in political economy of the nineteenth century, but also in the 'failed' sociological projects of Geddes and Wells. While Cole would have disagreed with much of what these writers said—Wells' focus on utopian visions would have alienated a man always driven by confronting what was and Geddes' environmental focus would have left him cold—he would have instinctively shared their view on the overall goal of sociology. Wells' (1906, pp. 366–367) claim that 'There is no such thing in sociology as dispassionately considering what *is*, without considering what is *intended to be*' chimes with Cole's (1957a, p. 171) claim that 'Sociology and social policy are intimately bound together at a thousand points; and it is well for humanity that this is so; for man, in order to live well, needs knowledge of good and evil as well as of the factually true and false'. While Cole sought to make a number of contributions to sociology as it was developing in Britain, his position outside the institutionalised core meant these were unlikely to take hold.

Therefore, Cole was born too late to encounter a sociology more congenial to his views and instead encountered one seeking the legitimacy of science. However, we can also suggest that he was born too early. Following these battles of institutionalisation, the notion of sociology driven by normative and political concerns, and one which theorises imperialism, comes to be much more accepted. In the next chapter, where I will discuss Cole's writings on the discipline, the canon and teaching, I will also argue he anticipates a number of debates on what sociology is for.

CHAPTER 4

Cole's Writings on Sociology, Normativity, the Canon and Teaching

In a letter dated 13 December 1956 Cole was invited, following a phone call the previous day, to address the 1957 BSA annual conference. The letter was written by the sociologist Ronald Fletcher, at that point teaching at Bedford College, later the first Professor of Sociology at York in 1964 (Scott, 2020, p. 27) and now perhaps best remembered for his history of the discipline, *The Making of Sociology* (Fletcher, 1971). In his letter, Fletcher (1956) notes that in their phone call Cole had suggested that he 'may not be a sociologist "officially"' but that, nevertheless 'most of us regard you as such'. He explained that the conference was seeking to broaden the scope of what, as outlined in Chap. 2, was an increasingly confident British sociology in the late 1950s. Fletcher notes they had already secured Robert Merton for the opening talk and wanted, in Cole, to have a speaker 'of similar status and international repute to bring the proceedings to a conclusion'. Cole was asked to speak on the relation of sociology and social policy, seeming to imply a broad definition of how sociology could relate to the normative. In his reply, Cole notes that his ill health makes it unlikely he could attend anything beyond his paper but agrees to speak. There then follows an exchange of letters on topics every academic will recognise—other speakers on the panel, the length of Cole's talk, an invite to lunch beforehand and so on. In this exchange, Fletcher

M. Dawson, *G.D.H. Cole and British Sociology*,
https://doi.org/10.1007/978-3-031-75484-5_4

notes the keynote papers will be published in the *British Journal of Sociology*, as Cole's paper, entitled simply 'Sociology and Social Policy', was (Cole, 1957a). Here Cole suggests:

> Because I hold strong subjective views on these and other social questions, and have always taken part and interest in social investigation primarily for the purpose of furthering causes in which I believe, I have always rejected the appellation of 'social scientist' and have been reluctant to accept that of 'sociologist' for fear of being expected to restrict my conclusions to what can be inductively demonstrated on the basis of purely factual studies. This does not mean that I reject, or seek to minimize, the importance of studying as impartially as possible all the relevant 'social facts' on the presence of which any effective action for change must needs rest to a very great extent. I want certain things because I believe them to be worth wanting, not because they are actually wanted. (Cole, 1957a, p. 167)

Following the conference there is a further exchange of letters between Cole and Fletcher. Fletcher's (1957a) handwritten letter notes how much he enjoyed the paper and thanks Cole for giving it. He then comments on how there appeared to be misunderstandings and disagreements in response to Cole's paper. But he agrees with Cole that sociologists should be forced to confront their 'naïve' attitudes towards normative questions. Cole responds to thank Fletcher and notes that he 'was a little disappointed that both the main speakers so completely misunderstood what I had said' but that 'one must accept that when the question of the relation between fact and value comes under discussion' (Cole, 1957b).

I have opened with this exchange between Cole and Fletcher since, in many ways, it is a microcosm of Cole's relationship to, and conception of, sociology. He is involved in sociology and while we can perhaps see Fletcher's comments on his standing being akin to Merton as the kind of overly generous comment one may offer to secure a speaker, given the breadth of his contributions at the time, it's not totally inaccurate. Indeed, as Chichele Professor of Social and Political Theory at a time when there are only a handful of professors of sociology in the country, he has one of the most significant institutional positions. It is perhaps a Freudian slip that in his write-up of the conference Fletcher lists Cole as 'Chichele Professor of *Sociology* and Political Theory' (Fletcher, 1957b, p. 96). Yet, he is outside the discipline, he is not an 'official' sociologist, despite what others may say about him. His paper then shows a deep knowledge of sociology, including multiple references to a figure who would be a frequent point of orientation for him, Durkheim, yet ultimately eschews sociology as his home since he feels it limits his potential to offer the visions of the good society he wants. This is then poorly received by a British sociology which wants to maintain, for this period at least, some separation of fact and values. Giving keynote lectures such as these are key intellectual interventions which have a performative power and, if well received, help position the intellectual and their claims within the field, pushing their project forward (Gross & Fleming, 2011; Baert & Morgan, 2018). Cole's poor reception indicates his positioning outside the dominant conception of British sociology, despite his initial prominence leading to him being invited to speak. In this sense, the story of Cole's paper to the BSA is the story of his relation to and thoughts concerning sociology which are the focus of this chapter.

This chapter has four sections. The first considers Cole's writings on sociology; this begins with Cole's definition of what sociology is before turning to his writings on what is now identified as the 'canon' in sociology. Significant focus here will be paid to Durkheim, whom Cole was as an early British commentator on, though I will also note Cole's engagement with other writers. The second section then considers Cole's relation to Marx and Marxism. As we shall see, Cole had a warm, though guarded, relationship to Marxism. This only furthered his semi-alienation from a British sociology which, at this point, wanted nothing to do with Marxism for fear of being seen as too radical. Building upon this, the third section then returns us to the question of normativity. Here I will discuss in some depth Cole's writings on the role of normativity and discuss how this differed from British sociology of the time, as well as before and after his death. Finally, I will discuss Cole's extensive writings on how sociology should be taught, as well as detailing his work seeking to establish sociology at Oxford.

While the last chapter sought to show Cole as a sociologist, this chapter shows how Cole was a commentator, supporter and critic of the discipline. The further expansion of sociology which begins just after Cole's death in many ways builds implicitly on the legacy that he left behind of a sociology more open to normative and critical questions, a topic I will return to in the Conclusion.

Cole's Writings on Sociology and the Canon

Cole defined sociology as:

> a *general* study of social organisation, designed to lay bare and to analyse the interrelations of the various ways in which men become organised in social groups of every sort and kind, from the family to the most embracing social groups that possess the beginning of an organised existence...In method, it is a fact-collecting, fact-analysing study, arriving at generalisation by the analysis and comparison of social factors, some of which it can take ready-made from other Social Studies, but many of which it must collect and digest for itself. (Cole, 1948a, pp. 266–267)

We can see here the marks of Cole's own sociological perspective discussed in the previous chapter, with its focus on how associations, or here 'social groups', act to create broader structures, or 'social organisation'. Beyond that, this definition reflects much of early definitions of the discipline in Britain. While, as Abrams (1968, p. 3) once noted, there were 61 definitions of 'Sociology' contained in *The Sociological Papers* alone, if we take Victor Branford's definition in the opening paper of this series with its claim that sociology is 'a theory of the origin and growth, of the structures and functions' of society (Branford, 1904, p. 16) then much of what Cole says here would be familiar to British sociology. Of course, Cole adds a methodological note here, concerning data collection. This reflected a broader tendency, where Cole would say sociology concerned itself with the collection of 'social facts' (Cole, 1946), using this term in a non-Durkheimian sense to mean simply 'facts about society'. Indeed, this discussion of sociology as empirical was frequent in Cole's discussion, with suggestions that its method was 'largely statistical' (Cole, 1947a, p. 26). He argued, as highlighted in Chap. 2, that this tradition of large scale social data collection had a rich history in Britain, as indicated by the Rowntree and Booth studies (Cole, 1946) and had left its mark on British sociology. As we saw in the last chapter, Cole was both a follower of this 'gentlemanly' approach to the discipline in the Nuffield Social Reconstruction Survey and someone who was not limited to empirical inquiry in his broader sociology.

This view of sociology as empirical did not mean Cole was unaware of, or ignored, the theoretical basis of the discipline. Indeed, he wrote broadly on these matters and here his lecture notes from his time as Chichele Professor, housed in the Cole Collection at Nuffield College, Oxford, are very instructive. Here, Cole shows a notable knowledge of French sociology, beginning with Comte. Cole's lecture on Comte (1948c) highlights a split between 'Comte I' the man who 'invented the word *sociologie* and was indeed the father of Sociology as a subject of study' through a positivist perspective (Cole, 1948c, p. 5). This Comte, despite Cole's own distance from positivism, was to be admired. 'Comte II', the writer who seeks to develop a religion of humanity is, for Cole, dismissed and, perhaps significantly, dismissed as not sociological enough. Therefore, Cole defends the early sociological Comte against his late theological form and sees him as important since 'in the succession of French thought...Comte [I] leads, on the strength of his earlier work, directly to Durkheim' (Cole, 1948c, p. 16).

With the exception of Marx, whom I will discuss below, there is no sociologist Cole discusses more than Durkheim. Indeed, it is probably fair to say he is treated as *the* sociologist par excellence in Cole's writings. Cole clearly read Durkheim broadly. In the aforementioned 'Politico-Economic Theories Part II' (Cole, 1952, see last chapter) Cole discusses Durkheim in some depth, including his 'big 4' books (Smith, 2020) of *The Division of Labour in Society*, *Rules of Sociological Method*, *Suicide* and *The Elementary Forms of Religious Life*. He also discusses, en passant, Durkheim's notions of individualism and conception of crime. Across this work he sees Durkheim's thought as having a 'dual character...stressing both solidarity as the basic factor, and the growing importance of groups in more advanced societies resting on complex division of labour' (Cole, 1952, p. 145). On the latter, Cole seems to have read the famed preface to the second edition of *The Division of Labour* since he notes Durkheim's interest, and faith, in occupational groups (Cole, 1952, p. 147).

Elsewhere, Cole notes how *Suicide* is one of the most significant examples of the statistical application of social theory (Cole, n.d.-c) and commented on how Durkheim reflected a broader virtue of sociology by refusing to recognise a distinction between political and economic theory, but rather treating them all as part of the sociological endeavour (Cole, 1934c, p. 3). This was, to Cole, a great virtue of sociology and one, as we shall see, he saw as a key justification to expand the teaching of the discipline. While, as noted above, Cole does not, curiously, fully understand Durkheim's notion of the social fact, seeing this simply as a claim that sociological claims should be 'defined and isolated from the general welter of facts and surmises', i.e. be empirically grounded (Cole, 1952, p. 140) he does consistently invoke the study of such social facts as a key basis of sociology (Cole, 1946, 1957a). He then invokes Durkheim's importance to the sociological understanding of rights given the weight given to the social environment (Cole, 1955b) and, reflecting a connection noted by later scholars (Ferguson, 1999, pp. 199–206), sees an echo of Durkheim in Freud's notion of the super-ego (Cole, n.d.-d).

Cole, reflecting the canon at the time, crowns Durkheim 'the most important French sociologist after Comte and LePlay' (Cole, 1952, p. 125), though he sees Durkheim as 'effectively' the person who founded the 'science of sociology' which pays attention to 'the social structures of societies as wholes' (Cole, 1949, p. 72). Therefore, Durkheim has a central position in Cole's view of sociology.

Despite this, Cole is critical of Durkheim on multiple grounds which reflect his broader sociological concerns. Firstly, Cole groups Durkheim with his main intellectual rival, Gabriel Tarde as theorists who start with social groups and see individuals as passive receivers of social and cultural life. Discussing the expansion of the division of labour he critiques Durkheim's argument that this happens 'not because individuals will it' but because 'there is growing scope for it, and society then passes it onto individuals' (Cole, 1952, p. 143). This is a theory, contrary to his Rousseauian structuration approach, of 'societies making men' (Cole, 1952, p. 141).[1] Here, Cole shared an approach to Durkheim with much of British sociology which, critical of what were termed 'group mind' approaches, tended to see Durkheim's approach as too structuralist and not sufficiently idealist (Studholme, 1995). In the most extreme version of this argument, Durkheim was cast as a 'scholarly forerunner of fascism' due to the supposed emphasis he gave to the sovereignty of the social (Ranulf, 1939).

Cole's other critiques differed from those offered in British sociology more broadly. This brings us to the concept of 'function'. As we saw in the previous chapter, this concept was central in Cole's sociology and, indeed, his model of 'functional democracy' raises this to the key organising principle of social life. However, whereas Cole drew his definition of function from Rousseau and therefore based it in a conception of will, he sees Durkheim's conception as too focused on a more literal depiction of what is 'functional for society as a whole'. Therefore, Cole suggests that

[1] Cole (1952) also sees Durkheim and Tarde as combined due to an 'emotional' approach to social life, by which he seems to mean an approach which sees emotions—in Durkheim's case anomie—as social products.

Durkheim follows Hegel in seeing 'employers and managers as united by their common function (Cole, 1952, p. 143). Therefore, functions were subordinate to broader social needs and, importantly, saw no internal conflicts. This view is, as we saw, anathema to Cole.

This then leads to Cole's broadest critique of Durkheim. While, as mentioned above, British sociology at this point was often critical of Durkheim's 'group mind' approach, this had not, as of yet, been grouped into a notion of Durkheim as a conservative writer as would later become dominant. Cole then is somewhat out of step, or perhaps one step ahead, when he says, with his concern of the impact of the division of labour on solidarity, that Durkheim 'is in a sense a conservative social thinker, because he emphasises the danger of new social tendencies coming into conflict with the existing moral order of a society, and so leading to its disruption' (Cole, 1952, p. 127). In particular, Cole is critical of Durkheim's 'denial' of the class struggle and focus instead on solidarity between employers and employees, rather than among workers. Here, reflecting a broader critique found in Marxist writers in later years (e.g. Bottomore, 1981), Cole sees Durkheim's lack of centring of the class struggle as a key impediment to his understanding of capitalism.

This assertion gives us a fascinating case of reception. As I have discussed elsewhere (Dawson, 2023), Cole and Durkheim share some significant overlaps which Cole misses by beginning with the notion of Durkheim as a conservative writer due to a lack of focus on class. Therefore while, like his own approach, Cole notes how Durkheim appreciates 'the demands in the modern world for occupational representation in politics' he sees this as a fundamentally 'corporative', rather than socialist position given it sits alongside this denial of the class struggle (Cole, 1952, pp. 129, 135). This also for Cole, while accounting for the fact that socially sanctioned moral judgements influence those of individuals, does not account for why particular moral judgements become dominant in society (Cole, n.d.-e). As I have also argued elsewhere (Dawson, 2023) this is a misreading of Durkheim, but one which is more understandable given that, despite his wide reading, Cole was working with a more limited collection of readings than that available to the contemporary reader.[2] Books, such as *The Division of Labour in Society*, are never received passively but rather are

[2] In particular, Cole suffered from not having access to Durkheim's *Professional Ethics and Civic Morals*, his most extensive discussion of class, the state and, their mutual source of inspiration, the guilds. This text was only published in 1957, at which point Cole had retired.

understood contextually and Cole's perception of Durkheim is undoubtedly a case of this (Da Silva & Vieira, 2019).

I have discussed Cole's thoughts on Durkheim in some depth since they are the most developed writings he offered on any sociologist (bar Marx) and given Durkheim's centrality to the discipline. In addition, Cole's distance from Durkheim, while both echoing and differing from the British sociology he confronted, suggests key elements of what Cole thought was both beneficial—the focus on the social environment and combination of the political and social—and negative—an overly structuralist approach—in sociology. This can be seen in the following quote:

> Durkheim put forward an entirely sociological theory of social development, in terms of the impact of the social environment…[which] is for Durkheim the source of social ideas and values, but only for their transmission. The changes, it would seem, can be accounted for only by social adaptation to changes in the environment brought about by forces acting on men rather than by man's own autonomous action. But do men merely respond to such changes, or do they in some instances initiate them by responding different to the same environmental forces? If differently, there is an individual as well as a social faction involved, arising out of individual differences of response and valuation…response to the environment is not uniform and fully determined but to some extent variable. Durkheim's theory resembles Tarde's in the stress laid on imitative or responsive conduct and valuation; but both regard determined (or normal) response as the main factor in social conduct and value judgements. The 'initiator' has to be 'imitated' for his initiation to alter the social pattern. (Cole, 1955b, pp. 17–18)

Therefore, Cole's sociology, with its political individualism and elements of voluntarism set him up on a fundamental collision course with many of Durkheim's claims, despite their potential sources of overlap on areas such as workplace democracy, individualism and the role of the state. Here we have a case of a 'missed connection' in the history of the discipline as one element of intellectual debate, in this case structuralism over voluntarism, dominates the reception of a writer.

Cole's writings on key sociologists went beyond Durkheim. He also discusses Tarde, LePlay and Sorel in the context of the development of French sociology. All of whom he sees as living in Comte's legacy. He also, perhaps reflecting his critical comments on Durkheim's work, sees virtue in Tonnies' separation of association and community as a way to analyse the political formations of different nation states (Cole, n.d.-f). Weber was also a frequent reference for Cole, including in discussion of elites and charisma (Cole, n.d.-g) and the Protestant Ethic thesis (Cole, 1948d). Also, in his activity as Chambers Encyclopaedia editor for Sociology, Cole wrote entries on the Durkheimian Francois Simiand and Georg Simmel. His Simmel entry (Cole, 1950c, p. 562), while brief, notes how 'his philosophy and his sociology were closely related' with 'social structure and behaviour being treated as the external manifestations of an inner spiritual life'. He also covered sociologists such as Follett, Pareto, Michels, Veblen and Parsons in his teaching (Cole, 1952). Given Cole began teaching Parsons in the early 1950s, he would have been one of the first teaching his work in Britain, where Parsons had not, at this point been well served, in spite of (or, in W.G. Runciman's (2004, p. 220) telling, because of) his pre-WWII period at the LSE and post-war year at Cambridge.

Cole and Marx(ism)

There is one major figure from the modern sociological canon we have not covered yet and it is one of Cole's most significant interlocutors: Karl Marx. Writing in similar terms to how he discussed his sociology, Cole had this to say about his socialism:

> I object to calling Socialism 'scientific' because I deeply mistrust the 'scientists', and not only the 'natural scientists' but fully as much the 'economic scientists' and the 'social scientists' and all the tribes of professors who attempt to wear the mantle of science...The choice of ends, among those which are practicable, is a matter not of science, but of the *art of living*, which can never be reduced to scientific terms. (Cole, 1947b, pp. 75–76)

As this indicates, Cole sought some distance between his socialist perspective and the 'scientific socialism' of Marxism including, significantly, in its social scientific form. However, while Cole may have kept a distance from Marxism, the writings of Marx are a different matter. As Wright (1979) notes, Cole's discussion of Marx shifted throughout his career as a reflection of changing political conditions. Nevertheless, I would suggest throughout these changing circumstances, what is important for our discussion is that Cole maintained a *sociological* reading of Marx.

In his earliest writings, roughly up to the early 1920s, Marx did not figure significantly in Cole's work. For example, in *Social Theory* Marx is only discussed in relation to the state (Cole, 1920a, pp. 145–149). Here, while Cole says he is offering 'an endorsement of a large part of the Marxian case', by this he simply means the claim that the state is 'perverted' by economic factors (Cole, 1920a, p. 149). While clearly, of course, a Marxist claim, Marxism contains much more than this. Meanwhile, Cole's great socialist statement, *Guild Socialism Re-Stated* only mentions Marxism, rather than Marx himself twice, each time en passant. Despite this, Cole certainly already had a close knowledge of Marx; in 1924 he ran an entire WEA course on Marx and Marxism. The course syllabus (Cole, 1924b) shows as extensive a knowledge of Marx's writings as could be possible for the English speaker at that time with Cole advising his students not 'to begin with a direct attack on the three massive volumes of *Capital*' but rather suggesting a list of secondary and primary readings followed by a different ordering of chapters across *Capital* (Cole, 1924b, p. 3). However, at this point, Cole's main published references to Marx were to rhetorically separate his approach from the Marxism of the Bolsheviks. This perhaps reflects Cole's goal of maintaining some peace between guild socialism and communism since the latter—despite Cole's claim that one could be a guild socialist *and* a communist (Cole, 1921)—greatly threatened guild socialism and eventually succeeded in converting many to their cause (Taylor, 2002).[3]

With the collapse of the guild socialist movement in the early 1920s Cole undertakes a significant engagement with Marxism. For Wright (1979) this reflects political pressure whereby, with the expansion of support for communism, Cole seeks to 'reclaim' Marx for his own vision of democratic socialism. There is some truth to this but it also reflects Cole's broader engagement with sociology.

Cole's most extensive engagement with Marx is his book *What Marx Really Meant* (Cole, 1934d), which was later republished, with some

[3] This helps explain a curious document found in the Cole archives. Entitled 'A Pioneer of Scientific Socialism' and published in 1920 this is a profile of Engels to mark the centenary of his birth. While largely a faithful description of Engels' life and work it does contain the interesting claim from Cole that Engels was an anti-state writer and that therefore 'when hostility of socialists to the state…is being more than ever exercised' it was fitting that Engels' birth was being marked (Cole, 1920c, p. 3). While, of course, Engels joined with Marx in condemning the class nature of the capitalist state, seeking to claim him as more broadly against the state, and therefore perhaps a supporter of guild socialism, seems to give credence to the idea that at this point Cole was trying to maintain a space for guild socialism as at peace, rather than in competition, with communism. This was perhaps a useful strategy for Cole to follow, since by this point many of his communist students had come to consider him a 'hopeless reactionary' (Rose, 2021, p. 308).

changes, as *The Meaning of Marxism* (Cole, 1948d). The former book could perhaps have been more faithfully titled *What Marx Should Have Meant* (Wright, 1979, p. 210) since Cole significantly reinterprets Marx's writings. By Cole's own acknowledgement, neither book was 'a summary of Marx's doctrines or merely an essay in interpretation of Marx's thought, but rather a revaluation of Marx's essential ideas and methods in relation to contemporary social structures and developments' (Cole, 1948d, p. 8). These reinterpretations, largely, seek to emphasise sociological elements of Marx's thought. There are some differences between the two books, most notably, *What Marx Really Meant* suggests a greater identification with Marx from the author. For example, compare these statements, which appear at the start of each text. First the earlier, *What Marx Really Meant*:

> I am conscious that my own thought has been deeply influenced by Marx – the more perhaps because I came to him after I had first received, and then repelled, the influence of the Hegelian doctrine. I am no Marxist, if to be one involves, as many of his followers seem to suppose, unquestioning acceptance of all his doctrine, and even a belief in the literal inspiration of all the Marxian scriptures. But I am Marxist, to the extent that I have found in certain of his doctrines, and above all in his methods of social analysis, clearer light than anywhere else by which to seek an understanding of the fundamental economic and political problems of to-day. In this sense alone, I claim, has anyone a sound Marxian title to call himself Marxist in 1934? (Cole, 1934d, pp. 7–8)

Now, the expanded and adjusted claim, which I have had to edit substantially given it now runs over three pages of *The Meaning of Marxism*:

> I am conscious that my own thought has been deeply influenced by Marx – the more perhaps because I came to him after I had first received, and then repelled, the influence of the Hegelian doctrine. I am no Marxist, if to be one involves, as many of his followers seem to suppose, unquestioning acceptance of his opinions, or any sort of belief in the literal inspiration of the Marxian scriptures. Indeed, in a good many respects my mind recoils from Marxism, as a system, both because I have a deeply-rooted mistrust of systems, one and all, and especially of systems which attribute everything of importance to a single cause...Over and above this, Marx's system hits right up against my conviction that it is a profound error to attribute to 'classes', of things or of men, any reality distinct from that of the individuals which compose them, or to regard the classes, as distinct from individuals, as active forces shaping the course of history...Nevertheless, despite this sharp dis-

> sent from certain of Marx's fundamental notions, I remain 'Marx-influenced' to a high degree, because I have found in certain of his doctrines, and above all in certain of his methods of social analysis, clearer light than anywhere else by which to seek an understanding both of certain key factors in the development of human societies and of fundamental economic and political problems of today. In this sense alone, I claim, has anyone a sound intellectual title to call himself Marxist in 1948? (Cole, 1948d, pp. 11–13)

We see here the key differences, now Cole is 'Marx-influenced' rather than simply, in some elements 'Marxist' and we have a more developed reason for his separation, based around the 'system' nature of his thought and consideration of class. Yet, each statement contains some affinity with Marx. In what follows, in addition to discussing Cole's broader writings on Marxism, I will focus on *The Meaning of Marxism* rather than its earlier sibling since in my view these shifting claims of Cole's personal allegiances do not change the key arguments of the book, the rest of which is not as edited as the above. Furthermore, Cole updated the discussion for the latter text, for example, including a discussion of how the Labour government of 1945 influences a Marxist notion of the state as well as expanded reflections on fascism.

For Cole, reflecting a later trend in sociology in which the value in Marx is seen to reside in a way of thinking rather than a set of political precepts (Giddens, 1981; Burawoy & Wright, 2001), Marx's 'methods [are] more directly helpful than his doctrines' (Cole, 1948d, 13, see also Cole, 1935a). This, of course is his materialist conception of history and it is here that Cole finds significant value, in two ways. Firstly, it reflects a key value of sociology in its desire to understand our current conjuncture as the result of historical conflicts and shifts (Cole, 1929b). Secondly, the focus on the relation and means of production as determinative is important since 'Every anthropologist or sociologist will agree that men's ways of getting their living have a profound effect on the structure of the societies in which they live' (Cole, 1933a, pp. xvi–xvii). Therefore, Cole wants to maintain the elements of a fundamentally sociological theory which emphasises the historical development of productive forces as helping to determine the structure of society, including its conflicts.

However, in doing so, Cole feels it necessary to redefine Marx's terms. Rather than a 'materialist' theory of history he favours a 'realist' theory. The reason for this is that this theory:

> as Marx describes it, cannot be truly regarded as 'materialist', in the most familiar sense of that term, because the forces upon which the entire movement rests – the 'powers of production' – are not forces of matter as opposed to mind, but embody the result of mind's action upon matter – man's command over nature, for short...Still more clearly, the struggle by which the process of historical evolution is carried on is not one of matter with matter, in any sense in which matter can be contrasted with mind, but of men with men. (Cole, 1948d, pp. 273–274)

Here we see a reflection of Cole's sociology. For him, to call this theory of history 'materialist' is to ascribe agency to the material forces rather than how these are used by humanity. The same is true for Marx's theory of class whereby, in addition to the changes in the class structure discussed in the last chapter and largely echoed in *The Meaning of Marxism* Cole rejects Marx's 'mystical' view of classes as being 'far more real and creative than individual persons' (Cole, 1933a, p. xxviii). Cole accepts the possibility that the sharing of class positions may generate common ways of thinking and of action, but that cannot automatically be understood as 'class action', rather a reflection of the agentic associative wills (Cole, 1948d). While the focus on the associative will is distinctively 'Cole-ian', the broader point of collective action by classes being a possible, perhaps even likely, though not automatic outcome of individuals being placed around class positions reflects much later Weberian understanding of class which would be so influential in British sociology (Goldthorpe & Marshall, 1992).

These changes then necessitate further adjustments in Marx's theory, most notably to the dialectic. Cole accepts the necessity of a dialectical way of thinking, including with reference to class when we can recognise such action occurring; however he rejects the notion of the 'dia' in the lectic, i.e. that conflicts will be two-sided. The rise of fascism and the role of the middle classes in this is, for Cole, a key example. Fascism both relied upon middle-class support to win power in a conflict framed around questions of class and race *and* then eventually destroyed this middle-class base, most notably in its petit bourgeois form (Cole, 1948d, pp. 130–152). Therefore, the dialectic as a way of thinking has significant sociological value, but it needs moving away from a focus solely on two classes facing each other.

As a result of these changes Cole acknowledges that many Marxists would argue he is not discussing Marxism at all but 'even if that were so, it would not matter, provided that my interpretation were the more valid basis for the formulation of a doctrine for today' (Cole, 1948d, p. 50).

This reflects a broader value Cole sees in Marxism as a theory which should never involve repeating 'parrot-fashion' what Marx said (Cole, 1933b) and instead must engage in constant revision:

> For it is the rankest injustice to Marx to suppose that he would have written exactly as he wrote in 1848, or in 1859, or in 1867, or even if 1883, if he had been alive and writing today. No sense was stronger in Marx than the sense of change...Only fanatics learn *The Communist Manifesto* and the key passages of *Das Kapital* by heart, and conceive themselves thereby to have unlocked the secrets of the capitalist world as it now exists. Only disciples who utterly misunderstood both the meaning and the method of their master. (Cole, 1948d, pp. 12–13)

This perspective then influences Cole's sociological reading of Marx as not a writer with a teleological theory of political development with reference to class, but rather as a sociological thinker seeking to understand the nature of society today with reference to a 'realist' theory which foregrounds the economy and the outcome of conflicts between diverse groups in society who each holds different positions of power.

Based upon this, *The Meaning of Marxism* discusses how this perspective is helpful in allowing us to understand a variety of social forces. Rather than recap the whole book, I will highlight two key factors. One is the development and future of capitalism. Here Cole conducts an exercise familiar to generations of sociology students by putting Marx in discussion with Weber's protestant ethic thesis. He argues that Marx's is superior given its emphasis on how humanity comes to dominate nature in material production. This analysis reflects later claims that the advance of modernity reflected the domination of humanity over nature (Leiss, 1972). In turn, he argues the expansion of joint-stock trading companies open new potential ways for socialising the economy, although in reality they are likely to embolden the middle classes who can now have more investment in the system (Cole, 1948d, pp. 51–107). The second concerns the state, where Cole argues the emergence of social democratic governments, such as the Labour government of 1945, shows the possibility for encroaching control to achieve a dictatorship of the proletariat rather than the smashing of the state (Cole, 1948d, pp. 181–210).[4]

[4] Cole here seems to be unaware of the writings of Marx which suggested the possibility of different national paths for the dictatorship of the proletariat which, in his defence, did largely come to be known after his death (e.g. note the publication date of Marx and Landor (1962)).

Therefore, Cole's engagement with Marx was deep and presented him as a historical sociologist with a method fit to understand society. Based off this we might say that Cole was closer to a sociological Marxist, in the terms of Burawoy and Wright (2001) than a political Marxist. His rejection of the latter was clear, as in this piece published after his death:

> I have never regarded myself as a Marxist. It has always appeared to me that to treat either the whole body of consumers – or working-class consumers – or the entire industrial proletariat as constituting in essence a single unified mass is inconsistent with real democracy because masses so large and amorphous are incapable of acting together except under a top leadership which is bound to substitute its own control for the control of the mass it is supposed to lead. In other words, so-called 'mass democracy' inevitably leads to bureaucracy and bureaucratic control in which the individual is unable to make his voice heard in shaping of policy. (Cole, 1959b, p. 282)

Yet, leaving aside this *political* disagreement, Cole's *sociological* perspective clearly had space for Marxist themes, as we have seen in his analysis of history, class and the state. Indeed, an acceptance of class warfare as an inevitable fact was central to his guild socialist sociology and, as we have seen, was a key point of disagreement with Durkheim. While this is befitting a British sociology which, after Cole's death, became much more comfortable with Marxist thought, it only furthered the semi-alienation from the discipline he experienced in his lifetime.

British Sociology and Marx(ism)

Canons, by their very definition, appear natural to those who encounter them, the sociological canon is no different here. However, Marx was for a long time not included in the canon at all, with his presence only secured in the 1970s at the expense of Parsons and functionalism (Alexander, 1987). Before this, Marx's fate internationally was either not to be discussed, or to be seen as someone outside the sociological tradition, perhaps with contributions to make on the question of class, but no broader insight to offer. Indeed, even Cole in his aforementioned course on Politico-Economic Theories (Cole, 1952) does not mention Marx at all in relation to sociology, but instead includes him under a discussion of political theory.

This denial of the sociological Marx took a particular form in Britain, as Rocquin (2014, 2019) has shown. It was not the case that British sociology totally ignored Marx and Marxism, but the way in which it was discussed was telling. Extra-mural sociologists, such as those who, like Cole, were teaching in the WEA were more willing to engage with Marx's writings than those at the LSE. In this sense, Cole's course on Marxism was indicative of a trend whereby, perhaps unsurprisingly, sociology for workers was more pro-Marxism than its institutionalised form. Marx only figures in the writings of Hobhouse or Ginsberg as a name cited to be dismissed. For Hobhouse, either we see Marx having a 'defective' economic theory (Hobhouse, 1966, p. 215) or as irrelevant to British conditions due to free trade (Hobhouse, 1994, p. 47). For Ginsberg, Marx is cited approvingly when he can provide rhetorical backing to his aforementioned theory of progress (Ginsberg, 1963, p. 299) but ultimately dismissed as inferior to 'non-Marxist sociological theories of social development, of which the most important is that of Hobhouse' (Ginsberg, 1961, p. 10). Consequently, given the failings of his perspective, 'it would be more sensible to banish it altogether from sociology' (Ginsberg, 1953, p. 40).

The broader sociology circles around the LSE and elsewhere were more willing to at least mention Marx but, in doing so, would state that 'they were going to discuss Marxist ideas although they did not agree with them' (Rocquin, 2019, p. 56). This was most common in discussions of class where Marx would figure as a thinker to argue against. Instead, unlike Cole, these writers would present Weber as a more appealing figure (Rocquin, 2019, pp. 56–58). Even here however, *any* mention of class was sometimes considered problematic precisely because it raised the spectre of Marxism. Ernest Barker, at this time Professor of Political Theory at Cambridge and a long-running critic of sociology—who, reflecting the precarious nature of sociology at the time, nevertheless was President of the Institute of Sociology from 1935–1937—reflected this in his claim that class was a 'dangerous word' (Rocquin, 2019, p. 47, 57). Therefore, as Rocquin notes, while Marxism was not absent from British sociology in its period, any mention 'was also raising fears and conservativism among British sociologists' (Rocquin, 2014, p. 198).

This then is further basis for Cole's semi-alienation from British sociology, although in this case exempting its extra-mural form in which Cole was active. Cole's distance from Marx was largely a political disagreement, a dislike of political Marxism in its communist form, with his view of the sociology of Marx, despite his differing thoughts on class, being much warmer. This perspective was not welcome in the British sociology of Cole's time since Marx introduced that dangerous word 'class' into the sociological lexicon. All of this, as we have seen, was anathema to Cole, though would have been welcomed later where, indeed, British sociology was sometimes accused of being *too* Marxist (Hammersley, 2016).[5]

Cole, British Sociology and Normativity

Of course, this distance from Marxism was part of a broader desire towards ethical neutrality in the attempt to build up sociology as a science and, therefore, a rejection of normativity. The question of normativity was a key part of the preceding chapter and there we saw how Cole rejected what he saw as the emerging rejection of normativity in British sociology. In this section, I will explore this in more depth, in particular, I will discuss Cole's writings on normativity and place him more clearly within the history of these debates in sociology.

As we saw in Chap. 2, the 'implicit' sociologists of the nineteenth century and the candidates for institutionalisation—bar Hobhouse—were comfortable with the notion of sociology as a normative discipline. However, it is also accurate to say that most of these writers, perhaps reflecting the 'gentlemanly' nature of the pursuit, did not contemplate in depth *why* sociology should, or should not, be normative or the balance of risks and rewards on either side. Instead, given they were largely pursuing sociology as a hobby and were often part of a governing liberal elite (Abrams, 1968) they took the normative and practical ends of a discipline focusing on the social for granted. There were exceptions to this. Wells (1906) in his defence of a utopian sociology places the discipline within the arts because, so he argues, scientific understanding cannot comprehend societal diversity; also, statements of what is in society are, in his view, inherently charged with what should be. Meanwhile Geddes' focus on the city and his desire for 'experimental solutions' (Branford & Geddes, 1919, p. 20) meant that inevitably for him sociology would have to be

[5] It could be claimed that the form of Marxism which became increasingly popular in British sociology after Cole's death, with a greater focus on cultural analysis via the entry of Gramsci, the Frankfurt School and Eurocommunist approaches would have been equally unappealing to Cole. There is perhaps some truth in this, and Cole's death meant we did not get his thoughts on this topic, though he does mention Gramsci briefly, albeit approvingly, in his *History of Socialist Thought* (Cole, 1958, p. 390).

'concrete' in developing plans for city improvement. In such a system it was inevitable that the 'departments of action and thought' had to be in an 'organic relation' as the city was adjusted in ways that proved most promising (Geddes, 1905, p. 80). However, these were the exceptions.

The institutionalisation battle being won by Hobhouse pushed sociology in a different direction. In 1908, Hobhouse opened the first issue of *The Sociological Review* with a piece discussing what sociology has been and should be (Hobhouse, 1908). There, in defending the notion of sociology as 'scientific' he makes a distinction between sociology and moral philosophy. When it comes to the former:

> sociological thinking must start with a clear cut distinction between the 'is' and the 'ought', between the facts of social life and the conditions on which society actually rests and the ideal to which society should conform...it must hold in full clearness from the outset that the question of fact is one thing and the question of right and wrong another...A science deals with facts and the interconnection of factors. It discovers laws and makes predictions. Hence it tells us what has been, what is, and what will be, but it has no concern with what ought to be. (Hobhouse, 1908, pp. 4–5)

This, for Hobhouse is contrasted with moral philosophy (or 'ethics' as he sometimes terms it) which is concerned with the 'art', not science, that adjudicates on the good life. Therefore, sociology as an empirical discipline is not concerned with what should be, with those questions being left to philosophers. Hobhouse is aware that the distinction between sociology—the 'science of society'—and moral philosophy is less clear than the distinction between other sciences and their normative counterparts. Indeed, he says that at some points 'the two come very nearly to the same thing', most notably when the sociologist 'proves' a certain element is required for social life, for example, solidarity, while moral philosophy is likely to hold the continuation of social life as a good. However, even here, Hobhouse suggests all sociologists should keep this distinction in their mind and keep to matters of fact. Sociology may be able to serve moral philosophy best by supplying those matters of facts which lead to ethical judgements, but those judgements are not its business (Hobhouse, 1908, pp. 5–7). This notion of scientific sociology and the ethical neutrality which is part of it then became a key principle of British sociology even though Hobhouse himself engaged in a separate programme of political reform advocacy, found most notably in his book *Liberalism*, which he defined as separate from his sociology. This view was further propagated by Ginsberg and broader LSE sociology (Abrams, 1968; Rocquin, 2014).

This, of course, holds some similarity to that of Weber, who separated out two kind of claims. Ascertaining the validity of facts relies upon evidence where a claim can be proven correct or incorrect according to universal judgement. However, value-judgements are 'practical evaluations of the unsatisfactory or satisfactory character of phenomena subject to our influence' (Weber, 1949a, p. 1) and therefore involve normative claims about what is good or bad about the world. Unlike facts, 'to *judge* the *validity* of such values is a matter of *faith*' (Weber, 1949b, p. 55). Therefore, value-judgements should remain outside of sociology, both in research *and* teaching. While Weber's discussion of value-freedom is much more complex than it is often given credit for and took place against the context of a politically split German sociology where being able to have some common ground on which to speak was essential (see Dawson, 2016, pp. 8–14), this split between facts and value-judgements is essential to his perspective and the form of value-free sociology it would give birth to. To quote Weber's famous rejection in *The Protestant Ethic and the Spirit of Capitalism*—a book which, as highlighted above, Cole had read and taught his students—of those who would seek to combine facts and value-judgements:

> He who yearns for seeing should go to the cinema…Nothing is farther from the intent of these thoroughly serious studies than such an attitude. And, I might add, whoever wants a sermon should go a conventicle…It is true that the path of human destiny cannot but appall him who surveys a section of it. But he will do well to keep his small personal commentarie to himself, as one does at the sight of the sea or of majestic mountains, unless he knows himself to be called and gifted to give them expression in artistic or prophetic form. In most other cases the voluminous talk about intuition does nothing but conceal a lack of perspective toward the object, which merits the same judgment as a similar lack of perspective toward men. (Weber, 1930, p. xli)

Therefore, Cole confronted a sociology, both within and outwith the UK which rejected normativity based on a distinction between claims to what is (the realm of science) and what ought to be (the realm of either moral philosophy or individual values).

Cole's position began with the acceptance of the distinction between facts and values Weber drew since, as he puts it, 'the true and the good are different things, and you can't *prove* anything to be good' (Cole, n.d.-h, p. 4). Therefore, in his discussion of 'social facts' Cole (1946) highlights that the use of statistics had gained greater appreciation in sociology due to its seeming claim towards such basis as 'fact'. However, Cole sees an impossibility of separating out facts and value-judgements as a basis for normativity. The reason for this is that unlike in the natural sciences where claims of fact and value can be clearly differentiated, in the social sciences all facts occur within the context of a society which must, for Cole, aim at some sense of human betterment and a good standard of living. As he puts it:

> We cannot do without value-judgements in Social Theory, however ardently we pursue scientific study of social facts – as we should do. For the purpose of understanding social facts, as in the natural sciences, is to control their working with a purpose in view; and in social studies this purpose is bound to be 'ethical' – the promotion of the good life...it is desirable to find out what people want and don't want, as well as to formulate ideas of what they ought to want. This is the case against keeping social science and normative social science in watertight compartments. (Cole, n.d.-i, p. 1)

Furthermore, Cole argues, unlike anthropology where scholars are more likely to be studying unfamiliar societies, where one has the advantage of distance, the same is not true to the sociologist studying their own society:

> no-one who studies his own or a like society can possibly help carrying his moral judgement with him into his work. They will be constantly in his mind, even if he leaves them out of his reporting and makes no mention of them in his analysis and summing up. This must be so because he is a citizen as well as a scientist. (Cole, 1950f, p. 9)

Therefore, both of these factors make the distinction between facts and value-judgements impossible. Cole does argue that sociologists can try, using contemporary language, to be as reflexive as possible about when they are discussing facts and when they are making value claims, but a separation between them is impossible (Cole, 1950e).

Not only is it impossible for Cole, but it is also inadvisable. A pure value-freedom position means that a sociologist cannot take a position on any political question and instead means he must accept any political form as equivalent to each other. Of course, the response to this from a Weberian position would be, reflecting Weber's claim that 'an *attitude of moral indifference* has no connection with *scientific* "objectivity"' (Weber, 1949b, p. 60), that this does not stop the sociologist holding views and expressing them as a citizen. But Cole sees this distinction as undermining the very value of sociology since it is as a sociologist, rather than a citizen, that the individual has something unique to say. Sociology and politics are for Cole are intimately bound together at a thousand points 'and it is well for humanity that this is so; for man, in order to live well, needs knowledge of good and evil as well as of the factually true and false' (Cole, 1957a, p. 171). Gouldner once spoke of the split Weber made between the scholar and the citizen as reflecting that he 'wanted the play to be written by a classicist and to be acted by romanticists' (Gouldner, 1962, p. 211). Cole wanted sociology to be jointly written and acted by classicists and romanticists. But, ultimately, in any conflict between the two, the romanticist should take the lead. We cannot for Cole be 'disinterested' when it comes to questions of what is right or wrong for the society we live in (Cole, 1950f).

This influences Cole's rejection of the Hobhouseian position. As we saw, while it shared significant ground with the Weberian position, this was also defined by seeing normative questions as beyond the scope of sociology and instead as questions for moral philosophy. As the above indicates, Cole would see moral questions, focused as they are on concerns of what is 'good' as at the same time political questions, reflecting how we can make a 'good' society and therefore, very much within the scope of sociology. Therefore, Cole's fundamentally normative vision of sociology was not befitting the sociology of his time which, in its attempt for scientific legitimacy in Britain and driven by Weberian notions of value-freedom internationally, saw no space for the kind of normative, both political *and* ethical claims Cole wanted to make in his sociology. Indeed, Cole's position would have been somewhat unique in both rejecting *and* accepting the Weberian distinctions between facts and values which, as others have noted, Hobhouse largely reproduced (Owen, 1974, pp. 174–178). Here, Cole was born too late since the earlier 'implicit' sociology of the nineteenth century would have been more accepting of this.

The case can also be made that Cole was born too early. The decade after his death, the 1960s, with the decreasing dominance of structural functionalist perspective and the emergence of new sociological perspective saw an expansion of claims against value-freedom. For example, in America, Gouldner engages in a debate with Becker which takes normativity as granted, but differs over whether it is to groups, or to values, that sociologists should claim allegiance (Gouldner, 1962, 1968; Becker, 1967). This is a debate in which Cole would have felt at home. For Becker, the impossibility of sociological research to cover all sides, along with the fact that claims of 'bias' inevitably follow any piece of sociological research due to this meant that, inevitably, one had to speak from a particular 'side'. The question then just becomes whose side we are on? Here, the political positioning of sociologists is significant since, as Becker puts it: 'We usually take the side of the underdog; we are for Negroes and against Fascists' (Becker, 1967, p. 244). Therefore, the requirement on the sociologist for Becker is take, and clearly state, their side as their commitments dictate. While should also try as hard as possible to not let this cloud one's statement, the sociologist also should not simply meekly accept the claims of 'bias' that immediately follow.

Gouldner, while having in an earlier piece critiqued the notion of value-free sociology (Gouldner, 1962) nevertheless strongly disagreed with Becker's argument, calling it 'the sociology of young men with friends in Washington' (Gouldner, 1968, p. 110). For Gouldner, Becker's 'smug' claims of partisanship sidestepped any question of the values sociologists should hold and instead allowed scholars such as Becker to side with the underdog against the 'middle dogs', the police on the street who harass them, the managers at work who demand too much, against the true 'top dogs' of capitalism, the state and oppressive structures. In turn, ambitious scholars could still seek the patronage of the top dogs—for example in government appointments or well-resourced funding bodies—to advance their work. Therefore, he argues sociologists should cleave close not to sides but to a notion of values, most notably the intolerance of suffering (see Dawson, 2016, pp. 14–18 for more on this debate).

Cole's position in this debate is an interesting note for reflection. On one hand, he would share much in common with Becker. As we have seen Cole clearly saw himself as having an allegiance to the working class and his public sociology was very much pitched with that in mind. On the other, Cole's commitment to the working class emerges as a result of his belief in socialism which, as we saw in Chap. 1, was originally ethical in focus and framed by him as a belief based 'on grounds of morals and decency and aesthetic sensibility' (Cole, 1951b, p. 90). He was also heavily critical of what he saw as the overly middle-class trends in the Fabian Society who proclaimed a belief in the working class until it inconvenienced them and their links to power (Cole, 1913b); he might perhaps have termed them 'young men with friends in Whitehall'. Therefore, as we have seen throughout this book, Cole sits in-between dominat sociological trends. Nevertheless, what is significant about the Becker and Gouldner debate is while Cole may have not agreed on the basis of normativity, unlike the time he was intellectually active, normativity was taken as a given.

Similar debates were occurring in Britain, where a number of factors meant the value-freedom consensus came to be questioned, including: the student protests of 1968 (Halsey, 2004); the increased electoral success of the Labour Party with its investment in social science (Butler, 2020) and increased attention paid to topics such as that 'dangerous word' class and the sociology of work (Scott, 2020). Also, the entry of new perspectives forced sociology to recognise that its previous claims of value-freedom were often, as Rocquin (2014) noted, attempts to maintain a conservative position. While the growth of Marxist work was significant here, the entrance of feminist, and later post/decolonial, perspectives were even more significant. Both, in different ways, forced British sociology to reckon with the perspectives it has produced (Evans, 2014). These perspectives all forced sociology to reckon not with *whether* values have a role in sociology, but rather *what* values have been present in sociology.

It is also the case that the expansion of sociology teaching encouraged this greater focus on values. For Bauman (2004) the expansion of sociology outside the metropolitan belt produced a group of students—what Halsey (1982) somewhat condescendingly terms the 'provincial' against the 'professional' sociologists schooled at the LSE—who being more likely to come from working-class backgrounds, pushed their lecturers to consider more normative and critical questions. The growth of polytechnics only encouraged this trend and, for Payne (2019), it is here that we see the most significant growth of critical, normative perspectives. In some ways, the polytechnics were the successors to the forms of extramural education, such as the WEA, which Cole had used as a forum to discuss Marx and sociology.

Therefore, Cole was in many ways ahead of the curve in seeing sociology as a fundamentally normative endeavour. Indeed, his view shares elements with the later claim of Levitas' (2013) notion of sociology being 'utopia as method' not only making value-claims inevitable but in which sociology has a unique contribution to make given its form of knowledge. As Levitas' (2010) work was, in turn, inspired by the earlier sociological work of H.G. Wells, what we see here is a uniting of the normative periods of British sociology which, unfortunately for Cole, occurred just before, and just after, his life.

Cole's notion of sociology was one which, while recognising the Weberian split between facts and values saw this as a spur to the political ends of sociology rather than an impediment. As he put it:

> It is often suggested that the sociologist will be endangering his objectivity if he identifies himself with the advocacy of any specific social policy, and that he ought in his investigations to set aside his personal beliefs and values and confine himself to a coldly impartial survey of facts. But what nonsense this is! Evidently, the investigator ought not to allow his beliefs or sympathies to lead him into falsifying facts; but in many fields of study sympathy is essential to understanding, and the investigator who remains coldly aloof will never discover some of the most essential facts-especially the facts about the value-judgments of the persons whose conditions and mutual relations he is setting out to study. His duty as a sociologist is to remain aware of his bias, and to correct it in arriving at his conclusions: his duty cannot be not to have a bias, for it is often his having one that is his strongest inducement to undertake his investigations. It is wrong to attempt to establish a sharp disjunction between the sociologist and the policy-maker; for a high proportion of sociological investigation has a practical purpose and is not worth doing unless it issues in conclusions about social policy; and it would be clearly absurd to have two separate teams, one of 'pure' sociologists and the other of policy-makers, investigating each aspect of social life in isolation from each other. (Cole, 1957a, pp. 170–171)

This view, readily accepted before and after his career is one which would have been anathema to the sociology Cole confronted, as he put it in a letter to the American political scientist Eugene Burdick: 'I hope you won't succeed in "unifying" the social sciences, especially since the last thing I want to be is to be regarded as a social scientist' (Cole, 1955d). As we have seen it is the 'scientist', rather than the social, which repelled Cole here.

Cole on the Teaching of Sociology

Thus far I have discussed Cole's contribution to sociology either through his publications or through his lecture notes. This section then turns the focus to Cole's activities to help establish sociology as a discipline in Britain and, more specifically, at Oxford.

Cole developed a number of links to British sociology beyond those already mentioned, including connections to significant sociologists, including Michael Young who was hired by Cole to work on the Nuffield Reconstruction Survey at the Ministry of Labour and who later said his move away from the Labour Party was driven by their lack of embrace of Cole's ideas (Cole, 1971, p. 231; Butler, 2020, p. 67) and Barbara Wootton, whom he worked with closely during his time at the WEA (Oakley, 2011, p. 96). Cole was active in the circles of sociology, including giving a paper to the LSE Sociology club, a discussion group, in 1929 (Rocquin, 2019, p. 77), publishing in sociology journals, including the *British Journal of Sociology*, the *American Journal of Sociology* and *The Sociological Review* (Cole, 1914b) as well as reviewing notable sociological texts, including aforementioned books by Ginsberg and Marshall, and a positive review of David Lockwood's *Blackcoated Worker* (Cole, 1959a). He was also commissioned to edit the 'sociology' section of the relaunched Chambers Encyclopaedia published in 1950. Here, Cole commissioned Ginsberg to write the actual 'sociology' entry which, perhaps frustratingly for Cole, claimed sociology was working towards discovering the universal laws of progress (Ginsberg, 1950). Therefore, it is perhaps unsurprising that Cole was one of the 24 people recruited in 1950 to act as sponsors for the forming of the BSA (Platt, 2003, pp. 18–20).

Unquestionably however Cole's strongest contributions to the institutionalisation of sociology can be located at Oxford. As highlighted in Chap. 2, both Oxford and Cambridge had remained resistant to sociology throughout the 1940s and 1950s as it began to gain a foothold elsewhere. Indeed, it was not until after Cole's death that something approaching a sociology department, the Department of Social and Administrative Studies, would be formed at Oxford (Scott, 2020, p. 38). Many explanations have been offered for this late take up of the discipline at Oxbridge. A form of snobbery against the discipline, including for its half Greek, half Latin origin mentioned earlier, played a not insignificant role.[6] Even worse, sociology was seen as somehow 'not British', with its practitioners 'looked upon as pariahs, as not better than Americans or Germans' (Shils, 1985, p. 168). This reflected a notion of sociology's empiricist and

[6] As outrageous as it seems in retrospect, this snobbery was very strong at Oxford during this period. Edward Shils gives us a story of Tawney's encounter with an Oxford contemporary; when Tawney informed his friend he was now teaching at the LSE the response came 'Yes, that's something like Selfridges, isn't it?' (Shils, 1985, p. 168).

continental origins being permissible at the LSE, but not befitting Oxbridge (Rocquin, 2019) with its 'education for gentleman' (Halsey, 2004, p. 102). There were also more pedagogical reasons why sociology did not initially find a home in Oxbridge. As Shils (1985) notes, the tutorial system, with its emphasis on logic expressed in dialectic debate without reference to the outside world did not match the concerns of sociology. Finally, political factors were also at work. I noted in Chap. 1 that Cole faced significant resistance when he launched the first student socialist newspaper at Oxford, similar political resistance was also directed to a discipline which, despite its attempts at achieving scientific legitimacy and open conservativism in Britain, was seen as overly left-wing and, perhaps even worse, tended to recruit working-class students (Shils, 1985). All of this led the historian Hugh Trevor-Roper to declare that sociology would only be taught at Oxford over his dead body (Halsey, 2004, p. 102).

Cole stood outside this Oxford view of sociology and strongly advocated the entry of the discipline to the university. This occurred as part of a broader concern with the teaching of the social sciences. For Cole (1944a, 1948a) the one 'success' in establishing social science teaching in the UK, economics, had demonstrated the folly of specialisation since the 'most jeered-at failings of contemporary economists' (Cole, 1944a, p. 354)—most notably the desire to reduce sociality to market exchanges—showed the failing of a lack of a general education (Butler, 2020, p. 33). Therefore, Cole advocates social scientific study beginning at school, with a general curriculum—running across sociology, politics, psychology, economics and anthropology—being taught before university. While Cole does not make this link, this is perhaps somewhat akin to the Scottish secondary school subject of 'modern studies'.[7] Then, at university, Cole believed that this generalism should continue, at least at undergraduate level. For him the ideal sociology degree would 'clearly include some Economics with a realistic bias, a broad course of Economic and Social History, Social and Political Theory, and, of course, some Anthropology and Social Psychology' (Cole, 1948a, p. 273). Here Cole sees the Oxford system of 'modern greats', more generally known as the PPE degree, to be the model to follow. He does however suggest this may not be best for

[7] Perhaps reflecting his—both fairly and unfairly—characterisation as a 'Little Englander', Cole speaks of an English education system which favours specialism without identifying a different case in the Scottish system, which favoured the generalism of the 'democratic intellect' (Davie, 2013).

everyone, especially those seeking to move into more 'applied' fields such as social work and that some earlier specialisation is preferable for those students.

When it comes to the content of such degrees, Cole notes the need for a grounding in social and political theory, but also argues there needs to be greater methodological expertise, especially in statistical techniques which he considered poorly developed in Britain, a long running concern for advocates of quantitative perspectives (Panayotova, 2019d). However, this would require the setting up of more sociology departments, with the funding that necessitates. Until then, Cole argues, the new universities emerging—which he suggests should be expanded by a number of extra-mural 'people's colleges' which aim to obtain university status—should use the model of the WEA, which can bring sociology to life with reference to students' surroundings. Because of this, Cole believed each department of sociological teaching should have a regional focus, focused on how sociology helped illuminate, and potentially solve, the issues in its regions (Cole, 1944a). There's an interesting link back to Geddes' notion of sociology as civics here and his setting up of the Edinburgh School of Sociology (Scott, 2007) though, of course, in Cole's case this would have focused on issues beyond remaking the built environment.

This need for more sociology departments also posed a problem: there was not enough people to teach sociology properly. As we have seen, even at the LSE in this period, ad hoc teachers with little to no sociology training had to be brought in to teach. Therefore, for Cole, this is a further reason, at least for the time being, to see sociology as part of a general degree rather than a specialism on its own, though hopefully that time will come:

> Some day, Sociology may come to loom as large here as it does in the United States. But that time is not yet. For the present, universities in Great Britain must advance slowly and tentatively along this line, for the simple reason that there is hardly anyone available, or being trained, to teach it. Except at the London School under Professor Ginsberg, Sociology, in the sense here given to the word, is hardly being taught at all. At Oxford we are just making a few tentative beginnings...I should like to go faster, but I would sooner go very slow than the subject inefficiently taught. There are, moreover, advantages in linking it closely to Social and Political Theory at the present stage, and thus to the whole group of Philosophy, Politics and Economics. We shall get a better standard thus, than if we started Sociology

off here and now on its own quite separate voyage. It still needs a convoy, if it is to have a fair chance of reaching port. (Cole, 1948a, p. 267)

Cole here mentions the 'tentative beginnings' of sociology at Oxford which, such as they were, owed much to his efforts.

For Carpenter, as soon as Cole returned to Oxford in 1925 'he began to participate in the variety of extension and delegacy activities which culminated in the broadening of the social sciences and the eventual acceptance of sociology' (Carpenter, 1973, p. 218). When it came to extension activities, he was a key figure in Barnett House, a social work training centre which bought some sociology training to Oxford as an extension to, and in 1958, full department of the university (Halsey, 2004, p. 103). Cole also devoted himself to Ruskin College, an adult, working-class education centre in Oxford (though not aligned to the university) which as a model of his 'people's colleges' included the teaching of sociology.

Within the university itself, Cole was instrumental in securing lectureships in fields such as criminology, anthropology, industrial relations and even, eventually, sociology (Carpenter, 1973, p. 219; Butler, 2020, p. 30). This lectureship went to John Mogey, whom Cole had previously employed as a researcher. Mogey became the first self-defined 'sociologist' to be employed at Oxford. Cole encouraged, and helped Mogey secure the funds for, his surveys of Northern Ireland and Oxford (Cole, 1971, pp. 239–240; Mogey, 1947, 1956).[8] Such activities became permissible due to Cole's work on the Nuffield Reconstruction Survey and his *Studies in Class Structure* which, whatever flaws we may now identify in the former, had done much to legitimise sociological approaches at Oxford. Indeed, Halsey argues the survey helped establish a certain 'investigative' way of thinking sociologically which would remain at Nuffield College (Halsey, 1996, p. 83). His position as the first Chichele Professor of Social and Political Theory, who used his teaching to discuss, and advocate, sociological perspectives, only added to this (Halsey, 2004, p. 103; Scott,

[8] Mogey's (1956) *Family and Neighbourhood: Two Studies in Oxford* includes a foreword from Cole due to his being chairman of the Social Survey Committee which oversaw the project. There (Cole, 1956b) thanks William Ogburn for his help with the project and argues that such a survey throws 'real light on a number of the problems of settlement in new housing estates as compared with those of residence in older, more congested and physically obsolete districts' (Cole, 1956b, p. vi). In the text, Mogey suggests that Cole was central in proposing that a WEA class in Oxford be considered part of the sample as a way to access working-class Oxonians.

2020, p. 37). In this role Cole 'was continually on the look-out for possible ways in which the teaching for, and the papers sat in, Modern Greats and other examinations could be improved' including by expanding the amount of sociology covered therein (Cole, 1971, p. 268). Indeed, many of Cole's lectures which have been cited throughout this book were for this programme.

Cole also sought to make Oxford a congenial place to explore sociological topics. As Butler (2020) details, the Coles, along with the Labour MP Evan Durbin were the key figures in establishing the 1945 Conference on the Psychological and Sociological Problems of Modern Socialism and the Politics of the Group. This conference sought to move socialism away from an overly economistic focus on the individual and instead build upon the emerging sociology of what would come to be called community studies to better think through its political ends. Among those attending, in addition to Cole himself who seemingly used these insights in his later work on how socialism needed to draw upon a notion of 'neighbourness' (Cole, 1950d), were Michael Young, T.H. Marshall and Karl Mannheim. But, even more significant here was the 'Cole Group'.

The Cole Group began as a continuation of the University of Oxford Strike Committee, set up by Cole to support the general strike. During the strike the Coles drove groups of undergraduates around to picket lines to offer solidarity and funds, as well as helping organise protests and fundraising. The future Labour leader, and Cole student, Hugh Gaitskell played a significant role in this, as did the poet C. Day Lewis (Gaitskell, 1960; Samuels, 1969). With the failure of the strike, the group formed into a discussion group, which met every week from 1925 to Cole's retirement 32 years later. Among its members were Labour politicians (Gaitskell, Durbin, Harold Wilson), academics and a number of other figures who would go on to renown in other fields (the psychologist John Bowlby and the poets John Betjeman and W.H. Auden). Members of the group would prepare a paper which would then be discussed. As time moved on the Cole Group turned its attention more and more to topics which could be considered sociological to the extent that, for Goodway (2021, p. 4) the Cole Group was effectively Oxford's Sociology Society. Stuart Hall was a later member of the group and wrote how much of the circle of what would become the New Left grew out of Cole's Group where they would meet and discuss the issues which would then become the sociological concerns of the New Left (Hall, 2010, p. 180). Hall highlighted how Cole's 'critique of bureaucratic "Morrisonian"-style nationalization was enormously influential in shaping the attitude of many socialists of my generation towards statist forms of socialism' (Hall, 2010, p. 178). Therefore the Cole Group was just one of the many ways that Cole brought sociological topics into Oxford and allowed connections to form between scholars. Hall would later return the favour by asking Cole to contribute to the first volume of the *Universities and Left Review*, to which he provided a reflection on the development of British capitalism (Cole, 1957c). In a note Cole would have appreciated, when a few years later the *Universities and Left Review* becomes *The New Left Review*, Hall introduces the journal with a tribute to William Morris (Hall, 1960). Perhaps those years in the Cole Group, listening to his passionate advocacy of Morris as the socialist par excellence, crossed Hall's mind when he wrote this piece.

Conclusion

This chapter has explored Cole's writings on sociology as a discipline as well as his efforts to help establish it in the UK. I began by highlighting Cole's definition of sociology along with his discussion of the canon. Significant was his discussion of Durkheim. Here Cole was one of the earliest, and most sophisticated early advocates for his work. However, he had significant areas of disagreements of him which both reflected his own sociological perspective along with some blindness to potential areas of overlap. I then turned to Cole's discussion of Marx(ism). Here I showed that, contrary to the British sociology of his time which sought distance from Marx in order to maintain a conservative response of scientific objectivity, Cole engaged in significant discussion of Marx and Marxism. In doing so, while he kept his distance from political Marxism, he reinterpreted Marx in a way which made him an explicitly sociological thinker, reflecting later interpretations of sociological Marxism. Finally, I explored Cole's normativity and its relation to the value-free perspectives of Hobhouse and Weber. Here I showed how, while sharing the belief that there is a distinction between claims of fact and claims of value, Cole rejects value-freedom as neither possible, nor advisable, for sociology. This furthered his semi-alienation from the discipline since his view of sociology was not practised at the time. I then showed how this perspective was more welcome in sociology after Cole's death as a mix of factors, including the expansion of sociology as an institutionalised discipline, encouraged more normative reflection from sociology. Finally, I discussed Cole's efforts to expand the teaching of sociology. As we saw, Cole was actively involved in efforts to expand the teaching of sociology at Oxford and elsewhere. This undoubtedly had an impact on Oxford's eventual embrace of the discipline and bore its mark on his students, such as Stuart Hall.

An inevitable question we face here is to what extent was Cole's semi-alienation specific to Britain? Would he have fit more in a different national sociology? Any counter-factual question such as this requires us to make a number of assumptions about how a person would travel across areas. For example, Cole may have been more at home with the pragmatist forms of theorising common in the US at the time, though the quest for 'scientific' recognition, strong during that period and the emergence of Parsonian functionalism would have been especially alienating (Turner & Turner, 1990). In turn, given Cole's extensive knowledge of, and interest in French sociology, perhaps this would have been more welcoming for him, despite the somewhat staid form of sociology which largely consisted of popularising Durkheim during his lifetime (Smith, 2020). The problem with this exercise, when it comes to Cole is that I would suggest his thought is distinctively English. He is part of a tradition of English socialism and radicalism, drawing on figures such as Morris which was idealist, libertarian and individualist. Cole's forms of inspiration come from these milieux and while he encounters figures from elsewhere such as Marx and Durkheim these are fed through, and understood in light of, these starting assumptions. Therefore, if Cole were elsewhere, he would have been a different Cole. In this sense we face the paradox of Cole, he is *too* English to have found an intellectual home abroad but yet those same English elements led to his semi-alienation from the form of sociology he confronted.

Cole had a vision of sociology as a discipline that would make significant contributions to the good society and broader political debates. This leads to an inevitable question: what exactly is the role between the sociologist and the broader political sphere? This aspect of Cole's work is explored in the next chapter, concerning the public role of sociology.

CHAPTER 5

Cole's Public Sociology

On 24 November 1934, *Time and Tide*, a political and literary magazine with left-wing leanings, published an article by St John Ervine,[1] the Irish novelist, playwright and essayist, as part of their regular 'Notes on the Way' series of commentaries. In it, discussing the rise of fascism and communism as 'enemies of freedom', Ervine makes the following claim:

> Mr G.D.H. Cole is the greatest enemy of freedom alive in this land. Compared with him, Sir Oswald Mosley is a devout lover of liberty. He has the mind of the worst sort of tyrant: the academic bureaucrat, that is to say, a man whose essays in oppression have never been checked by practical experience of men and women. (Ervine, 1934a, p. 3)

As part of an attack both on Cole personally and academics, Ervine claims that the issues with Cole's work stem from his being cut off from 'ordinary' people. He concludes his piece with the claim that Cole does not know people 'only Postgates', referencing the comfortably middle-class family of his wife, Margaret and collaborator, Raymond.

Come the 8th December issue of *Time and Tide*, Cole (1934e) responds. He reacts angrily, perhaps understandably, to his wife's name

[1] Confusingly, the writer in the magazine is listed as St John *I*rvine, however it does appear from references therein to be St John *E*rvine, which is how I have referenced it here.

M. Dawson, *G.D.H. Cole and British Sociology*,
https://doi.org/10.1007/978-3-031-75484-5_5

being brought up, but makes a more fundamental point, Ervine exaggerates the significance he and other intellectuals have in Britain:

> St. John Irvine [sic] still does me too much honour. I am sure I am not 'the greatest enemy of freedom' alive on this island. I am neither the greatest enemy of freedom nor its greatest friend, but I hope I may be ranked among the friends of freedom rather than among its enemies. (Cole, 1934e, p. 5)

Finally, on 22 December, Ervine sends in the final exchange in the series. In a brief piece he adopts a tone of surprise and 'I think he doth protest too much' attitude to Cole's response. He defends his comments about Cole's views and his influence, saying that 'I have no doubt whatever of his authority or his influence among a large number of ardent politicians and sociologists, especially among those who are young' (Ervine, 1934b, p. 5).

This exchange is telling for the arguments in this chapter. Here we see a 'public' debate, beyond the realms of academia, in which Cole figures prominently as both a sociologist and the representative of a certain political position. This is a debate in which Cole is an active participant. Indeed, the very fact Cole had to defend himself against Ervine's attacks is because, as we shall see in this chapter, he had become such a prolific public commentator in the years leading up to it. In short, my argument in this chapter is that Cole is one of Britain's foremost 'public sociologists' (Burawoy, 2005a).

The historiography of public sociology in Britain has reflected many of the earlier assumptions discussed in the Preface: that any 'history' is a story of absence. This has been tied to claims of the lack of academic sociology creating a lack of public sociology (Anderson, 1968), a stable social order (Turner, 2006) or the notion that Britain is distinctively unreceptive to 'public intellectuals' more generally (see below). As we have seen across this book however, early British sociology was distinctively concerned with its public and political status and scholars have increasingly begun to highlight this. This has included discussion of figures such as Robert Owen (Pūras, 2014), Geddes (Law, 2005), Young (Butler, 2020) and Hobhouse (Collini, 1979) as early public sociologists. A scholar such as Young is then part of the broader sociological 'moment' which Savage (2010) traces to the 1960s which saw the flowering of public interest in sociology suggested in a publication such as *New Society*. Further to this, Scott (2005) has highlighted that while sociology may not have a hugely significant public presence in Britain, it does teach a large number of students across A-Level and university degrees which, by making more people aware of the sociological perspective, has a clear public role. Meanwhile, Urry (2005) argues that sociology has had significant impact on governmental policy, perhaps most notable in this instance would be the NS-SEC, the national economic classification schema used by the government which is based on the work of Goldthorpe and his collaborators to measure social mobility. In addition to this, a provocative argument from Rocquin (2019) suggests that the earliest sociological survey work on poverty and inequality was a distinctively British form of public sociology which had immense impact indicated by the public concern with, and debate about, inequality in the UK. Therefore, the claim that somehow sociology in Britain has had no public presence is, at the very least, highly questionable.

Many of these claims reflect the broader literature about public intellectuals and their place in British life. For Collini (2006) much of British writings on intellectuals has been marked by 'Dreyfus-envy' where the lack of a particularly engaged, political and powerful intellectual class is bemoaned in comparison with their counterparts across the channel. As Collini (2006) also notes, such a claim has been largely fictitious with Britain, reflecting most countries, taking an exceptional case in France at the turn of the century as the representative case. This has not stopped writers engaging in the 'declinist' notion of intellectuals (Baert & Shipman, 2012) whereby intellectuals such as Owen, Geddes and Hobhouse are seen as figures from the past with no contemporary comparison. Various explanations are offered for this, including the specialisation of academia leading to fewer people able to make general contributions (Small, 2002); the tying of intellectuals to universities with their pressures of expertise and career advancement (Bauman, 1992; Said, 1994); and the increased influence of market mechanisms as determining the value of cultural exchange (Bourdieu, 1989). While many of these points are true, as the accounts of both Baert and Shipman (2012) and Misztal (2007) put it, they force us to reckon with the transformation, rather than eradication, of intellectuals and their need to 're-earn' the position of the public intellectuals. While many of the above forces may conspire against this, certain factors may also advance it, including an increasingly well-educated public able to engage in and critique intellectual claims and the new roles of interpreter and mediator opened up by this and new forms of media (Bauman, 1987, Baert & Booth, 2012). Such a discussion then encourages us to think about how public intellectuals have operated in Britain and to move away from the tendency Collini notes for British intellectuals, expressed most prominently by Orwell, to define intellectuals as 'other [objectionable] people' (Collini, 2002).

My argument in this chapter is that by not including Cole British sociology has not accounted for one of its most significant public advocates and more broadly we have not accounted for a notable public intellectual. This significance covers not just the extent of Cole's public sociology but also the nature of how he did it. Given what has come before and above, the reader will not be surprised to hear that Cole's public sociology always had a normative point to make. Nevertheless, it did this in a way which grounded it in the everyday experiences of the publics he confronted. Cole took this so seriously that, as we shall explore below, he would adjust his thought in order to maintain public relevance. Therefore, Cole's public sociology has, I will suggest, three key points of interest for the current day: (1) his mode of communication; (2) in its normative focus blurring the lines between 'policy' and 'public' sociology; and (3) Cole's prioritising of public relevance in the shaping of his political agenda.

This chapter will begin with this final point where I will discuss the twists and turns of Cole's political agenda. Following Wright (1979), though questioning some of his strongest claims, I will suggest that Cole's shifting political positions reflects a desire to fit his normative sociological claims to the shifting tides of public reception. From here, I will go on to discuss the nature of Cole's public sociology contributions. This will include books, newspaper articles, poems, songs, film strips and other activities. Following this, I will conclude the chapter by putting Cole's public sociology work in discussion with the literature on sociology's public commitments and that on public intellectuals more generally. I will suggest that knowledge of Cole's public sociology is not only significant for sociology's historical record, but also gives us a different way of considering how sociology can and should be public.

The Desire for Relevancy: Shifts in Cole's Politics

By the mid-1920s, the guild socialist moment had passed. Therefore Cole, at this point only in his mid-thirties, was suddenly head of a moribund movement. As many scholars have noted (Wright, 1979; Carpenter, 1973; Riddell, 1995) this precipitates a change in Cole's work. The fact this work changes is, largely, undisputed, what is disputed is the extent and reason for it. Let us first explore the changes before offering judgement upon them.

These changes are seen to have three components. A first shift is in the topics Cole discussed. A look at his books from 1924 to 1935, a period in which he published or edited 47 books (18 of which were detective novels),[2] shows a shift away from a focus on guild socialism and union organisation and to a mix of labour history (his Owen and Cobbett biographies along with his *Short History of the British Working Class Movement* all come from this period), literary texts (*Politics and Literature* (1929), poetry collection *The Crooked World* (1933), collection of Morris' stories (1934)), texts on economics aimed at a broad audience (*Gold, Credit and Employment* (1930), *Economic Tracts for the Times* (1932), edited *What Everybody Wants to Know About Money* (1934)), the beginning of his contributions to the 'The Intelligent Man's Guide to…' genre (*The Intelligent Man's Guide Through World Chaos* (1932) and *The Intelligent Man's Review of Europe Today* (1933), the latter co-written with Margaret Cole) and programmatic texts, aimed at crafting a policy platform of the Labour Party (*The Next Ten Years in British Social and Economic Policy* (1929) and *Principles of Economic Planning* (1935)).

It is that last set of books, most notably in *The Next Ten Years…*, which indicates the second, and perhaps, most significant shift. This book, as the title indicates, set out a policy platform for the Labour Party which was remarkably lacking in the form of workplace democracy and decentralised control previously favoured by Cole. The text is a largely statist account of the steps a Labour government should take. It is Fabian, strikingly so for a man who, as we saw, in Chap. 1 stormed out of this organisation. Cole had rejoined the Society in 1928 and Beatrice Webb commented that the book 'does not differ substantially from what we should advocate' and that Cole had 'matured alike in intellect and character; he has lost all that childish petulance and hypercriticism and he is thinking hard' (Webb, quoted in Cole, 1971, p. 162). This quasi-Fabian embrace of state planning and action, without significant reference to workplace democracy, was then repeated across other texts (Riddell, 1995).

Thirdly, and related to this, Cole becomes more of a 'party intellectual' than at any other point in his career, indeed, as Wright (1979, p. 186)

[2] Cole was always prolific, but the 1930s saw a rate of production which can only be described as Herculean. In her biography of her husband, Margaret Cole (1971) traces this to his 1931 diagnosis of diabetes discussed in Chap. 1. The result was that he redoubled himself to his work and, she notes, became less willing to revise texts, preferring to write and move on. There is inevitably a drop in quality which comes with that quantity.

notes, by the late 1920s, the contemporary record sees Cole as 'the' Labour intellectual. This reached its apotheosis with Cole serving on Prime Minister Ramsay MacDonald's Economic Advisory Council, producing a broadly Keynesian economic line, who was now a colleague on the council. Reflecting this position, and with strong encouragement from comrades in the movement, Cole was, reluctantly, adopted as Labour candidate for the King's Norton parliamentary seat in Birmingham. He had to resign before the 1931 election due to ill-health, though, in any case, the seat remained comfortably Tory.[3]

The above indicates a significant shift in Cole's politics and intellectual positioning which, as we have seen, was shaped by hostility towards the Fabian tradition, an investment in non-parliamentary organisation and a driving concern with libertarian democracy. So, why the shift? Some, such as Houseman (1979) and Goodway (2021), have argued there was no shift at all and, even during this period, Cole maintained a libertarian focus on the freedom of the individual.[4] There is some truth to this, particularly when we look across Cole's writings where, for example, his discussion of Morris sits alongside his more programmatic texts. However, such a claim can overlook the extent to which his political programme changed. A contrasting perspective argues this shift reflected the wider context in which Cole worked. Riddell (1995) terms the years 1929–1933 the 'age of Cole' in the labour movement where, being intellectually homeless after the collapse of guild socialism, Cole follows the broader trend in the movement towards an embrace of state socialism and, in so doing, becomes its leading intellectual. For Riddell, this shift is driven by a mix of Cole losing faith in liberatory democracy and a desire to occupy the position of Labour Party intellectual (see also Holthaus, 2014). In so doing, while he anticipated later Labour moves towards the mixed economy (Riddell, 1995, p. 942) he, in Riddell's view, did the cause of industrial democracy great harm. In addition, while Riddell (1995, p. 957) notes that later in life Cole came to talk of himself as 'remaining' a guild socialist (Cole, 1958,

[3] The eventual Labour candidate, Gilbert Mitchison, would later be MP for Kettering from 1945–1964. With this initial victory he dislodged John Profumo, who would later be elected to the Stratford-on-Avon seat, the seat he represented at the time of the eponymous affair.

[4] Scholars who discuss Cole purely as a 'pluralist' tend, unlike Houseman and Goodway who at least recognise a shift in topics, not to recognise any shift in Cole's work at all. This is largely since they, incorrectly, see Cole's pluralism as his key defining feature whereas this is actually his socialism (see, e.g. Runciman, 1997; Milani, 2020).

p. 10) and speaking once again in a libertarian mode, this perspective tends to see this a somewhat cynical return.

There is a different way to frame this shift by drawing upon positioning theory of intellectuals. Developed most notably by Patrick Baert and colleagues (e.g. Baert, 2015) and reflecting a broader shift from the sociology of intellectuals to the sociology of intellectual interventions (Eyal & Buchholz, 2010) this approach focuses on how 'through their work writers position themselves intellectually and that this positioning affects whether their ideas are taken up by others' (Baert, 2015, p. 16). This approach is, therefore, innately relational, with these interventions also given a performative element since they are seen 'as *doing* something – bringing something about' (Morgan & Baert, 2015, p. 6), while also not reducing these relations simply to the intellectual field. This is especially the case for public intellectuals who, in making interventions across different media, are invested in winning over an audience for their position. As Baert puts it:

> intellectual interventions, whether through writing or speaking, always involve positioning...The basic intuition underlying our theory is that any such intervention locates the author(s) or speaker(s) within the intellectual field or within a broader socio-political or artistic area while also situating other intellectuals, possibly depicting them as allies in a similar venture, predecessors of a similar orientation or alternatively intellectual opponents. (Baert, 2015, pp. 165–166)

For example, Baert discusses how the 'existential moment' found in the immediate post-war period in France allowed that school of philosophy, and Sartre as its representative, to reach a level of fame in the country. Sartre's interventions, not just his books and articles but public lectures, allowed him to position himself as an 'authoritative public intellectual' (Baert, 2015, p. 112) who responded to the trauma of WWII. This perspective, which draws from notions of performativity, moves away from understanding the actions of intellectuals as driven by factors such as social position, motivation or 'authenticity' and instead theorises the relational placing of intellectuals achieved via their interventions.

Therefore, the shifting nature of Cole's interventions are an attempt to win an audience to his socialist project in changing circumstances, both politically and within the intellectual field. We can see this in how *The Next Ten Years...* with its focus on what an incoming Labour government should pursue is an attempt to position Cole's work in relation to changing political circumstances. In doing so, certain 'performative tools', to use Baert's (2015, pp. 170–173) phrase, such as the changing format of the books Cole writes are used to advance this agenda.

Positioning theory provides a more convincing explanation for Cole's shift than Riddell's more cynical approach. After all, if Cole's goal was to obtain the position of party intellectual why did he then 'return' to more libertarian means of expression which would then undercut that? There are, however, two elements of Cole's interventions it does not fully account for. Firstly, Baert wants to reject the 'motivational bias' whereby an idea of what an intellectual intends to do via their interventions is not incorporated unless we have strong evidence for it (Baert, 2015, pp. 159–161). I would argue, as we shall see below, in the case of Cole we do have such evidence. Secondly, while Baert does focus on question of allegiance of intellectuals, this tends to be framed more in questions of their allegiance to intellectual groupings, as suggested in what he theorises as the tension between 'co-operation' and 'individualization' (Baert, 2015, pp. 177–179). In Cole's case this allegiance is to a class and a cause. Consequently, the most convincing perspective on Cole's shift is one which while identifying a shift in focus, and recognising that these interventions are seeking to position Cole in changing political times, sees this as reflecting Cole's notion of what an intellectual, particularly a *socialist* intellectual should do. For Carpenter (1973, p. 30):

> Cole always felt that middle-class intellectuals should place themselves at the disposal of the movement, and provide it with the long-range thinking guided by research which it so desperately needed.

This need to 'place themselves at the disposal for the movement' meant, for Wright (1979), that Cole inevitably had to shift his intellectual focus and policy programme to fit changing political needs. In the 1920s and early 1930s, Cole confronted the rise of fascism, the increased electoral prospects of the Labour Party, the collapse of alternative political mechanisms, the failure of the general strike, the economic crash and the rise of communism. All of these factors meant he had to change his focus in order to maintain this relevance and usefulness to the labour movement and the working class. He had to speak to how fascism could be confronted and what a Labour Party just entering government for the first time, with the backdrop of economic crisis, should do. Hence, Cole begins writing to that end since it is where, he believed, he could be useful. Cole therefore, in response to events sought to combine a dual position as proclaiming allegiance to a class and a cause while also seeking the autonomy of action and thought—most notably the ability to change one's mind—of what Bourdieu termed the intellectual as the 'defender of the universal' (Bourdieu, 1989, p. 103).

Reflecting this conception of the intellectual, Cole was immensely critical of what he termed 'university socialists' (Cole, n.d.-j) who sought a purity of thought and intellectual coherence over the ability to speak to a broader public and, hopefully, change the world for the better. While we can perhaps see a slight element here of the trend Collini (2002) noted for British intellectuals to see intellectuals as 'other people', there is a basis to Cole's differentiation from others. This can be seen in a book review he offers of Herbert Samuel's *Unknown Land*, a utopian tale (Cole, 1942; Fordham, 2016). He condemns the book's intellectual snobbery and, in doing so, argues there is a difference between a utopian who simply makes his readers think and those who persuade them to action. Cole clearly favoured the latter. He then offers this perspective on how being tied to speaking to an active public may negatively impact purity of thought and intellectual coherence: 'It is my humble conviction that high philosophy is all rubbish – failure to answer questions which are unanswerable because they are not real questions at all' (Cole, 1942, p. 8).

Leaving aside Cole's glibness, it is hard to deny this desire to adapt to changing circumstances, to make one's self relevant to an audience, did impact the coherence of his intellectual project across his career. Indeed, multiple commentators have suggested that, after his guild socialist period, Cole lacked any 'systematic' or 'core' theoretical system (Carpenter, 1973; Wright, 1979; Riddell, 1995). This is perhaps to push the case a bit too far. As I have shown in this book some key sociological tenets run across Cole's work. This is his political individualism which sees structure and agency as dual achievements expressed by the democratic will. While some immediate political questions and modes of orientation may change in Cole's work, this sociological perspective remains solid.

As mentioned Cole would, in his later work, claim he had in fact always been a guild socialist (see Cole, 1947b), including a defence of his innately libertarian beliefs. Take, for example, his election address in his second attempt at standing for parliament, for the Oxford University seat, this time seen through to the end though even in the Labour landslide of 1945, the seat remained solidly Tory:

> my Socialism is, and has always been, of a strong libertarian brand. In my political faith I put foremost recognition of the value of tolerance, kindness of man to man, variety of social experiment, and encouragement of voluntary as well as statutory activity over the wide field of social service. I believe that public ownership of key industries and services can be so arranged as to admit of wide variety, to exclude bureaucracy, and to enlarge instead of limiting freedom, alike for the manager, the technicians, and the manual worker. I believe in wide freedom for local government, and in the utmost freedom of voluntary association and expression of opinion as essential ingredients in the making of a real democracy. (Cole, 1945b, p. 70)

This willingness to openly advocate a libertarian perspective can, however, be linked to the above points of how the changing political context impacted Cole's position. With victory in war the threat of fascism had been defeated, communism had solidified itself elsewhere but had not fully broken through in the UK and the Labour Party had become institutionalised as one of the two main parties with experience of government. This last factor, which had helped secure the idea of 'socialism' as meaning 'state socialism' required Cole to, once more, reassert its libertarian form and to push the Labour Party to go further; his positioning as a public intellectual had changed. Here is a further example of such a position, which also reflects the claims concerning class and the welfare state discussed in Chap. 3, taken from a pamphlet produced by *The New Statesman* for a mass audience:

> the Welfare State is, all the same, not Socialism: in the form in which we have been attempting to move towards it in recent years it is at most only socialistic – if even that. For what we have been doing is not to put people on an equal footing, but only to lessen the extremes of inequality by redistributing grossly unequal incomes through taxation; and even this redistribution has quite largely taken the form of making the poor pay for one another's basic needs. No doubt, the taxation levied on large incomes has been severe: no doubt, it would have been quite impossible to develop even such services as we have developed without putting the major part of the cost on the workers and the middle classes, for the simple reason that the income of the rich, even had it been possible to take it all, would not have been nearly enough. Nevertheless, we need only the evidence of our senses to assure ourselves that the rich are still among us and that the class structure of our society remains, if not intact, very much in being. (Cole, 1954, pp. 204–205)

Therefore, I largely share a position with Carpenter (1973) and Wright (1979) that there is a shift in Cole's work during this period, but this reflects the changing political context Cole has to respond to rather than a loss or faith or a cynical move. This is perhaps reflected in the fact that while Cole always had a public presence, he was most active in the 1920s and 1930s. Where I have a difference from these writers in that, as we shall see below, it is possible to see a consistency in Cole's sociology which still influences this public work. Let us now then turn to the content of Cole's public sociology.

Cole's Public Sociology Writings

Cole's public sociology primarily takes the form of what Burawoy (2005a) termed 'traditional' public sociology, i.e. pieces of writing designed to bring sociological insight to a wider audience. What is significant about this output is its extent, variety and modes of communication. I am going to theme them by this final category, moving from books to newspaper articles and then finally to other modes of presentation.

Books

Although Cole could write in a particularly academic form (his early articles on Rousseau being the best example, Cole (1914a, 1926)) or even on occasion with a romantic flourish, mostly when discussing William Morris, his writing tended towards more everyday usage. While writing is always a matter of taste, and Cole's penchant for the encyclopaedic could make his style a bit ponderous at points, there is nothing in how he writes to deter a broader audience. This was a conscious attempt on his part and one which, as Margaret Cole explains, was made partly with reference to sociology:

> he believed and said that economic statements could and should be made in plain and intelligible English, with the assistance of straightforward charts and diagrams...he did maintain that the experts were set on coining, continually, neologisms that were not in the least necessary. He said this even more strongly of sociologists, particularly German and American sociologists, attacking both their language and their methods – all the more bitterly since the matter of their study was one which, he recognised, claimed his support. (Cole, 1971, p. 208)

Therefore, all of Cole's books could, without stretching Burawoy's claim too far, be considered a form of 'public' sociology. More realistically though, we can identify a series of books, published across his career, which fit this criteria more clearly. It is worth noting before we start that these books did enjoy some level of circulation and renown. Cole was identified at the time as a public intellectual and, with his link to the Labour Party, was cast in the role of a powerful 'legislator' with direct access to power and the state (Bauman, 1987). For example, in the 1935 general election, the Conservative Party sought to capitalise on Cole's increased fame by drawing on writings in which he advocated nationalising banks to argue that Labour, with Cole's steer, would nationalise the building societies and take savings away from the working class (Houseman, 1979, p. 37). More forebodingly, Cole's name was among those of the prominent people the Nazis listed as requiring immediate arrest in case of a successful invasion of Britain (Schellenberg, 2006, p. 174).

As examples of Cole's more 'public' books take his two contributions to 'The Intelligent Man's Guide…' genre popular at the time, whose titles form part of the 'paratext' which we need to understand for how books are positioned and received by audiences (Da Silva & Vieira, 2019). *The Intelligent Man's Review of Europe To-Day* (Cole & Cole, 1933) presents itself as helping to facilitate 'better knowledge of the facts and tendencies of to-day' which 'may help to create in men's minds that international understanding' (Cole & Cole, 1933, p. 15). It then proceeds to detail the broad history across the continent, a breakdown of each country's position, history and politics, then provides a broader look at the economics, political systems and international relations of Europe. The book runs to over 800 pages and clearly is intended to be a kind of political encyclopaedia. It represents the politics of the Coles, for example ending by advocating the abolishing of capitalism and imperialism, but throughout its goal is to inform and provide key details. *The Intelligent Man's Guide to the Post-War World* (Cole, 1947c), even bigger at over 1100 pages, does something similar, with sections on the difference between capitalism and socialism, the demographics and institutions of post-war Britain and international comparisons. Again, the politics of Cole are clear here; the first section is entitled 'The Right to Work' and he makes clear his socialist beliefs early[5] but the book is presented as an exercise in creating an

[5] Cole, perhaps unable to help himself, may have undercut his reception with some members of the public by, while declaring his socialist beliefs, stating that whatever quibble one may have on the means, the ends 'are good, in a thoroughly and finally objective sense' and that 'anyone who denies their truth is blind, or mad, or wicked, or at least purblind' (Cole, 1947c, p. 38). See the conclusion for the full quote.

informed democratic citizenry, since it aimed especially at 'men and women coming out of the armed forces of the public services, to workers set free from munition factories or other forms of war work, and to young people…in short, it is meant for intelligent electors' (Cole, 1947c, p. 33). Similar claims could be made of other books; without wishing to give an exhaustive list, examples could include the co-written *The Condition of Britain* (Cole & Cole, 1937) which detailed the demographics, education system, financial regulation and politics of the UK; *The Simple Case for Socialism* (Cole, 1935b) which put forward the broad principles of those advocating socialism and the group of *Gold, Credit and Employment: Four Essays for Laymen* (Cole, 1930a); the edited *What Everyone Wants to Know About Money* (Cole, 1933c) and *Practical Economics* (Cole, 1937a), all of which sought to make economics understandable to a lay audience.

Cole's historical writings are driven by a similar public commitment. For Wright (1979, pp. 144–145), Cole's turn to history can be traced to the failure of guild socialism and the general strike. Here Cole saw the need for an 'educative process' or 'education for socialism' in which the workers were provided with the tools and skills to produce successful action informed by the ideas and history of Labour. Therefore, Wright (1979, p. 145) suggests, Cole's historical writings were of a part with his lifelong commitment to working-class adult education and the WEA. As with his 'popular' books discussed above, this goal can be seen in his historical texts. There are his biographies, his volume on William Cobbett presents its subject as the 'tribune of the transition' for the contemporary labour movement who 'taught the workers to think for themselves' (Cole, 1924a, p. 12, 13) while his biography of Robert Owen highlights his role as the 'consciousness of co-operative capacity among the workers' (Cole, 1930b, p. 35). Cole also produced a collection of *Chartist Portraits* (Cole, 1941a) which, in capturing what Cole termed the 'unrecorded' and 'unknown' history of Chartism, also defended the value of social history as a way of 'caring about the past' (Cole, 1941a, p. 30). This concern with social history then drove books capturing the history of Labour and the working class. Most famous here, and perhaps his best-selling book,[6] is *The Common People, 1746–1946*, co-written with his brother-in-law Raymond Postgate (Cole & Postgate, 1956). This text focuses on the

[6] At least, in my experience, it is the book of Cole's that one is most likely to find in second-hand bookshops. Including, in one experience of mine, finding it in a bookshop on the lower East Side of Manhattan.

history of inequality between workers and capitalists, the attempts of the labour movement to fight it and their successes in lessening it. The book ends with somewhat of a rallying call, linking current conditions to the history it has told in highlighting that:

> two nations still confronted each other in 1946, though much less starkly than in the days of the Chartists when Disraeli wrote *Sybil*...But there has been no equivalent change in the distribution of property...The great majority of those who died still had almost nothing to leave to their successors. (Cole & Postgate, 1956, p. 688)

Later a companion text, by Cole and A.W. Filson (1951), republished with commentary many of the texts drawn upon in that volume and, in doing so, made many of them available to lay readers for the first time. Similar political links can be found in *A Short History of the British Working Class Movement, 1789–1927* which advocated historical knowledge for a 'wise' Labour leadership (Cole, 1932a, p. xvii). *A Century of Co-operation* (Cole, 1944b) sees Cole argue the co-operative movement should be 'proud of its hundred years of democratic development' and draw on this in adapting to modern conditions. Both *British Working Class Politics, 1832–1914* (Cole, 1941b) and *A History of the Labour Party from 1914* (Cole, 1948b) urge workers, in the words of the latter text, to be aware that 'even if at times the stress of events may beat hard upon their hopes' for socialism they should realise that through their combined historic efforts 'the poor and weak in Great Britain are getting a fairer deal than ever before' (Cole, 1948b, p. 478). All of these books, as we can see, reflect Cole's dual purpose, firstly 'to shape history through Socialism' (Owen, 1966, p. 181), to give the workers and socialists more broadly a history which to that point had been unrecorded, and secondly, as a 'socialist educator...helping people develop their thoughts about a better society' (Carpenter, 1973, p. 112, 114).

The reader may at this point question the extent to which, worthy as the above texts maybe, they count as public *sociology*. Might we instead frame them as the interventions of the classic 'authoritative' public intellectual whose is defined by a general, rather than disciplinary, knowledge, and who speaks not from a formal academic position but from a moral one (Baert & Shipman, 2012)? It is certainly the case that Cole's distinctively sociological contributions to public debate come out more clearly in the articles I will discuss below. However, I would suggest that to ascribe Cole purely to the authoritative model, leaving aside the point that many of Cole's interventions highlight his role of, at that point, a Reader in Economics, is to overlook the sociological basis to the above texts in two ways. Firstly, we can identify sociological content whereby, if we see historical sociology as done by those 'who investigate the mutual interpretation of past and present, events and processes, acting and structuration' (Smith, 1991, p. 3), much of Cole's work is a form of historical sociology, perhaps most notably his discussions of the formations of labour movements. Secondly, and perhaps more significantly, these texts are shaped by a broader normative goal which links them directly to his sociology. As we have seen in this book, Cole's sociology takes as its starting position the individual who, immersed in a web of associations, can exercise collective agency through these associations and thereby enacting a role in producing the structures which then shape their experiences. We have also seen that a normative goal of Cole's work is to make that agency real through the enactment of libertarian forms of socialist organisation which allows for devolved democratic control. Following the same logic, Cole's desire to write 'popular' books is, as we have seen, an attempt to provide actors with the knowledge to allow them to exercise that democratic agency to the best of their abilities. In doing so, Cole reflects the broader goals of sociology others later set. In *The Sociological Imagination* Mills argues that, in his famous notion of sociology providing a way for individuals to link private troubles to public issues has the political goal 'to make society more democratic' (Mills, 1959, p. 189). Meanwhile Bauman (2000) argues that an engaged sociology is one which helps create the critical, questioning citizens of an 'autonomous society' and that ultimately 'the job of sociology is to see to it that the choices are genuinely free' (Bauman, 2000, p. 89). These perspectives share with Cole the notion that a key public role of sociology is to help lay readers place themselves into a broader social and political context, all of which Cole's 'public' books attempted.

Of course, as Cole himself would acknowledge, such a lofty goal is not simply one which can be furnished by the developing of knowledge. Broadly transformative change, often pushed by the collective agency of social movements, was required. I will now turn to how Cole sought to advocate this in his broader writings.

Newspaper and Magazine Articles

One of the most remarkable items held in the Cole archives is a collection of articles Cole wrote across his career for newspapers and magazines. Most of these are held as clippings from the original publications and likely, all in told, run into dozens of pieces.[7] This collection is, in effect, a forgotten collection of some of Britain's foremost public sociology since Cole's style of writing in these pieces, mostly published in regional newspapers, is to take an everyday event the reader can relate to and then link it into a broader sociological critique which, unsurprisingly given what we have seen in this book, tends to focus on questions of class, inequality, freedom or the state. In this section, I will detail just a few of these.

The first piece appears in Cole's regular slot in *The New Statesman* and is titled 'A Place Called Carradale' (Cole, 1939a). Here Cole details how he and his wife recently holidayed in Carradale and Campbeltown, which are located on the Firth of the Clyde, west of Glasgow. Hoping to get away from politics, Cole encounters a local campaign to keep a ferry service between the towns and Glasgow running. Both the local council and the private company operating the ferries want to stop them on grounds of financial feasibility and claimed that people could easily travel by car instead. Cole notes that by needing to travel around, rather than across, the firth, driving adds significant time to any journey, even for the small number of people who own a car. He then links the attempt to stop the ferries into a broader transformation in how public services are increasingly being run for profit and public collective travel is being transformed into private, individualised travel. Arguing that stopping the ferries will just leave a poor council having to fund expensive road building rather than help the poor citizens who live in the towns he notes that 'the people here are victims of large-scale capitalism which regards their ways of living as obsolete' and suggests that, even if they don't name it as such, the residents are becoming socialists 'because the capitalist system is leaving them to rot away in their isolation and enforced poverty' and is 'exposing its disregard for human values' (Cole, 1939a, p. 269). Therefore, for Cole,

[7] These are in addition to the numerous pieces that Cole and his collaborator William Mellor produced for the *Daily Herald*, the left-wing newspaper (and forerunner of *The Sun*), most notably in 1914. Nuffield College also house these. One example, entitled 'The Class War and the State', sees Cole and Mellor castigating 'old' trade unionists who 'call themselves socialists' but who aim for 'at the best, a benevolent bureaucracy, and, at the worst, a bureaucracy minus the benevolence' (Cole & Mellor, 1914).

this decision to cut a ferry line, which was eventually successful, shows the broader changes in how public services are disregarded under capitalism.

Similar themes are found in an article entitled 'Freedom to Choose One's Job', published in the *Brighton and Hove Weekly News* on 26 June 1930 which concerns a classic topic of sociology: the division of labour. Cole begins by noting that most people, like his readers, will have just the one profession across their life. While acknowledging that some specialism is required Cole argues this indicates how 'modern civilization wants to put me in a particular box, label me neatly and keep me there for the rest of my life' (Cole, 1930c) even as our work becomes increasingly more specialised, less fulfilling and we come to tire of it. Instead, for Cole, true freedom should allow for the ability to move between jobs, try out different occupations and develop our talents. Here, however, Cole introduces a class angle. Some people, in which category he includes himself, have the 'luck' to change their job when they get bored. For most however 'the power to chop and change does not exist in any effective sense'. Therefore, for Cole, allowing for the freedom to choose one's job requires a transformation of the economic system and the class system which it produces, or, as he puts it:

> What appals me most about modern civilization is that most people do not enjoy their work...Choice of job is freedom and doing a job you do not want to do and see no good reason for doing is servitude. In that sense most people are slaves, or at least serfs, to-day. The biggest object we sought to set...is to set men free to range from job to job...We shall not, I am sure, reach that result, even approximately, until we have made a much better approach to social and economic equality...Get rid of the economic scramble, and we shall be a long way to getting the square pegs into square holes and the round pegs into the round. But, at present, I believe the pushing of men into the wrong jobs, and the holding of men to the same job all their lives, are responsible for as much human unhappiness as anything in the world. (Cole, 1930c)

Here we see Cole combine elements of a Marxist approach to the division of labour as causing alienation with the Durkheimian claim of a 'forced division of labour' (Durkheim, 1984). Even if some division is required, what we have now is a 'forced' one which allows some, due to their class position, the freedom to move and others are condemned to stay in one boring, alienating job.

A similar concern with class and freedom is discussed in 'The Case for Going One's Own Way' published in the *Kensington News* on 8 September 1933. This begins with the notion, which Cole suggests is commonly held, that people have too few tastes (Cole, 1933d). He argues there is some structural interest in maintaining this situation, since it means advertisers have more ready receivers of their messages and governments are able to direct activity more freely. More fundamentally though, the reason tastes are not able to grow is class:

> One reason – a very big one – why most people have so few real tastes of their own is that most people have too few opportunities to gratify them. For tastes are things that grow by feeding; and most of them cost money. The very words 'hobby' and 'amateur' are middle class words. (Cole, 1933d)

Cole goes on to note that inequity in access to leisure activities has been enhanced by an education system which, while it outwardly seeks to promote a 'gentlemanly' way of acting, has reduced the development of 'tastes' to simply those that provide economic advantage on the labour market and which fit the 'correct set of outward tastes' (Cole, 1933d). Here of course we see an early echo of Bourdieusian arguments on both the social construction of tastes and their relation to a class system requiring both cultural and economic capital. Therefore, for Cole, there is a need to battle the class system not just for the inequities of money it produces, but for the fact that it shuts off leisure activities from the working class. As he puts it: 'making the many less poor is one of the two most important things in the world. The other one is making the rich less rich' (Cole, 1933d). Similar themes are discussed in a piece entitled 'The No-Sayers', published in the *Oldham Evening Chronicle and Standard* on 27 April 1936 in which Cole uses the example of his children asking for money to go to the cinema as a starting point to argue that increasingly there has been an expectation of legislating away what are seen as 'bad' or 'problem' forms of leisure activities which, inevitably he argues, tend to be the leisure activities of the poor (Cole, 1936a).

Cole developed these links between class and politics in a piece entitled 'Employers who are a Menace to Democracy', published in *The Manchester City News* on 11 May 1935. This starts with a story of a schoolteacher who was sacked from his job after running as a Labour candidate for his local council. From here Cole makes a broad point of principle, that employers should not be able to limit what their employees do outside working hours, but also notes a classed contradiction in how these principles are implemented. Many businesses support their executives taking on council roles in the hope of furthering their company. This is seen as 'non-political', as is the case of Oxford academics who, like Cole, are encouraged to seek political office (often, incidentally, as Tories). However, for working-class employees, or even the middle-class employee such as the schoolteacher who follows personal beliefs and/or a desire to serve their community (most frequently not as Tories), this is seen as 'political' and therefore not compatible with their work (Cole, 1935c).

Finally, there is a piece entitled 'Freedom's Garden' published in the London-based *Inquisitor* on 7 September 1936. Here Cole notes a trend towards gardens which are increasingly ordered, well presented and in which the gardener is always 'sweeping and cutting and rolling and paving and pruning and binding, in order that everything may obey his law' (Cole, 1936b). These are different from the increasingly less popular 'natural' garden in which 'flowers and shrubs and trees are let grow, as nearly as they may be, in their own way'. These latter gardens in turn cause outrage from the 'lovers of trimness and symmetry' who regard them as 'unkempt wilderness' (Cole, 1936b). For Cole, we see a reflection of this mentality in the increased use of state power for an 'enforced uniformity'. While, of course, most notable in the fascist countries, Cole argues the same can be seen in Britain via increased police powers and government surveillance. Here, we can see a forerunner of an argument of the potentially totalitarian formations of modernity, with its quest for order and desire, which can be seen in Arendt (1951) and Bauman (1989b) the latter of whom, interestingly, uses the metaphor of the gardener to describe the role of the modern authoritarian state.

The above is just a small selection of Cole's contributions in this format. I could also cite his defence of the 'jack of all trades' as reflecting the possibility for free development (Cole, 1937b), the ways in which our daily habits make us more, or less, susceptible to fascism (Cole, 1939b) and his reflections on how travelling to the countryside make Cole question the shape city living takes, reflecting what Simmel would call the 'blasé' attitude (Cole, 1931b, 1940). What they all share is a desire to connect everyday concerns facing the reader, whether this be the changing shape of gardens, the lack of hobbies people have the resources to pursue or a closed ferry service, to broader sociological concerns. Reflecting the fact that much of this activity was undertaken in the 1930s, there are across these pieces a concern with defending freedom against fascism but much of their sociological messages remain ones that are significant today. Indeed, what is 'The Case for Going One's Way', with its discussion of the classed nature of leisure time, if not a proto-Bourdieusian attempt to explain access to, and construction of tastes, according to the distribution of capital?

I will return later in this chapter to the lessons to be taken from across Cole's public sociology in which these newspaper articles are central. Before that, however, I want to turn to a final group of Cole's public activities, which were presented in a more creative medium.

Cole's Creative Public Sociology: Poems, Songs and Films

In her discussion of successful public intellectuals, Misztal (2007) highlights the role of 'creativity'. A public intellectual has to be creative in a literal sense, their goal from their interventions is to bring something new into being, as well as in the sense of moving beyond narrow means of expression in order to obtain a public audience. Cole was an excellent example of this creativity in the varied ways he sought to get his message across, which I will explore in this section.

As highlighted in Chap. 1 Cole took to writing poetry when he arrived in Oxford as a student. Composing poetry was a lifelong concern for Cole. He published a volume of his poems, *The Crooked World*, in 1933 with many other verses published in the magazines and newspapers that would also take his articles. While many of these poems are romantic tales and/or contemplations of one of Cole's greatest loves, the English countryside, it is perhaps unsurprising that many have a political focus and, much as his newspaper articles, sought to convey sociological messages, only this time in verse.[8]

The best place to begin is *The Crooked World* (Cole, 1933e). This is a 135-page volume containing dozens of poems. How these are structured is telling, with Cole seemingly attempting to present the volume as a

[8] The reader may remember that in the Chap. 1 I referenced Margaret Cole's claim that her husband's early poems were 'bad, though not abysmal' (Cole, 1971, p. 46). Not being a literary critic or an appreciator of poetic verse, I will not seek to assess the value of Cole's poems *as poems*. However, it is perhaps fair to say that while he seemed to have improved as a poet from his undergraduate days, it is maybe unlikely his poems would have attracted much attention, or even been published, had they not been written by G.D.H. Cole.

political account of Britain in the 1930s through verses. The book begins with poems which explore working class' lives, poverty and inequality. Take, for example, 'Mean's Test' which presents the two sides of a person seeking assistance from the Public Assistance Committee, who applied a means test to such claims. First, we have the voice of the applicant as he confronts the Chairman of the Public Assistance Committee:

> I hate you, because you dole me out my pittance
> As if of all human claims it was more than a quittance
> God, if only I could afford to fling your dole
> Back in your ugly face and solve my soul
> I should have no need to hate you – you and your charity. (Cole, 1933e, p. 22)

Then the poem shifts to the perspective of the Chairman who, hiding his own hate from the claimant who he 'supposes I have to keep you and your brats from starvation/or else you'll be breaking windows, hell and damnation', ends the poem without any reflection on his position:

> Three years on the dole, his skill at his trade destroyed
> He'd have to manage on two bob no less, now the nation
> Was reduced to a state of complete financial prostration
> Which done, he went off to his club, and made a good dinner
> And it never occurred to him that *he* was the sinner. (Cole, 1933e, p. 23)

Another poem, 'Factory Dirge', considers the alienation felt from the repetitive manual labour of the factory. Here Cole talks of how the:

> Power of metal, steam and evil
> Soulless soul-destroying devil
> How you drive, how you race me
> How you torture me and haunt me
> In my sleep
> How you dominant and taunt me. (Cole, 1933e, p. 16)

The poem then ends with the worker, unable to recall the last time they saw the countryside, lamenting that:

> In this Polyphemus cave
> Unresisting I attend
> To the end. (Cole, 1933e, p. 17)

While these poems attend to the sense of alienation in working-class lives, in the next section of *Crooked World* Cole moves to discussing how resistance happened, with poems dedicated to politics. These were often satirical of the respectable politics of the Labour Party. One example is 'Proletarian Ditty', a short poem which runs:

Put the thing through quickly;
Wage the class-war slickly
'Ang the rich from lampposts 'igh
But don't 'ang me
Stick to Marx me 'arty
Damn the Labour Party
Keep the 'Ell fires burning
For the *Bourgeoisie.* (Cole, 1933e, p. 51)

Having commemorated labour, if not Labour, politics in verse, Cole moves in the next section to the threat of fascism, an example of which can be found in the poem Hail Hitler which, condemning the violent, racist nature of fascism, speaks of 'myriad blind followers after leaders blind' and 'to hate, to joy in hating and to dare' (Cole, 1933e, p. 94). This section also touches on war and reflects the broadly anti-war sentiment the early 1930s British socialist Left held dearly.

Cole then ends the book with a collection of love poems. But, even here, what is remarkable is Cole's implicit claim that the issues of class, alienation and fascism make experiencing true love difficult. For example, the collection ends with a poem entitled XXX which says:

Someday I mean, when the world is mended
And no one's a slave and no one's poor
And the ceaseless wrangle is over
By one alone, who loves me, attended
For, being with her, I shall need no more
To slip away, and live in clover. (Cole, 1933e, p. 135)

And ends with:

But while there's work to be done, how shirk it?
Brace ourselves first for a strong endeavour
To leap a bound right over the moon
It's a difficult feat; but we've got to work it

And then, when it's done, we can do as we list
And no one need play the philanthropist. (Cole, 1933e, p. 135)

Therefore, *The Crooked World* attempts to put over similar messages to those found in Cole's sociological works in lyrical verses. Cole's poems published elsewhere aim at something similar. For example, the 1934 edition of *New Britain* contained two poems by Cole. One, entitled 'The Song of the Farmers', bemoaned the conditions of farmers living a life where 'wheat's too cheap' for them to get a fair wage yet 'bread's too dear' for them to be able to live. The second poem, 'The Invocation', is, as the title indicates, a call to action to resist the evils of capitalism, with its ending claim that 'The future lies in you/why then do you linger/to make life anew?' (Cole, 1934f).

Cole also expressed similar sentiments in song. Notable here is *The Striker Stricken* (Cole, G.D.H., 1977a), an operetta written by Cole in 1926, at the end of the general strike. As Margaret Cole (Cole, M., 1977b) details, this piece was originally written as entertainment for working-class students attending the summer school of the Tutorial Classes Committee at the University of London, for which Cole was in his final year as director. Following a tradition at such gatherings, the school ended with a day of entertainment and Cole wrote the operetta for the students to perform. It was not published at the time, given it was considered libellous, but the programme was toured around the Durham coalfields later that year and would be played at Labour/socialists gatherings for years afterwards (Cole, M., 1977b, p. 58). Therefore, while it would only be published in 1977, it was a piece of public, oral, sociology.

The Striker Stricken concerns itself with the politics of the General Strike. The first two acts focus on trade union leaders, the government, the royal family, the middle classes and press barons. Here Cole portrays a general strike being betrayed by trade union leaders desperate for status, a government eager to crush trade unionism while looking reasonable in public, a royal family with no beliefs beyond defending privilege, middle classes who are comfortable with charity work to support the poor but hate when the working class practice resistance and a press eager to promote the establishment's political position. The strike eventually ends and these 'leaders' are eager to claim their respectable positions. For example, here are the words of J.H. Thomas, a Labour MP from the time who previously was head of the rail unions and had become known for his desire to be seen as a moderate figure of the governing class (see Elliott, 1993, pp. 36–44, *passim*): 'Peace, perfect peace, the Constitution's sound/ Statesman like us are never wanting found' (Cole, G.D.H., 1977a, p. 91).

Act three then takes place at the pearly gates of heaven. The ghost of Karl Marx arrives and, after an argument with St Peter concerning whether heaven could exist (in Cole's telling, Marx utters 'By heaven, I swear this place does not exist/My whole conception is materialist') leaves for hell, or the LSE,[9] but drops a copy of *Das Kapital* on the way. Peter begins to read the book and seemingly convinced by it rejects heavenly entry to all the characters of the first two acts given their lack of allegiance to the workers. Only the working class and two of their leaders who faithfully represented their cause are allowed in, joining St Peter in a drink. Before the end of the operetta Marx returns—apparently rejected by the LSE—and the whole cast sings this song to conclude:

> The angels' flag is deepest red;
> As Conrad Noel always said;
> And while the wicked squirm and roast
> We give you this parting toast;
> Then raise the scarlet standard high,
> O'er heaven it waves in empery,
> To pay off every earthy debt
> We give you GOD's OWN SOVIET! (Cole, G.D.H., 1977a, pp. 99–100)

The Striker Stricken, while undoubtedly something written to be enjoyed and laughed at, reflecting its original intent, is also an attempt to show the various competing forms of power at work in the general strike and explain its eventual demise with reference to the role of media, class, the increasing 'elite' positioning of trade union leaders and the role of government. In many ways therefore, it continues Cole's desire to put over scholarly arguments in a popular form.

[9] The position of LSE in the operetta is intriguing for our argument. One of the treacherous trade union leaders, weighing up options for his soul, utters 'Hell, or the London School of Economics? Not much in it' (Cole, G.D.H., 1977a, p. 96). It seems at this point Cole was riffing on how the LSE was viewed, with its desire for respectability and its emphasis on objectivity and science suggesting it was not a friend of the labour cause. Also, given it was originally performed for a summer school for University of London extension students, some may have been, or would be, associated with the LSE and thus there could be a bit of an 'insider's joke' about this reference.

Cole also published a collection of songs in a co-edited collection with Margaret Cole entitled *The Bolo Book* (Cole & Cole, 1921). While the preface to the book says neither Cole can claim sole authorship of all the songs, many of them reflect Cole's broader public sociology goals. For example, 'The Building of Houses' concerns itself with post-WWI house building in the UK, especially 'workmen's house' for the ever-increasing number of industrial workers. Here the Coles take the perspective of a young worker being put in such a house:

> A vision of a street of houses
> Danced before young David's eyes
> And he saw the curly smoke-wreaths
> From a thousand chimneys rise.
> It was a miracle of rare device;
> A thousand houses and not one was nice. (Cole & Cole, 1921, p. 25)

Another song, 'The Social Scheme', satirises the Fabians and the emerging connection of socialism to the welfare state, with its desire to 'completely abolish the unemployed' and leave 'only a modicum of freedom for everybody' (Cole & Cole, 1921, p. 52). Finally, 'Wanglo-Persian Oil Lyric' discusses the entwining of imperial domination and mercantile capitalism in the case of the Anglo-Persian Oil Company, later BP, with the claim 'The profiteers has all the oil in freight/Because the British Empire had a new mandate' (Cole & Cole, 1921, p. 51).

The final medium Cole operated in is film. As Margaret Cole details (Cole, 1971, pp. 273–274) he had a lifelong interest in the proper, pictorial, representation of data and therefore, when a company named Common Ground contacted him with the offer of producing film strips made up of Cole's lectures with representations of data, art and other visuals alongside it, Cole was eager to take it up. The Cole archives at Nuffield College contain film strips for a number of topics, including the class structure, the Industrial Revolution, an introduction to Economics and trade unionism, among many more. While these strips were primarily aimed at schools and colleges, they were also made available for the interested lay viewer. In this sense, they serve as a visual accompaniment to Cole's 'popular' books discussed above.

The above has detailed how across songs, poems and film, Cole sought to take his sociological perspective into the public realm in mediums beyond the classic book and/or essay format.[10] Befitting his moving between multiple media, the format of his messages differ—from the talking of everyday experiences of newspaper articles, to the romantic appeals to humanity of the poems, to the satirical form of the songs—but in each case there is a desire to highlight key elements of his sociological critique based around factors such as class, alienation, the state, welfare and individualism. The means of intellectual interventions are important, with different means creating new relationships with audiences (Baert & Booth, 2012). By exploring these different means of communication Cole is engaging, in the words of Bauman (1992, p. 95), in 'building that bridge' between intellectual ideas and lay experience and, in this sense, to again use the terms of Bauman, is adopting the role of intellectual as interpreter which 'consists of translating statements…so that they can be understood…this strategy is aimed at facilitating communication between autonomous (sovereign) participants' (Bauman, 1987, p. 4).

What is then remarkable about Cole's public sociology is not only its extent and goal, but its consistent message, even in a time when he engages in some political shifts. Reflecting his broader sociological perspective, Cole's consistent focus was the ways that capitalism and liberal democracy do not allow for people to express their will, and act, in the ways they would desire. Instead, activity is directed in such a way so that the general will, rather than reflecting all the associative wills, takes particular expressions, reflecting dominant class interests, as its focus. Therefore, there is a need to bring in a socialist system, for Cole, to allow these different wills to express themselves. As this indicates, Cole's public sociology work is also political, and the next section considers the relation between these two.

[10] One format I have not discussed here is Cole's detective fiction novels. He wrote 38 with his wife Margaret and they, seemingly, could be his most 'popular' form of writing. As Evans (2015, pp. 184–222) details, the novels bore the influence of their joint politics with any Tory character clearly guilty and any socialist inevitably innocent. Furthermore, the novels touched on themes such as industrial relations, war and class. However, I have not discussed these here since they do not seem to reflect Cole's *sociological* contribution and are more narrowly political. In addition to this, Margaret was the more committed of the two to detective fiction. Therefore, while the novels may well be valuable for a discussion of how Cole presented political arguments in a popular format, they are less useful for my discussion. I am grateful to my colleague Robert Gibb for bringing Evans' book to my attention.

Assessing Cole's Public Sociology

Above we have seen the broad scope of Cole's public sociology. At this point however we need to bring this story back to the start of the chapter. As I noted there, while maintaining some core beliefs, Cole changed his political focus and favoured means of implementation to fit changing times and priorities. This, then, highlights the significance of Cole's public interventions as also political interventions, driven not just by a desire to critique, in Cole's case to critique capitalism and liberal democracy, but an advocacy for a socialist alternative. This makes us reconsider the nature and purpose of public sociology and the broader debate on the activity of public intellectuals.

Burawoy, in his programme for public sociology, raises and never quite solves two political contradictions. These both relate to Burawoy's argument concerning the division of labour within the discipline, which for him is made up of four parts (Burawoy, 2005a). The first of these is professional sociology, the institutionalised part of the discipline, made up of university departments, graduate training courses, ethics boards, methodological debates and journals behind paywalls. Here, sociologists talk to other sociologists in a technical form. The second is policy sociology, where sociologists talk to an (select) outside audience. This is mostly governments and private organisations who commission sociologists to conduct a piece of research and/or offer advice on a policy they are implementing. Significantly here, the ends are already decided, an organisation or government knows what they want, the sociologist is only advising them how to get it. The third form is critical sociology. This, like its professional form, is largely inward looking, with sociologists talking to other sociologists. Here sociologists from critical perspectives—Marxists, feminists, queer studies and so on—critique the claims of their professional counterparts for their omissions and/or biases. Finally, there is public sociology, where sociologists talk to a broader public audience. This can be in a 'traditional' form, where sociologists make their research known through top-down mechanisms of writing public texts, appearing on television and more generally being a 'public' intellectual. Or, it can be an 'organic' form, where sociologists work with/are part of social movements.

For Burawoy, these forms of sociology then inform each other; the conducting of good professional sociology, informed by the critique of critical sociology, provides rich material for public sociology whereby a scholar can write for a public audience with the insights their professional/

critical activity has given them. Meanwhile, policy sociology conducted well must build upon the tools of the professional sociologists. Therefore, as he puts it one does not 'have to be a public sociologist to contribute to public sociology, one could do so by being a good professional, critical or policy sociologist. The flourishing of each sociology would enhance the flourishing of all' (Burawoy, 2005a, p. 17).

Here however we run into our first political contradiction, while Burawoy claims each sociology has its own intrinsic worth, he clearly thinks that public sociology is a more acceptable form than policy sociology. Indeed, he claims that public sociology is the 'conscience' of policy sociology (Burawoy, 2005a, p. 10). This has led critics to question the basis for this split; if the goal is to take sociological insight beyond sociology, why is there a distinction between working for governments/organisations and other forms of public engagement? Burawoy argues this is due to a shift in the type of knowledge each draws upon, while policy sociology uses 'instrumental' knowledge—largely based around the problem/puzzle-solving of scientific research—public sociology uses 'reflexive' research, which involves a 'dialogue about ends' (Burawoy, 2005a, p. 11). While this could perhaps reflect a question of the means used for public communication (Baert & Booth, 2012), for Burawoy's critics, this reflects an implicit equation of public sociology with his Marxist politics and against right-wing policy sociology (Abbott, 2007; Calhoun, 2005) which in turn gives shape to an anti-state politics (Brady, 2004). This overlooks not just the successes sociology has had in improving governmental practice (Urry, 2005) but also the ways in which policy sociology *can* be critical, for example producing governmental reports to show that increasing social mobility requires more drastic changes (Goldthorpe, 2016). In short, it could be said that Burawoy is drawing on an implicit notion of the Dreyfusardian or 'exilic' intellectual, as one who hates '*all* systems, whether on our side or theirs, with equal distaste' (Said, 1994, p. 55). That maybe a normative position Burawoy wishes to hold, but it is a normative claim which involves seeing some other means of 'public' intellectual intervention as lesser. These critics were willing to accept that there may be differences between each activity, they just reject the valuing of one over the other.

The example of Cole however should make us question the extent to which this distinction needs to hold true. Cole did both policy sociology, working for the Labour Party, including in government, conducting the Nuffield Survey on Social Reconstruction, writing policy documents, etc. and public sociology, as discussed above, without any real change in tenor or argument. As indicated above, Cole is both legislator *and* interpreter

(Bauman, 1987). This is because his sociological activity refused to accept any notion that the ends could be decided by anyone but him. Cole defined policy as 'what *ought* to be done' (Cole, 1957a, p. 158) and held that one could be both 'scientific *and* moral' (Cole, 1950e, p. 249), that you could decide means *and* ends. Therefore, Cole's public activity is innately tied to his role as a policy intellectual, his public books, such as *The Next Ten Years in British Social and Economic Policy* and his other public publications, such as the advocacy of public transport in 'A Place Called Carradale', offer *both* sociological account *and* policy programme.

The second key point of contention in Burawoy's argument is the politics of public sociology. Burawoy himself is inconsistent here. On one hand, he values pluralism, arguing that since public sociology simply involves taking sociological knowledge to a broader audience it 'can as well support Christian Fundamentalism as it can Liberation Sociology or Communitarianism' (Burawoy, 2005a, pp. 8–9). On the other hand, Burawoy argues that, due to the 'scissors movement' (Burawoy, 2005a) sociology has become more left-wing as society has moved to the right. The reason for this is that sociology is, uniquely among academic disciplines, invested in the civil sphere as a space for debate and discussion, a sphere which is increasingly facing privatisation and/or state authoritarianism (Burawoy, 2007). Therefore, Burawoy sees public sociology increasingly defining itself against the market (Burawoy, 2007) and measuring itself by some notion of 'democratic socialism' (Burawoy, 2005b, p. 325). Again here, we see some implicit Dreyfusardian notion of intellectuals as inevitably left-wing. This then has left Burawoy open to criticisms on both sides. One side considers his pluralism naïve, arguing that public questions have innately political contestations and sociologists will be placed within these (Etzoni, 2005; Piven, 2007), especially if we engage with publics via the media (Ericson, 2005), with journalism operating by different political rules of engagement (Ehrenreich, 2007). In turn, this means public sociology needs to move even more into its organic form, becoming activist in focus (Ghamari-Tabrizi, 2005; Aronwitz, 2005). This once more reflects Said's (1994) notion of the 'exilic' intellectual, defined by their marginality and resistance to power. Indeed, this position argues that adopting this exilic position would have the benefit of correcting a mistake in Burawoy's initial argument wherein the long tradition of organic public sociology undertook by marginalised groups, most notably by women and/or people of colour, has been overlooked (Katz-Fishman & Scott, 2005; Collins, 2007). The other side however criticises Burawoy for the political links he draws to public sociology. This is seen to impose a political homogeneity on a diverse discipline (Holmwood, 2007), a position overly determined by a hatred of markets and a desire to do Marxist work without saying what had become, especially in US sociology, an unfashionable word (Nielsen, 2004). In turn for these critics, Burawoy's claim of public sociology being part of civil society hides an 'arrogance' whereby sociology is seen to have a unique and special voice within this (Tittle, 2004; Stacey, 2007) and ultimately public sociology will fail as its politicised message speaks only to the converted and exposes that sociologists agree on very little (Brady, 2004).

The example of Cole shows us the significance of politics to public sociology. Cole's public sociology only has its power because of its political position and, in line with the first group of critics, since he is willing to engage in normative questions of what should happen. For example, the newspaper article 'The Case for Going One's Way', with its condemnation of class-based inequities in leisure and alienation at work only has its power because it suggests that this does not have to be, that a democratisation of work and leisure is possible. Therefore, while his perspective is innately political, it also reminds us of the possibility, reflecting the work of Wells, whom, as discussed in previous chapters, Cole would share much with, of sociology being utopian and suggesting what could be. While, in response to the second group of critics, Cole would likely have argued that public sociology can indeed take many different political forms, he would not have shared their concern about this showing that sociologists agree on very little, or that it implied some level of 'arrogance' in terms of its access to the civil sphere.

Therefore, I would suggest that Cole's public sociology informs us about the ways that political sociology can, and most likely *has to* be done. This will innately involve political questions since critiquing what is automatically presupposes what could be and, in turn, can run across the public and policy forms of sociology. Central to this is a different conception to Burawoy. While the latter places the sociology on the ground of a dialogue-heavy civil society, Cole sees the sociologist as defined foremost by intellectual autonomy. Those who worked with Cole such as Worswick (1960) and Briggs (1960) continually emphasise that his desire was to maintain a sense of autonomy from power and from institutions and, in so doing, to further political discussion and outcomes. As Briggs put it:

> as an intellectual Cole believed that there were 'real disagreements' and that there was a need for socialists to air them. 'Freedom to *choose*' he would argue, was not granted to large numbers of people within the framework of

> a capitalist society; socialists should not deliberately limit the freedom to choose in a socialist society. (Briggs, 1960, p. 671)

This perspective on the role of the intellectual as an autonomous individual reflects Said's (1994) notion of the intellectual as an 'amateur' who raises moral and political questions without seeking to align one's self with a project or institution as well as Bourdieu's (1989) notion of intellectual autonomy being defended on the grounds of the autonomous field of intellectual life.

Of course, this is not to pretend such a position is easy to fulfil. Leaving aside the question of to what extent the pure autonomous individual was ever really available to men (Oakley, 2011) and, as mentioned above, the changes in the placing of public intellectuals, such a position becomes even more challenging in times of increased audit found in British academia (Pardo-Guerra, 2022). Cole himself showed the difficulties that could arise. Despite his desire for autonomy, he was, as we noted, strongly linked to the Labour Party, including as a parliamentary candidate. His changes in political programme were, in turn, often linked to the positioning of this party. Therefore, Cole had to walk a difficult middle path. This could, on occasion, lead to him being criticised from both sides. As we saw, his time as head of the Nuffield Reconstruction Survey comes to an end partly due to his criticisms from those not on the Left concerning political allegiances. Meanwhile, for many politicians in the Labour Party his aloof intellectual manner made him a figure of suspicion as even his pupil, and future Labour leader, Hugh Gaitskill noted (Gaitskell, 1960). It is claimed, for example, that when Cole visited Clement Attlee, he would be greeted with the claim 'give me a pair of starry eyes Douglas and I will do what you say' (Foot, 1968, p. 53).

As we have seen, the 'implicit' sociology of the time before Cole often had a public, or perhaps in Burawoy's term, policy focus, in its desire to use it for a normative end. In turn, despite the claims of sociology's precarious position in the UK we can point to a number of figures, such as member of the Cole Group, Stuart Hall as constituting a public sociology in the UK. While the nature and actions of public intellectuals may change, we should not fall for the fallacy that Britain has never had them (Collini, 2006). Cole's value here is to show us particular ways of being a public intellectual and doing public sociology across different medium and with a desire to link it to everyday activity. It is a rich tradition we have not fully appreciated.

Conclusion

This chapter has summarised Cole's public sociology. I began by noting the shifts in Cole's political claims and, building upon explanations by others, argued this reflected Cole's notion that a socialist intellectual such as himself should be useful to the public and respond to the different context. I have also suggested however that we can identify a consistency in Cole's sociological outlook across this work. I then detailed Cole's public sociology. This began by highlighting his many encyclopaedic and labour history texts which sought to provide an informed, democratically engaged citizenry, who could fulfil the traditional sociological goal of placing their personal troubles into public issues. From here, I turned to Cole's newspaper articles, which took a different approach of starting with the discussion of an everyday issues, a ferry service on the West coast of Scotland, the design of gardens, what Cole's children wanted to spend their money on, and linked them into broader sociological critiques on matters such as capitalism, class, the state, leisure and the division of labour. From here I outlined what I have termed Cole's 'creative' public sociology, expressed in formats such as poems, songs and film strips which drew upon similar themes to the newspaper articles.[11] Finally, I put this work in discussion with Burawoy's notion of public sociology and broader debates on public intellectuals, highlighting how Cole would question the split between public and policy sociology while also asserting the need for autonomy in order to engage in the political debates public sociology produces.

As also noted at the start of this chapter, British sociology's notable achievements in public intellectual life are increasingly being commented upon. Here, however, we see another case of Cole's poor timing, since in the period he was active sociology was its least 'public' in Britain. While this is perhaps understandable given in this period it is seeking to establish itself as an academic discipline, it is notable that while Hobhouse had some public profile due to his background as a journalist, Ginsberg had

[11] Amazingly, despite the depth of my discussion, I have not yet noted Cole's most significant public impact. Cole was, along with Bertrand Russell the co-inspiration for the character of Professor Yaffle in Bagpuss. Oliver Postgate, Cole's nephew by marriage and creator of the show, justified his choice by saying he wanted a character who 'had no sense of humour and wasn't a bit ridiculous' but who also was a 'distinguished academic personage who would claim to know everything and would go "*nerp, nerp, nerp*" in a birdy way' (Postage, 2010, p. 296).

none at all. Indeed, it was the Politics Department at the LSE that produced the most significant socialist intellectual of this period, in Harold Laski.[12] Cole misses what Savage terms the 'sociological moment' of the 1960s when a flowering of popular outlets, such as *New Society*, give the kind of earlier public sociology Cole favoured a natural outlet.

I began this chapter saying the three significant elements of Cole's work were (1) his mode of communication; (2) in its normative focus blurring the lines between 'policy' and 'public' sociology; and (3) Cole's prioritising of public relevance in the shaping of his political agenda. We have seen this here and I would highlight in particular Cole's desire to meet the public on an everyday level, for example in asking what they like to do for hobbies. Nevertheless, reflecting one of the key themes of this book, it is the normative element of Cole's work which is most significant here. It is shaped, and dedicated, by the desire to change the world. For Cole, the only reason to be 'public' was to seek to make things better, that, for him, is the only justification for public sociology. His interventions were precisely that, attempts to do something, in this case to make society better. In contemporary British academia, with its justification of 'impact' as a worthwhile goal to be pursued no matter what 'impact' one is trying to achieve, it is a timely message.

[12] Interestingly, as Margaret Cole notes (1971, pp. 201–203), despite some similarity in political outlook Cole and Laski, perhaps the pre-eminent socialist intellectuals of their period in Britain, had a 'mutual antagonism' towards each other. Partly this reflected some petty squabbles common to academia and left-wing politics—Laski, the younger of the two, was put off by the fame Cole amassed at a young age in the guild socialist movement, while Cole felt Laski let his work slip as *his* fame increased. But, it also reflected some difference in personality. As Margaret tellingly puts it, her husband 'cherished a certain contempt for certain aspects of Laski – for his liking to meet and gossip with great names, for example, and for his telling of tall stories which he expected to be believed' (Cole, 1971, p. 202).

CHAPTER 6

Conclusion

This book has put the work of G.D.H. Cole and the history of British sociology into discussion with each other. Doing so, I have argued, allows us to look at each anew. There are three arguments that come from this discussion.

Firstly, while the golden age we are currently experiencing for research on the history of British sociology has been hugely fruitful it should pay more attention than it currently does, with some notable exceptions, to the period between 1920 and 1960. While the earlier and latter periods have some natural appeal for historians, this intervening period is also hugely significant. As we have seen in this book, it is a time where the vision of what British sociology might be, having been so vociferously fought over during the battles for institutions, is being determined. This is occurring within the LSE but also beyond it, including in the extramural teaching such as the WEA in which Cole was active. Indeed, it is this 'official' vision for the discipline found at the LSE which loses out to other competitors in the end. While events after 1960, such as the expansion of universities, the radical movements which reached a pinnacle in 1968, the greater acceptance of Marxism and so on, inevitably play a significant role the future direction of sociology they had something to build upon and did not emerge from nothing. Greater attention, therefore, needs to be paid to this part of British sociology's history.

M. Dawson, *G.D.H. Cole and British Sociology*,
https://doi.org/10.1007/978-3-031-75484-5_6

Secondly, this book has presented Cole as a sociologist. As mentioned in Chap. 1, it is not my goal here to say that Cole was 'really' or 'only' a sociologist; his work is too broad and covers too many areas to make that claim. However, I have shown in this book how Cole has a sociological perspective. This is grounded in a form of Rousseauian structuration theory and political individualism which, while being more voluntarist than much of contemporary sociology would be comfortable with, is the basis of his normative guild socialist project. Furthermore, Cole makes sociological contributions on topics such as class, imperialism and the state in ways that have been suggested in this book. His sociological contribution is not only limited to his intellectual output but includes his work helping to establish the discipline, especially in Oxford, his discussion of the teaching of sociology and his prominence as a public sociologist. This last category is especially significant to how we should see Cole today as discussed in Chap. 5. Therefore, while I think alternative readings of Cole—as a political theorist, socialist theorist and historian most notably—remain valid, I do think he can be placed clearly within the sociological tradition and that sociology was important to him. While, as mentioned above, Cole's voluntarism sits uncomfortably in contemporary sociology and his treatment of gender may now be unacceptable, we can see that he was one of the most significant sociologists of his time and did anticipate many later developments, most notably around debates on structure and agency, class and imperialism.

Thirdly, by presenting Cole and the history of British sociology together I have told a story about semi-alienation. I have used this concept to indicate Cole's liminal position as neither insider nor outsider to sociology. This is not due to Cole's social positioning, as a concept such as 'optimal marginality' suggests (McLaughlin, 2000), but rather due to intellectual positioning. As we have seen, Cole is alienated from much of what he saw in the practice of sociology—its value-freedom, its overly technical research projects, its evolutionism, its ignorance of class and politics—but this is only a 'semi' alienation since he is very welcoming of the notion of sociology, as indicated by his broader writings on the discipline and efforts to expand it. Therefore, part of my claim is that Cole's rejection of the label of sociologist is a rejection of a particular form of the discipline and, leaving aside that Cole disliked any label except for that of 'Socialist', may well have been different had he been born later or earlier. In each of these periods, British sociology was much closer to Cole's ideal of the discipline. This concept of semi-alienation may well help capture instances when a scholar's distance from a discipline is reflected not of the nature of their thought per se but rather to the particular historical/national form of the discipline they confront. In Cole's case, as we have seen, the question of normativity was particularly strong here. Also, by looking at the history of this period of British sociology through the person of Cole we can relativise and question it. For example, its avoidance of Marx and Marxism comes to be seen much more clearly as a choice when at the same time Cole is developing a notion of a sociological Marx that would later become dominant in the discipline.

These then, are the three main arguments which I have offered in this book and I hope the reader has looked at Cole and/or the history of British sociology afresh as a result of reading this text. In what follows I want to turn the focus away from history to the current day and discuss (a) the value in using the term 'semi-alienation' for a case such as Cole; (b) Cole's continuing impact in British sociology; and (c) what relevance Cole has for sociology today.

Semi-Alienation and the Sociology of Intellectuals

This notion of semi-alienation may be useful to further studies on the history of disciplines and, more broadly, on the sociology of intellectuals. Take, for example, positioning theory as applied to intellectuals which was discussed in the last chapter. What is notable for our discussion is that positioning theory seemingly involves a positioning as clearly *within* a field. To use Baert's (2015) example, Sartre becomes the voice of *philosophy*, indeed, as Baert accounts, it is partly his positioning within the humanities which hastened his downfall as the social sciences gained increasing prominence. Elsewhere, writing with Marcus Morgan, Baert draws on an account of the 'MacCabe affair', whereby a debate over whether a temporary lecturer in English be made permanent at the University of Cambridge as a broader debate on the nature of English literature (Morgan & Baert, 2015). There is a similarity here between positioning theory and other studies of intellectuals, such as Lamont's (1987) account of how Derrida became a dominant French philosopher via legitimation and diffusion, or Camic's (1992) discussion of how Parsons' 'predecessor selections' reflected the particular reputations in the field at the time and allowed Parsons to become a key figure in sociology. All these, understandably, share a focus in successful positioning within a field, such as philosophy, English or sociology.

It could be responded, of course, that a positioning which does not give an intellectual a clear positioning within an intellectual discipline, and the legitimacy and resources which come with this, is a 'failure'. Therefore, when it comes to Cole, his lack of positioning within a discipline may in fact explain his decreased renown as no one single subject has taken up his mantle. An alternative explanation would suggest that Cole sits on the borderline between what Baert and Shipman (2012) term the 'authoritative' intellectuals—who speaks not from a discipline but as an intellectual of general and superior knowledge—and the 'professional' intellectuals, whose renown is given to them due to their positioning in a field and the university posts which come from it. In short, as so often in our story, Cole is between eras, too young for the positioning of the authoritative intellectual of John Dewey and too old for the professional intellectual of E.P. Thompson (Baert & Shipman, 2012). Or, in the terms of Bauman (1992), between the shift from 'intellectuals' who seek to enlighten the masses and 'experts' who use their university position to supply their 'expertise' to a public unable to penetrate their speciality.

While there are elements of truth to each of these claims, I would argue we can understand Cole's semi-alienation from sociology as its own form of positioning, whereby Cole's interventions are focused on positioning himself as both of and not of the sociological field in a relational sense. It is the work that has been ascribed the label of 'Sociology' from which Cole is alienated, while he holds up the position of true 'sociology'. Importantly, however, Cole does not do this to seek to present his alternative positioning as the replacement—never does Cole present his vision as what sociology should be for instance—instead it is an attempt at positioning as sympathetic to but outside the discipline, a position I believe we can capture as 'semi-alienation'. Here, using the Marxist language I drew upon in Chap. 1, we see a rejection of sociology as actually existing, though not of it internally. As mentioned above, one value in using this concept is that it does not automatically link this positioning to one's demographics, as a concept like 'optimal marginality' or the 'exilic' position does (McLaughlin, 2000; Said, 1994) nor is it simply a model of 'failure'. While, as Baert notes (2015, p. 181) we should be hesitant to discuss the intention of intellectual actors, there is enough evidence available in Cole's case, I would suggest, for us to say he would have been content with this position. I say this not because of any direct evidence of how Cole felt about his semi-alienation. Indeed, I am not aware of any writings where Cole reflects on his feelings of his semi-alienation, but rather because of the material I have cited in this book concerning what Cole said about his positioning vis-à-vis sociology. Therefore, while it is possible that Cole could be content with his positioning as an intellectual fact, but regret it as a man, we don't have evidence for the latter claim. Semi-alienation therefore has value as a descriptor of positioning as neither of nor outside a discipline as well as the nature of the intellectual interventions which mark out this position.

While I have applied this concept to Cole and sociology, there are potentially other cases where it may be useful. To stick solely with instances from sociology, we might wish to classify the relationships of scholars such as John Carroll, bell hooks and Edward Said as marked by some element of semi-alienation.

Cole's Influence on British Sociology After His Death

I began this book noting that Cole is restricted to the footnotes in contemporary sociology. While, as also highlighted earlier, Cole maintained a significant level of renown in intellectual life after his death; this marginal relationship to sociology was established very soon after his death. For example, while as we saw in Chap. 3 Cole had made significant contributions to the sociology of class, his work does not appear in prominent texts on the topics that would emerge in the years after, such as the 'Affluent Worker' studies, Bottomore's *Classes in Modern Society* or Giddens' *The Class Structure of the Advanced Societies.* Cole does appear in Lockwood's *Blackcoated Worker* but even here the reference is to statistical information about trade unionism (Lockwood, 1958, p. 161). As previously noted, the tradition of social stratification and mobility studies which begins under David Glass and the LSE and which was so central—either as a point of agreement or dissent—to the above studies made no place for Cole. While Glass himself was a socialist and open to Marxism, it is likely this was at least partly due to the desire to remain 'officially' distant from this form of politics (Mills, 2019). It is also difficult to find any sociology which took inspiration from Cole's broader work, such as his structuration theory. Even Stuart Hall who, as we saw previously, gave Cole great credit for the insights he bequeathed himself and the broader New Left, saw this as largely a political lesson, the rejection of an overly statist British Labour Party (Hall, 2010), though Gotzler (2019) argues this lesson in anti-statism did much to shape the field of cultural studies in Britain. Therefore, while we can identify some areas of indirect influence, I would say that Cole had no significant long-term direct impact on the content of British sociology, much to its loss.

There is however one exception to this and it is a telling one, the work of Paul Hirst. Hirst, having been educated at the centre of 1960s sociology, Leicester, later went on to Professorship of Social Theory at Birbeck College. He began his intellectual career as an early British advocate of structural Marxism and ended up, in collaboration with Graeme Thompson, as a groundbreaking 'sceptic' of the strongest claims for globalisation (see Hirst & Thompson, 1996). However, between these activities he developed a theory of 'associative democracy' (Hirst, 1994) which drew heavily on Cole.

Hirst framed Cole as part of an English tradition of political pluralism, of which he, along with John Figgis and Harold Laski were the most significant figures. Hirst edited a collection of their writings which, in the case of Cole, reproduced a significant part of *Social Theory* and introduced his writings to a new audience (Hirst, 1989). In the context of the late 1980s/early 1990s where Thatcherism and the rise of the New Left was encouraging socialists to rethink the nature of their political project it was this interpretation of Cole, as a social theorist, that Hirst turned to. He wrote of him as a 'social theorist who sought to retain the benefits of modern industry, division of labour and social pluralism without a separate public power' (Hirst, 1990, p. 65). Later, as part of an argument that democracy was socialism's 'best reply to the right', he emphasised Cole's belief in 'voluntary co-ordination' as both a description of individuals and the associations of which they are part as a way to challenge notions of 'laws of the market' (Hirst, 1997). This work then culminated in *Associative Democracy*, his 1994 text which outlined a new model of society in which democratically run associations fulfil the diverse needs and lives of modern society. Hirst here differs his model from Cole on some basis—most notably he is critical of Cole's notion of representation and argues his guild system was too rigid—yet, the work is presented as very much in the tradition of this 'pluralist' tradition, and most significantly, of a tradition of associations, of which Cole is part (Hirst, 1994, pp. 45–48, 103–112).

Why, it may be asked, was Hirst this exceptional sociologist who drew so significantly on Cole? The reason for this brings us to a topic I will also explore below. Hirst, at this point, was not just seeking to advance a sociological case of explanation or even critique, but of an alternative. His project of associative democracy was seeking to use sociological insight to outline a normative project. It is here where Cole was so valuable to Hirst, even when he disagreed with him. Cutting across sociology and politics this kind of sociology is now a rare one, even as the discipline becomes more comfortable with normativity, as I will explore below. This has meant that Cole has figured in rare sociological accounts primarily as a touchstone for a pluralist alternative, such as in McLennan (1989, p. 39) or that sought an alternative more generally, for example as a response to the challenge of intersectionality (Masquelier, 2023).

Therefore, Cole remained a figure in British sociology when attempts were made to think through an alternative project, but remained outside of it when they were not. This, as I will explore below, is a misfortune for sociology, which has much to learn by returning to Cole, including, though not limited to, the role of alternatives.

Cole and Contemporary Sociology

Adorno, writing of the pressures for critical intellectuals to develop blueprints, condemned the pressured to be 'terrorised into action' (Adorno, 1998, p. 292). Anyone who is not by vocation a historian and is writing a history of sociology may feel the pressure to be 'terrorised into the present', to justify their historical topic in light of contemporary concerns. I would suggest that most historical questions, including the history of British sociology, is innately interesting in and of itself. Indeed, much of what has been called the 'New Sociology of Ideas' has sought to reject the notion that the sociology of ideas is a means to an end and rather has advocated seeing it as an end in and of itself (Camic & Gross, 2004). However, when it comes to Cole and British sociology we are lucky that there are five areas where we can speak to contemporary concerns in sociology. Perhaps unsurprisingly, many of these return us to questions of normativity.

Rejecting Origin Myths (Especially About Normativity)

Origin myths, stories of how something came to be which are at best a one-sided account, are common when discussing the emergence of disciplines. Such myths can exist for multiple reasons. They can be used to 'celebrate the heroes who slew the dragon of metaphysics and rescued the fair maiden of empirical science, the lawgivers who proclaimed the end of ideology' (Samelson, 1974, p. 228), to justify contemporary views by giving them an 'honourable past' (Platt, 1996, p. 268) or to exclude certain figures who do not fit the image of a school we wish to present today (McLaughlin, 1999). What unites all these different myths is that they are 'used to legitimate contemporary preferences' (Platt, 1996, p. 267), whether this be our continuing on a valiant mission began by our forebearers, or, by overcoming flaws which blighted our past.

Sociology is no stranger to the construction of origin myths. These are especially strong, I would suggest, when discussing the role of politics and normativity in the discipline where two contemporary ends are justified by four different myths. The first story celebrates the current embrace of critical sociology as a kind of 'returning to our roots' as we fulfil the original mission of sociology which was later lost due to the actions of those wishing to turn sociology into a professional discipline in service of power (Burawoy, 2005a; Feagin et al., 2015). In this story there is some innate radicalism, both intellectual and political, within sociology which has been 'betrayed' by events since then (Bottomore, 1984). The second story which welcomes this radicalism frames this differently, namely, the radical perspective we now take requires conquering our forefathers. This story is, understandably, especially strong in feminist and decolonial perspectives which highlight the innate conservativism of classical sociology (with some exceptions) which we should then supersede (Sydie, 1987; Bhambra & Holmwood, 2020). However, it can be found in other schools, think of Gouldner's (1962) claim, befitting an origin myth, that value-freedom is a minotaur that needs slaying. Therefore, each of these stories welcome our current comfort with critique as either a return to a past we have forgotten, or as a way of superseding our problematic past.

The second two stories go to the past to condemn our current comfort with critique. For the third group of writers, the embrace of normativity has too readily given up the appeal of value-freedom (Hammersley, 2024) in a desire to be fashionably political and a concern with social justice (LeRoux et al., 2023). This has been achieved through either an ignorance or active bastardisation of what classical sociology said, especially concerning the role of values (Black, 2014). Finally, a fourth group of mythmakers see the problems rotting in early. It was when sociology began to be directed into Sociology, as a named discipline, that the rigour of earlier attempts were lost in an idealist attempt for relevancy. Therefore, we need to turn to an alternative parentage to secure our legacy, such as in the tradition of statistical science (Goldthorpe, 2021) or humanist cultural analysis (Carroll, 1980).

While all four of these origin myths contain elements of truth and in their narratives of slaying demons and defending our principles against powerful forces fit the mode of 'dramatic' intellectual interventions likely to attract followers (Alexander, 2016) it is obvious that not all of them can be fully true. They are indicative of what can sometimes be the narrow parameters of any disciplinary history which 'consists in writing history backwards' (Collini, 1988, p. 389). The relationship between a sociology today which is comfortable with critique and politics and its forms in the past is immensely complex and depends which era/form one chooses. What if we take the period between 1920 and 1960 as our starting point, where do we stand today? It seems British sociology has 'slayed its minotaur' of value-freedom and the split between sociology and ethics suggested by Hobhouse, yet also seemingly would be eager to make imperialism as significant a factor as it was for him. But, if we go even further back, we are actually seeking to return to the past with the great comfort with normativity in the nineteenth century; although perhaps their belief in positivism means that for the other side of the debate we should return to them instead as a guide for good science. In this story, Cole is one of the people who betrayed this vision of sociology in his desire for political relevance. However, for those seeking to justify a critical sociology, Cole is someone who can be invoked as a voice for such a subject which was betrayed by its professionalisation. And on and on.

The lesson from this is that we look at the history of a discipline as varied as sociology we can find antecedents and anticipation of probably all the positions we take in the current day. It is the duty of historians of the discipline to trace those legacies. However, in so doing, we should never seek to replace this story of pluralism with one where the past is seen simplistically. We should reject any account which, as Platt puts it in her discussion of origin myths in American sociology, sees a simplified past 'leading directly to a glorious present, or as error which has now been triumphantly overcome' (Platt, 1996, p. 270).

Critique as Involving Both Criticism and Alternative

Sociology is now very comfortable with being critical; indeed, Levitas is surely right when she claims that in classifying sociological work '"uncritical" is a criticism verging on the insulting' (Levitas, 2013, p. 99). The idea that our discipline is 'critical' has adopted almost a shibboleth status in Britain, the type of thing all first-year sociology students are taught alongside an encouragement to read *The Sociological Imagination* and a comparison of Marx and Weber.

But, as Levitas (2013) also notes, in a view shared by Sayer (2009), the form of critical sociology which has become dominant is lacking in significant respects. Most notably, while this form of critical sociology is comfortable with normativity when it comes to values and/or positionality, it is much less comfortable with normativity of visions, with providing visions of alternative societies.[1] As I have discussed elsewhere, there is a long history of 'sociological alternatives', or sociologically informed and grounded ideas for different types of societies (Dawson, 2016). These, due to a variety of factors I have also outlined elsewhere, perhaps most notably increased political agreement and an awareness of the problem of some previous alternatives, have become much less popular in sociology (Dawson, 2015).

Nevertheless, a critique without an alternative is lesser. The main reason for this is that to be critical, to set out to question what does exist, implicitly implies not just that another world is possible but also that is *desirable*; we could live both differently *and* better. This is what Levitas sees as the implicit utopianism found within the sociological project, contained in the realisation that:

> Those of us who work on inequalities of health, of class, of gender or in the field of ethnic relations frequently – I would say usually – work with the embedded assumption that such inequalities are wrong and should as far as possible be eliminated. And in so far as *any* implications for politics or policy may flow from sociological work, it is, implicitly, future-oriented, and about the education of hope. (Levitas, 2005b, p. 14)

In turn, there is a clear goal for sociology here in reclaiming what I call its history of alternatives and what Levitas sees as utopianism:

> Sociology must reclaim utopia, those normative, prescriptive, future-oriented elements that have suffused the discipline from the beginning, but are too often a cause of embarrassment rather than celebration. It needs to be released from damaging self-censorship, and turn to the vision of a better world that is so often what draws people to the discipline in the first place.

[1] A good example of this can be found in Sayer's (2009, p. 784) account of an exercise he set for students taking a class on critique. Asked what defined a critical sociology almost all students emphasised reflexivity or positionality, rather than values or ideals.

> If sociologists have no claim to superior imagination or ethical competence, they are no less capable of or responsible for this than anyone else. They should have something to contribute to understanding systemic connections and thus mapping alternatives. If sociology has nothing to offer here, I really don't know quite what it is for. (Levitas, 2013, p. 217)

Cole, I would suggest, is a timely reminder of this. His critical sociology is unimaginable without its link to a normative vision in guild socialism. Indeed, I would say this vision enriches his critique. Would Cole, for example, hold to the critique of a lack of functional democracy if he did not believe that forms of functional political representation were possible? Would he, as we have seen in this book, be so critical of the alienating impacts of work and the deadening of potential brought about by class inequality had he not also believed that society could be so structured so as to allow all to excel across multiple spheres, as in his favourite utopia *News from Nowhere*? The answer to these, and related questions I could offer, is clearly no. In that sense, Cole is an example of the inevitability of critique being tied to an alternative. This alternative enriches his critical sociology.

I would also suggest that while the role of alternative in critique is a long-running issue for sociology, Cole's specific alternative is very pressing. The issues Cole identified are: of a capitalism which blunts human potential and perpetuates human suffering; of a politically alienated citizenry who, not given the power to really influence decisions, are apathetic; of the long legacy of (territorial) colonialism and facing new (economic) imperialism; of how to ensure collective goods are protected and provided for the collective and so on (see also Masquelier & Dawson, 2016). Now, in light of the emerging climate crisis, we face calls to rethink our economy and, in particular, to think about how smaller forms of economy, perhaps even 'degrowth' (Latouche, 2009) may help solve the crisis. Cole's focus on devolved power and the unit of association may hold greater relevance, including for its ability to account for intersectional inequalities (Masquelier, 2023). As Martell (2023, p. 181) argues forms of what he terms 'pluralist socialism...a perspective based on socialism, collective ownership, and the state with pluralism and complexity within this. Not a utopian of many utopias, but a utopia with plurality within it...socialism with pluralism' is well placed to solve our contemporary issues and Cole's socialism—a sociological alternative—should be part of this.

Structure and Agency as a Political Problem

There was a period when the question of structure and agency was considered *the* key theoretical occupation of British sociology and, via the work of Archer and Giddens, the work that 'helped establish British sociology internationally' (King, 2010, p. 259). As is the case in sociology historically, focus has since moved on and the question of structure and agency no longer occupies the central place in the discipline it once had. However, I would suggest the legacy of these debates remain in the national discipline. Indeed, perhaps one reason why Bourdieu has become so dominant in the UK is because his sociology promised to 'solve' this question while also maintaining an awareness of class, so central to British sociology but somewhat lost in both Archer and Giddens' theories. This may explain why, as Reay (2004) has noted, there is a tendency to 'namecheck' rather than theorise with Bourdieu; somehow, in invoking his name, the British problem of structure and agency was seen to have been 'solved' without any further discussion.

Cole, however, encourages us to think again, and differently, about structure and agency. His unique contribution here is not to think of it as a question about how we are positioned in social space (as in Bourdieu); or how we relate to the world (Archer); or how we maintain a sense of self (Giddens) but rather as a question of politics: how do we, individually and singularly, create the world we want and how, in turn, do the fruits of those political struggles then relate to how we see the world? Therefore, for Cole, structure and agency become as much a question for political sociology as for sociology more generally.

It could be argued that this political reading of structure and agency, by somewhat limiting its scope to politics and removing question of selfhood, action and consciousness, is not an improvement on the other models and may indeed be a step back. I think there is merit in that argument generally, though would refer the reader back to my defence of Cole in Chap. 3, and it is not my goal here to claim that, in Cole, we have finally 'cracked it'. Instead, reflecting that a sociological 'question' as multifaceted as how structure and agency relate to each other can only inevitably have multiple 'answers', I would present Cole's as another approach, perhaps complementary, on this central question of sociology. This is especially so when other attempts at 'solving' this problem have been criticised for their inability to account for political outcomes (Stones, 2005; Burkitt, 2016).

Relativising the Decolonial Critique

The decolonial critique has become increasingly significant in British sociology and while I would not want to claim it has obtained total acceptance, it has become a part of the British sociological lexicon (Bhambra & Holmwood, 2020; Meghji, 2021). Indeed, it has been suggested that this perspective may have had a ready audience in Britain given the contribution of post-war scholars from formerly colonised countries to sociology (Valluvan & Kapoor, 2023). One key contribution of this critique has been to revisit the history of the discipline, exploring the omissions and biases in classical sociology and the ways this has been reproduced down into the current day (e.g. Connell, 2007). However, with the notable exception of Steinmetz (2014) there has been little attempt to do this with British sociology. The reasons for this appear to be twofold. Firstly, Britain is presumed to be part of a 'European sociology' with common assumptions due to its Europeanness (e.g. Savransky, 2017). Secondly, many such accounts are based on classical theorists and here Britain's supposed failure, mentioned earlier in the book, to produce a 'great theorist' means it is not considered (e.g. Bhambra & Holmwood, 2020). This is, however, problematic when we consider the centrality of British empire to the imperial project. Therefore, we are well overdue for a specifically British interrogation of our discipline's history and the role of empire.

The case of Cole has shown us the potential interesting outcomes that can come from this exercise. One drawback of the tendency to speaking in terms of 'European sociology' is that it can encourage a catch-all approach which Julian Go (2016) has termed racial/geographic essentialism, i.e. reading one's political beliefs from one's social position, as in this case that being 'European' means an active support for, or at the very least toleration of, the principles of empire. The case of Cole shows the complexity here; someone otherwise spoken of as a 'Little Englander' who for most of his life showed little interest to travel and lived a fundamentally English middle-class life (Cole, 1971) was not just implacably opposed to empire, but also willing to theorise it and treat writers from the Global South as experts on their own worlds. There may be an initial temptation here to link this to Cole's socialism, however being a socialist in Britain at that point was no guarantee of being anti-empire, with strongly pro-Empire (Elliott, 1993) views to be found, especially among the Fabians (MacKenzie & MacKenzie, 1977) combining with anti-imperial currents, often emerging from the broader labour movement (Gupta, 1975). Indeed, Hobhouse, coming from a liberal position, shared Cole's anti-imperialism. However, it should be noted, Cole's theorisation was more sophisticated, with economic and political considerations while Hobhouse, perhaps reflecting his background in journalism, was more willing to link it to a kind of delusional mind state (Tan, 2024). Therefore, there is real need for a specifically British interrogation of these imperial relations within the history of its national discipline. Such an interrogation would follow on from the initial work of Steinmetz (2014) by foregrounding the role imperialism played in the discipline, without assuming this was a one-sided relationship. As Steinmetz (2023, p. 354) puts it: 'colonial-era thinkers should not be condemned without careful reading of all of their work, situating writing in its historical contexts and relations to earlier writings'.

How to Do Public Sociology

I discussed this extensively in the preceding chapter, so will not repeat the main elements of that argument here. As we saw there, Cole does provide suggestions for how public sociology can be done, most notably concerning the role of creative expression and the divide between policy and public sociologies. I would add here however that the example of Cole reminds that when sociology, as it often does, undergoes a new process of considering what it is and what direction it should take, it is a requirement for that to include some historical consideration. For example, Beer's (2014) *Punk Sociology* with its call for sociology to embrace new forms of communication that speak directly to people and to favour quick, direct forms of dialogue shares significant elements with Cole's work. However, Beer misses any discussion of historical antecedents since he cites only four sociological texts published before the year 2000 and only one before 1977 (*The Sociological Imagination*) across the whole book. Any attempt at a programmatic statement of what sociology should be needs to be much more attentive to the discipline's history than we have been to this point.

A Final Word: Cole on Being a Sociologist

Therefore, as we have seen above, Cole has potentially much to offer to contemporary debates within sociology, most notably around the nature of what the sociological endeavour should be and the role of normativity therein. Let us end by giving the final word to Cole.

In his 1950 *Essays in Social Theory* Cole includes an extract from his earlier book *The Intelligent Man's Guide to the Post-War World*, here retitled as 'What I Take for Granted' (Cole, 1950e). The extract is in effect a personal credo, with Cole listing the beliefs he holds. He argues that while he has never shied away from saying what he believes, doing this during teaching where students can question, prod and challenge is different from writing a book, where the audience does not have the same opportunity. Therefore, there is an especial obligation for what Cole terms 'frankness' on behalf of an author, who must set out their assumptions clearly (Cole, 1950e, p. 246). Cole does this, highlighting 12 values he holds to, ranging from an increased standard of living, personal and political freedom, the right to go one's one way, morality and truth among many. He then concludes with this:

> I am, in effect, a Socialist. By Socialism I mean fundamentally, not a particular economic arrangement by which the State owns and runs industry, but the entire body of principles I have set out on the foregoing propositions...Without a high degree of economic equality, we cannot have freedom and self-government for all, or a satisfactory standard of living for all. At any rate, that is my view: why it is so, I have done my best to make clear in my writings. I may be wrong about this; for about means one may at any time be wrong. But I am not wrong about the ends I have laid down as good. They *are* good, not merely for us, at the present point of our historical development, and not merely in relation to the particular pattern of living which our civilization has worked out. They are good altogether and *for good*, from the moment of their conception in any man's mind. Their goodness cannot be altered...they will be no less true in a hundred or a thousand years than they are to-day. Anyone who denies their truth is blind, or mad, or wicked, or at least purblind. They are the postulates from which I set out; and I am not arguing with anyone who denies them: I am simply telling him. (Cole, 1950e, pp. 250–251)

As the reader will have learnt, this is distinctively Coleian, from the definition of socialism through to the significance of belief and his willingness/bluntness in expressing them. It is that bluntness, the claims that some things just are *good*, no matter what anyone says, which will perhaps strike the contemporary sociologist, more open to notions of relativity than Cole ever was. I am not seeking to fully defend this as an anthropological claim (though I would wish to at least partly defend it) but I would say it has something worth defending when it comes to practising sociology. While we may inevitably quibble and change our minds on ends there are, surely, some values we hold that we hold precisely because we—as humans, citizens or sociologists, or perhaps all three—believe they *are* good for all. Those goods can potentially be achieved in lots of different ways, and ultimately that is a matter for debate and discussion but, while being open to this, Cole would encourage sociologists to never shy away from the values they hold. There is a need for sociologists, in his words 'to never conceal a weakness' (Cole, 1950e, p. 245), to still seek to discuss the facts as they are, including the 'inconvenient facts' that Weber once encouraged teachers to pass onto to their students (Weber, 1922, p. 147). Yet, while being honest in the weaknesses of our case we should not shy away from talking about how things should be. This is a daunting task for sure and, faced with it, other options maybe appealing, whether that is value-freedom or the emaciated critique that comes without an alternative. But, Cole's final words remind us that this is the only way to do sociology and, more fundamentally, the only way to be in the world.

References

Abbott, A. (2007). For Humanist Sociology. In D. Clawson et al. (Eds.), *Public Sociology* (pp. 195–209). University of California Press.

Abraham, J. H. (1973). *Origins and Growth of British Sociology*. Penguin.

Abrams, P. (1968). The Origins of British Sociology. In P. Abrams (Ed.), *The Origins of British Sociology 1834-1914* (pp. 3–153). The University of Chicago Press.

Adorno, T. (1998). *Critical Models: Interventions and Catchwords*. Columbia University Press.

Alatas, S. F., & Sinha, V. (2017). *Sociological Theory Beyond the Canon*. Palgrave Macmillan.

Alexander, J. (1987). The Centrality of the Classics. In A. Giddens & J. Turner (Eds.), *Social Theory Today* (pp. 11–57). Polity.

Alexander, J. (2016). Dramatic Intellectuals. *International Journal of Politics, Culture and Society, 29*(4), 341–358.

Anderson, K. B. (2016). *Marx at the Margins: On Nationalism, Ethnicity and Non-Western Societies*. University of Chicago Press.

Anderson, P. (1968/1992). Components of the National Culture. In P. Anderson (Ed.), *English Questions* (pp. 48–104). Verso.

Archer, M. (2000). *Being Human: The Problem of Agency*. Cambridge University Press.

Arendt, H. (1951). *The Origins of Totalitarianism*. Penguin.

Aronwitz, S. (2005). Comments on Michael Burawoy's "The Critical Turn to Public Sociology". *Critical Sociology, 31*(3), 333–338.

M. Dawson, *G.D.H. Cole and British Sociology*,
https://doi.org/10.1007/978-3-031-75484-5

Baert, P. (2015). *The Existentialist Moment: The Rise of Sartre as a Public Intellectual.* Polity Press.
Baert, P., & Booth, J. (2012). Tensions Within the Public Intellectual: Political Interventions from Dreyfus to the New Social Media. *International Journal of Politics, Culture and Society, 25*(4), 111–126.
Baert, P., & Morgan, M. (2018). A Performative Framework for the Study of Intellectuals. *European Journal of Social Theory, 21*(3), 322–339.
Baert, P., & Shipman, A. (2012). Transforming the Intellectual. In P. Baert & F. D. Rubio (Eds.), *The Politics of Knowledge* (pp. 179–204). Routledge.
Banks, J. A. (1967). The British Sociological Association – The First Fifteen Years. *Sociology, 1*(1), 1–9.
Barnes, H. E. (1948). Leonard Trelawney Hobhouse: Evolutionary Philosophy in the Service of Democracy and Social Reform. In H. E. Barnes (Ed.), *An Introduction to the History of Sociology* (pp. 614–653). University of Chicago Press.
Bauman, Z. (1972). *Between Class and Elite: The Evolution of the British Labour Movement, A Sociological Study.* Manchester University Press.
Bauman, Z. (1987). *Legislators and Interpreters: On Modernity, Post-Modernity and Intellectuals.* Polity Press.
Bauman, Z. (1989a). Hermeneutics and Modern Social Theory. In D. Held & J. B. Thompson (Eds.), *Anthony Giddens and his Critics: Social Theory of Modern Societies* (pp. 34–55). Cambridge University Press.
Bauman, Z. (1989b). *Modernity and the Holocaust.* Polity Press.
Bauman, Z. (1990). Effacing the Face: On the Social Management of Moral Proximity. *Theory, Culture and Society, 7*(1), 5–38.
Bauman, Z. (1992). Love in Adversity: On the State and Intellectuals, and the State of the Intellectuals. *Thesis Eleven, 31*, 81–104.
Bauman, Z. (2000). On Writing: On Writing Sociology. *Theory, Culture & Society, 17*(1), 79–90.
Bauman, Z. (2004). Zygmunt Bauman. In A. H. Halsey (Ed.), *A History of Sociology in Britain: Science, Literature and Society* (pp. 206–208). Oxford University Press.
Becker, H. (1967). Whose Side Are We On? *Social Problems, 14*(3), 239–247.
Becker, H., & Barnes, H. E. (1952). *Social Thought from Lore to Science: Sociological Trends Throughout the World.* Harren Press.
Beer, P. (2014). *Punk Sociology.* Palgrave Macmillan.
Bell, G. (2016). *Hesitant Comrades: The Irish Revolution and the British Labour Movement.* Pluto Press.
Bhambra, G., & Holmwood, J. (2020). *Colonialism and Modern Social Theory.* Polity Press.
Black, A. (1984). *Guilds and Civil Society in European Political Thought from the Twelfth Century to the Present.* Methuen and Co.

Black, D. (2014). On the Almost Inconceivable Misunderstandings Concerning the Subject of Value-free Social Science. *British Journal of Sociology, 64*(4), 763–780.
Bloch, M. (2015). *Closest Queens: Some 20th Century British Politicians.* Little Brown.
Boos, F., & Boos, W. (1990). *News from Nowhere* and Victorian Socialist Feminism. *Nineteenth Century Contexts, 14*(1), 3–32.
Bottomore, T. (1981). A Marxist Consideration of Durkheim. *Social Forces, 59*(4), 902–917.
Bottomore, T. (1984). *Sociology and Socialism.* St. Martin's Press.
Bourdieu, P. (1989). The Corporatism of the Universal: The Role of Intellectuals in the Modern World. *Telos, 81*, 99–110.
Brady, D. (2004). Why Public Sociology may Fail. *Social Forces, 82*(4), 1629–1638.
Branford, V. (1904). On the Origin and Use of the Word Sociology. In *Sociological Society, Sociological Papers 1904* (pp. 1–24). Macmillan.
Branford, V., & Geddes, P. (1919). *The Coming Polity.* Williams and Norgate.
Brewer, J. (2007). "We Must Protest That Our Inheritance Is Within Us": Robert Morrison MacIver as Sociologist and Scotsman. *Journal of Scottish Thought, 1*(1), 1–24.
Briggs, A. (1960). Intellectuals and the Labour Movement: G.D.H. Cole. *The Listener*, October 20, 671–672.
Briggs, A., & Saville, J. (Eds.). (1960). *Essays in Labour History: In Memory of G.D.H. Cole.* Macmillan and Co. Ltd.
Bulmer, M. (1985). The Development of Sociology and of Empirical Social Research in Britain. In M. Bulmer (Ed.), *Essays on the History of British Sociological Research* (pp. 3–36). Cambridge University Press.
Burawoy, M. (2005a). For Public Sociology. *American Sociological Review, 70*(1), 4–28.
Burawoy, M. (2005b). The Critical Turn to Public Sociology. *Critical Sociology, 31*(3), 313–326.
Burawoy, M. (2007). Public Sociology vs. the Market. *Socio-Economic Review, 5*(2), 356–367.
Burawoy, M., & Wright, E. O. (2001). Sociological Marxism. In J. Turner (Ed.), *Handbook of Sociological Theory* (pp. 459–486). Springer.
Burkitt, I. (2016). Relational Agency: Relational Sociology, Agency and Interaction. *European Journal of Social Theory, 19*(3), 322–339.
Butler, L. (2020). *Michael Young, Social Science, and the British Left, 1945-1970.* Oxford University Press.
Calhoun, C. (2005). The Promise of Public Sociology. *British Journal of Sociology, 56*(3), 355–363.
Camic, C. (1992). Reputation and Predecessor Selection: Parsons and the Institutionalists. *American Sociological Review, 57*(4), 421–445.

Camic, C., & Gross, N. (2004). The New Sociology of Ideas. In J. R. Blau (Ed.), *The Blackwell Companion to Sociology* (pp. 236–249). Blackwell.
Carpenter, L. P. (1973). *G.D.H. Cole: An Intellectual Biography*. Cambridge University Press.
Carroll, J. (1980). *Sceptical Sociology*. Routledge and Kegan Paul.
Caute, D. (2022). *Red List: MI5 and British Intellectuals in the Twentieth Century*. Verso.
Cole, G. D. H. (1913a). *The World of Labour*. G. Bell and Sons.
Cole, G. D. H. (1913b). Fabian Excursions: What Rebels in the Society are Doing. *The Herald*, Cole Collection, Nuffield College, University of Oxford. Document A1/45/1.
Cole, G. D. H. (1914a). Conflicting Social Obligations. *Proceedings of the Aristotelian Society, 15*(1914–1915), 140–159.
Cole, G. D. H. (1914b). Discussion on Scientific Management. *The Sociological Review, 7*(2), 119–120.
Cole, G. D. H. (1917). *Self-Government in Industry*. Hutchinson.
Cole, G. D. H. (1920a). *Social Theory*. Methuen & Co.
Cole, G. D. H. (1920b). *Guild Socialism Re-Stated*. Leonard Parsons.
Cole, G. D. H. (1920c). A Pioneer of Scientific Socialism. Cole Collection, Nuffield College, University of Oxford. Document A1/1/3/1-3.
Cole, G. D. H. (1921). Guild Socialism and Communism. Lecture, Cole Collection, Nuffield College, University of Oxford. Document A1/51/1/1-16.
Cole, G. D. H. (1922). Labour in Ireland: A British Comment. *The Irish Economist*, Cole Collection, Nuffield College, University of Oxford. Document A1/53/3.
Cole, G. D. H. (1923). *Social Theory*. Course Syllabus, Cole Collection, Nuffield College, University of Oxford, Document E2/1/21.
Cole, G. D. H. (1924a). *The Life of William Cobbett*. W. Collins Sons and & Co.
Cole, G. D. H. (1924b). *Marxism*. Course Syllabus, Cole Collection, Nuffield College, University of Oxford, Document E2/1/9.
Cole, G. D. H. (1926). Loyalties. *Proceedings of the Aristotelian Society, 26*(1925–1926), 151–170.
Cole, G. D. H. (1929a). *The Next Ten Years in British Social and Economic Planning*. Macmillan.
Cole, G. D. H. (1929b). The Kink in History. *The Listener*, Cole Collection, Nuffield College, University of Oxford, Document A1/28/25.
Cole, G. D. H. (1930a). *Gold, Credit and Employment: Four Essays for Laymen*. Allen & Unwin.
Cole, G. D. H. (1930b). *The Life of Robert Owen*. Macmillan.
Cole, G. D. H. (1930c). Freedom to Choose One's Job. *Brighton and Hove Weekly News*, 26th June, Cole Collection, Nuffield College, University of Oxford, Document A1/36/1.

Cole, G. D. H. (1931a). William Morris. In L. Abercrombie et al. (Eds.), *Revaluations: Studies in Biography* (pp. 131–154). Oxford University Press.
Cole, G. D. H. (1931b). Reflections on a Walking Tour. *King's Norton Labour News*, February, Cole Collection, Nuffield College, University of Oxford. Document A1/43/12.
Cole, G. D. H. (1932a). *The Short History of the British Working Class Movement, 1780-1927*. George Allen & Unwin.
Cole, G. D. H. (1932b). *Economic Tracts for the Times*. Macmillan.
Cole, G. D. H. (1932c). An English View of the Indian Labour Problem. Cole Collection, Nuffield College, University of Oxford, Document A1/75/1/1-6.
Cole, G. D. H. (1933a). Introduction. In K. Marx (Ed.), *Capital' Everyman's Library* (pp. xi–xxix). J.M. Dent and Sons.
Cole, G. D. H. (1933b). Marx's Place in Socialist Theory: A Symposium. *The Plebs*, March, Cole Collection, Nuffield College, University of Oxford. Document A1/4/2/1-2.
Cole, G. D. H. (Ed.). (1933c). *What Everybody Wants to know About Money*. Victor Gollancz Ltd.
Cole, G. D. H. (1933d). The Case for Going One's Own Way. *Kensington News*, 8 September, Cole Collection, Nuffield College, University of Oxford. Document A1/36/4.
Cole, G. D. H. (1933e). *The Crooked World*. Victor Gollancz Ltd.
Cole, G. D. H. (1934a). Introduction. In G. D. H. Cole (Ed.), *William Morris: Selected Writings* (pp. xi–xxiv). Bloomsbury.
Cole, G. D. H. (1934b). *William Morris and the Modern World*. Lecture, Cole Collection, Nuffield College, University of Oxford. Document A1/5/3/1-28.
Cole, G. D. H. (1934c). *Some Relations Between Political and Economic Theory*. Macmillan & Co.
Cole, G. D. H. (1934d). *What Marx Really Meant*. Victor Gollancz Ltd.
Cole, G. D. H. (1934e). Response to Mr. Irvine. *Time and Tide*, 8 December, Cole Collection, Nuffield College, University of Oxford. Document A1/36/6/5.
Cole, G. D. H. (1934f). Two Poems. *New Britain*, 29 August, Cole Collection, Nuffield College, University of Oxford. Document A3/7/1.
Cole, G. D. H. (1935a). The Marxian Method. *New Statesman*, 9 February, pp. 182–183.
Cole, G. D. H. (1935b). *The Simple Case for Socialism*. Victor Gollancz Ltd.
Cole, G. D. H. (1935c). Employers Who Are a Menace to Democracy. *Manchester City News*, 11 May, Cole Collection, Nuffield College, University of Oxford. Document A1/36/7.
Cole, G. D. H. (1935d). The Problem of Colonial Empire – I. *New Statesman*, 12 October, pp. 472–474.

Cole, G. D. H. (1935e). The Problem of Colonial Empire – II. *New Statesman*, 19 October, pp. 550–551.
Cole, G. D. H. (1936a). The No-Sayers. *Oldham Evening Chronicle and Standard*, 27 April, Cole Collection, Nuffield College, University of Oxford. Document A1/36/8.
Cole, G. D. H. (1936b). Freedom's Garden. *Indicator*, 7 September, Cole Collection, Nuffield College, University of Oxford. Document A1/36/17/6.
Cole, G. D. H. (1937a). *Practical Economics*. Penguin.
Cole, G.D.H. (1937b). Jacks of all Trades. *Brixton Free Press*, 2 April, Cole Collection, Nuffield College, University of Oxford. Document A1/36/14.
Cole, G. D. H. (1938). Thoughts on Reading Ghandi's Hird Swaraj. Cole Collection, Nuffield College, University of Oxford. Document A1/29/11/1-9.
Cole, G. D. H. (1939a). A Place Called Carradale. *New Statesman*, 19 August, pp. 268–269.
Cole, G. D. H. (1939b). The Habit of Freedom. *Blackley Guardian*, 10 June, Cole Collection, Nuffield College, University of Oxford. Document A1/36/21.
Cole, G. D. H. (1940). Another Sort of Freedom. *Worksop Guardian*, 1 March, Cole Collection, Nuffield College, University of Oxford. Document A1/38/1.
Cole, G. D. H. (1941a). *Chartist Portraits*. Cassell.
Cole, G. D. H. (1941b). *British Working Class Politics, 1832-1914*. Routledge and Kegan Paul Ltd.
Cole, G. D. H. (1942). The New, New Atlantis. *The Fortnightly*, 7 October, Cole Collection, Nuffield College, University of Oxford. Document A1/31/26/1-12.
Cole, G. D. H. (1944a). The Social Studies in the Universities. *The Political Quarterly*, *15*(4), 353–364.
Cole, G. D. H. (1944b). *A Century of Co-Operation*. Co-Operative Union.
Cole, G. D. H. (1945a/1950). Scope and Method in Social and Political Thought. In G. D. H. Cole (Ed.), *Essays in Social Theory* (pp. 1–16). Macmillan.
Cole, G. D. H. (1945b/2021). G.D.H. Cole's Election Address for the University of Oxford Constituency, 1945. In G. D. H. Cole (Ed.), *Towards a Libertarian Socialism: Reflections on the British Labour Party and European Working-Class Movements* (pp. 69–71). AK Press.
Cole, G. D. H. (1946). The Study of Social Facts. *American Journal of Sociology*, *52*(2), 147–149.
Cole, G. D. H. (1947a/1950). Sociology and Politics in the Twentieth Century. In G. D. H. Cole (Ed.), *Essays in Social Theory* (pp. 17–30). Macmillan.
Cole, G. D. H. (1947b/2021). What Socialism Means to Me. In G. D. H. Cole (Ed.), *Towards a Libertarian Socialism: Reflections on the British Labour Party and European Working-Class Movements* (pp. 73–79). AK Press.
Cole, G. D. H. (1947c). *The Intelligent Men's Guide to the Post-War World*. Victor Gollancz Ltd.

Cole, G. D. H. (1948a). The Teaching of Social Studies in British Universities. *Universities Quarterly, 2*(3), 262–274.
Cole, G. D. H. (1948b). *A History of the Labour Party from 1914*. Routledge and Kegan Paul.
Cole, G. D. H. (1948c). August Comte, Lecture, Cole Collection, Nuffield College, University of Oxford, Document E3/26/1-18.
Cole, G. D. H. (1948d). *The Meaning of Marxism*. Victor Gollancz Ltd.
Cole, G. D. H. (1949). Political Theory. Westminster Book Review, August, Cole Collection, Nuffield College, University of Oxford, Document A1/34/1/1-89.
Cole, G. D. H. (1950a). *Essays in Social Theory*. Macmillan.
Cole, G. D. H. (1950b). Rousseau's Political Theory. In G. D. H. Cole (Ed.), *Essays in Social Theory* (pp. 113–131). Macmillan.
Cole, G. D. H. (1950c). Simmel, Georg. In *Chambers Encyclopaedia New Edition*, Volume XII Róskilde-Spahi (p. 562). George Newnes Limited.
Cole, G. D. H. (1950d). The Essentials of Democracy. In G. D. H. Cole (Ed.), *Essays in Social Theory* (pp. 97–112). Macmillan.
Cole, G. D. H. (1950e). What I Take for Granted. In G. D. H. Cole (Ed.), *Essays in Social Theory* (pp. 245–251). Macmillan.
Cole, G. D. H. (1950f). The Subject Matter of Social Theory. Lecture, Cole Collection, Nuffield College, University of Oxford, Document E3/3/2/1-10.
Cole, G. D. H. (1951a). Review of *Citizenship and Social Class* by T.H. Marshall. *The Economic Journal, 61*(242), 420–422.
Cole, G. D. H. (1951b/2021). The British Labour Movement: Retrospect and Prospect. In G. D. H. Cole (Ed.), *Towards a Libertarian Socialism: Reflections on the British Labour Party and European Working-Class Movements* (pp. 89–106). AK Press.
Cole, G. D. H. (1952). Politico-Economic Theories Part II. Lecture, Cole Collection, Nuffield College, University of Oxford, Document E3/13/1/1-172.
Cole, G. D. H. (1953a). The Idea of Progress: Review article of *The Idea of Progress: A Revaluation* by Morris Ginsberg. *British Journal of Sociology, 4*(3), 266–285.
Cole, G. D. H. (1953b). *A History of Socialist Thought: The Forerunners, 1789-1850*. Macmillan & Co..
Cole, G. D. H. (1954/2021). Is This Socialism? In G. D. H. Cole (Ed.), *Towards a Libertarian Socialism: Reflections on the British Labour Party and European Working-Class Movements* (pp. 199–229). AK Press.
Cole, G. D. H. (1955a). Introduction. In J. J. Rousseau (Ed.), *The Social Contract and Discourses* (pp. v–xxxviii). Everyman's Library, J.M. Dent and Sons.
Cole, G. D. H. (1955b). Rights, Lecture, Cole Collection, Nuffield College, University of Oxford, Document E3/4/4/1-36.
Cole, G. D. H. (1955c). *Studies in Class Structure*. Routledge.

Cole, G. D. H. (1955d). Letter to Eugene Burdick, 4th April, Cole Collection, Nuffield College, University of Oxford, Document C/1/66/1.
Cole, G. D. H. (1955e). National and Racial Equality, Cole Collection, Nuffield College, University of Oxford, Document E3/17/4/1-5.
Cole, G. D. H. (1956a). *World Socialism Restated.* New Statesman and Nation.
Cole, G. D. H. (1956b). Foreword. In J. Mogey (Ed.), *Family and Neighbourhood: Two Studies in Oxford* (pp. v–vi). Greenwood Press.
Cole, G. D. H. (1956c). *A History of Socialist Thought: Volume III, Part I: The Second International, 1889-1914.* Macmillan & Co.
Cole, G. D. H. (1957a). Sociology and Social Policy. *British Journal of Sociology, 8*(2), 158–171.
Cole, G. D. H. (1957b). Letter to Ronald Fletcher, 29th March, Cole Collection, Nuffield College, University of Oxford. Document C/1/61/1.
Cole, G. D. H. (1957c). What Is Happening to British Capitalism? *Universities and Left Review, 1*(1), 24–27.
Cole, G. D. H. (1958). *A History of Socialist Thought: Volume IV, Part I: Communism and Social Democracy, 1914-1931.* Macmillan & Co.
Cole, G. D. H. (1959a). Review of *The Blackcoated Worker* by David Lockwood. *British Journal of Sociology, 10*(1), 71–73.
Cole, G. D. H. (1959b/2021). Socialism, Centralist of Libertarian? In G. D. H. Cole (Ed.), *Towards a Libertarian Socialism: Reflections on the British Labour Party and European Working-Class Movements* (pp. 279–290). AK Press.
Cole, G. D. H. (1960). *William Morris as a Socialist.* William Morris Society.
Cole, G. D. H. (1961a). *A History of Socialist Thought: Volume IV, Part II: Communism and Social Democracy, 1914-1931.* Macmillan & Co.
Cole, G. D. H. (1961b). *A History of Socialist Thought: Volume V: Socialism and Fascism, 1931-1939.* Macmillan & Co.
Cole, G. D. H. (1977a). The Striker Stricken or The Thirty Sleepers of Eccleston Square being The Operartives' Opera in Three 'Ops. In A. Briggs & J. Saville (Eds.), *Essays in Labour History, 1918-1939* (pp. 61–101). Crom Helm Ltd.
Cole, G. D. H. (n.d.-a). Lectures on Rousseau's Politics, Cole Collection, Nuffield College, University of Oxford. Document E3/18/12/143.
Cole, G. D. H. (n.d.-b). The Social Contract, Lecture, Cole Collection, Nuffield College, University of Oxford. Document E3/18/1/1-9.
Cole, G. D. H. (n.d.-c). Social and Political Theory, Second Version, Lecture, Cole Collection, Nuffield College, University of Oxford, Document E3/6/1/1-3.
Cole, G. D. H. (n.d.-d). Politics and Human Nature, Lecture, Cole Collection, Nuffield College, University of Oxford, Document E3/3/3/1-37.
Cole, G. D. H. (n.d.-e). Sociology and Politics in Relation to Political Theory, Lecture, Cole Collection, Nuffield College, University of Oxford, Document E3/2/4/1-7.

Cole, G. D. H. (n.d.-f). The Foundations of Political Theory, Lecture, Cole Collection, Nuffield College, University of Oxford, Document E3/8/1/1-12.
Cole, G. D. H. (n.d.-g). Equality: Rights, Lecture, Cole Collection, Nuffield College, University of Oxford, Document E3/8/5/4.
Cole, G. D. H. (n.d.-h). Concepts of Freedom and Democracy, Lecture, Cole Collection, Nuffield College, University of Oxford, Document E3/2/5/1-7.
Cole, G. D. H. (n.d.-i). Good and Bad in Social Theory, Lecture, Cole Collection, Nuffield College, University of Oxford, Document E3/2/8/1-8.
Cole, G. D. H. (n.d.-j). Untitled Article, Cole Collection, Nuffield College, University of Oxford, Document A1/23/22/1-6.
Cole, G. D. H., & Cole, M. (1921). *The Bolo Book.* George Allen and Unwin.
Cole, G. D. H., & Cole, M. (1933). *The Intelligent Man's Review of Europe To-Day.* Victor Gollancz Ltd.
Cole, G. D. H., & Cole, M. (1937). *The Condition of Britain.* Victor Gollancz Ltd.
Cole, G. D. H., & Filson, A. W. (1951). *British Working Class Movements: Selected Documents, 1789-1875.* Macmillan.
Cole, G. D. H., & Mellor, W. (1914). The Class War and the State. *The Daily Herald,* 3 March, Cole Collection, Nuffield College, University of Oxford. Document A1/47/2.
Cole, G. D. H., & Postgate, R. (1956). *The Common People, 1746-1946.* Meuthen and Co Ltd.
Cole, M. (1971). *The Life of G.D.H. Cole.* Macmillan.
Cole, M. (1977b). The Striker Stricken, G.D.H. Cole. In A. Briggs & J. Saville (Eds.), *Essays in Labour History, 1918-1939* (pp. 57–60). Crom Helm Ltd.
Collini, S. (1979). *Liberalism & Sociology: L.T. Hobhouse and Political Argument in England 1880-1914.* Cambridge University Press.
Collini, S. (1988). "Disciplinary History" and "Intellectual History": Reflections on the Historiography of the Social Sciences in Britain and France. *Revue de Synthése, 109*(3–4), 387–399.
Collini, S. (2002). "Every Fruit-juice Drinker, Nudist, Sandal-wearer...": Intellectuals as Other People. In H. Small (Ed.), *The Public Intellectual* (pp. 203–223). Blackwell.
Collini, S. (2006). *Absent Minds: Intellectuals in Britain.* Oxford University Press.
Collins, P. H. (2007). Going Public: Doing the Sociology that had no Name. In D. Clawson et al. (Eds.), *Public Sociology* (pp. 101–113). University of California Press.
Collison, P., & Webber, S. (1971). British Sociology 1950-1970: A Journal Analysis. *The Sociological Review, 19*(4), 521–542.
Connell, R. (2007). *Southern Theory: The Global Dynamics of Knowledge in Social Science.* Polity Press.
Cook, H. (2005). *The Long Sexual Revolution: English Women, Sex, and Contraception 1800-1975.* Oxford University Press.

Cristi, M. (2012). Durkheim on Moral Individualism, Social Justice, and Rights: A Gendered Construction of Rights. *Canadian Journal of Sociology, 37*(4), 409–438.

Crompton, R. (1989). Class Theory and Gender. *The British Journal of Sociology, 40*(4), 565–687.

Crompton, R. (2008). *Class and Stratification.* Polity Press.

Da Silva, F. C., & Vieira, M. B. (2019). *The Politics of the Book: A Study on the Materiality of Ideas.* Pennsylvania University Press.

Dahrendorf, R. (1995). *LSE: A History of the London School of Economics and Political Science 1895-1995.* Oxford University Press.

Dalla Costa, M., & James, S. (1971). *The Power of Women and the Subversion of Community.* Falling Wall Press.

Davie, G. (2013). *The Democratic Intellect: Scotland and her Universities in the Nineteenth Century.* Edinburgh University Press.

Dawson, M. (2010). Bauman, Beck, Giddens and our Understanding of Politics in Late Modernity. *Journal of Power, 3*(2), 189–207.

Dawson, M. (2015). On the (Alternative) Worlds That We Have Lost: Sociology and the Third Way Revisited. In M. Dawson et al. (Eds.), *Stretching the Sociological Imagination: Essays in Honour of John Eldridge* (pp. 101–119). Palgrave Macmillan.

Dawson, M. (2016). *Social Theory for Alternative Societies.* Palgrave Macmillan.

Dawson, M. (2023). *The Political Durkheim: Sociology, Socialism, Legacies.* Routledge.

Devine, P. (1988). *Democracy and Economic Planning.* Polity Press.

Dresvina, J. (Ed.). (2021). *Thanks for Typing: Remembering Forgotten Women in History.* Bloomsbury.

Du Bois, W. E. B. (2000). Sociology Hesitant. *Boundary, 27*(3), 37–44.

Durkheim, E. (1970). *Montesquieu and Rousseau: Forerunners of Sociology.* University of Michigan Press.

Durkheim, E. (1973). The Dualism of Human Nature and Its Social Conditions. In E. Durkheim (Ed.), (pp. 149–163). *On Morality and Society*, University of Chicago Press.

Durkheim, E. (1984). *The Division of Labour in Society.* Palgrave Macmillan.

Ehrenreich, B. (2007). A Journalist's Plea. In D. Clawson et al. (Eds.), *Public Sociology* (pp. 231–238). University of California Press.

Eldridge, J. (2000). Sociology and the Third Way. In J. Eldridge et al. (Eds.), *For Sociology: Legacies and Prospects* (pp. 131–144). Sociology Press.

Elliott, G. (1993). *Labourism and the English Genius: The Strange Death of Labour England?* Verso.

Ericson, R. (2005). Publicising Sociology. *British Journal of Sociology, 56*(3), 365–372.

Ervine, S. J. (1934a). Notes on the Way. *Time and Tide*, 24 November, Cole Collection, Nuffield College, University of Oxford. Document A1/36/6/3-4.
Ervine, S. J. (1934b). Reply to Mr. Cole. *Time and Tide*, 22 December, Cole Collection, Nuffield College, University of Oxford. Document A1/36/6/6.
Etzoni, A. (2005). Bookmarks for Public Sociologists. *British Journal of Sociology, 56*(3), 373–378.
Evans, C. (2015). *The Spectrum of English Murder: The Detective Fiction of Henry Lancelot Aubrey-Fletcher and G.D.H. and Margaret Cole.* Coachwhip Publications.
Evans, C. (2017). "The Man with the Laughing Eyes": Socialism and Same-Sex Desire in G.D.H. Cole's *The Death of a Millionaire.* In C. Evans (Ed.), *Murder in the Closet: Essays on Queer Clues in Crime Fiction before Stonewall* (pp. 114–125). MacFarlane and Company.
Evans, D. F. T. (1986). *Le Play House and the Regional Survey Movement in British Sociology, 1920-1950.* MPhil Thesis, City of Birmingham Polytechnic.
Evans, M. (2014). Feminism in Sociology, Feminism as Sociology. In J. Holmwood & J. Scott (Eds.), *Palgrave Handbook of Sociology in Britain* (pp. 260–281). Palgrave Macmillan.
Eyal, G., & Buchholz, L. (2010). From the Sociology of Intellectuals to the Sociology of Interventions. *Annual Review of Sociology, 36*, 117–137.
Feagin, J., Vera, H., & Ducey, K. (2015). *Liberation Sociology.* Paradigm.
Ferguson, H. (1999). *The Lure of Dreams: Sigmund Freud and the Construction of Modernity.* Routledge.
Fletcher, R. (1956). Letter to Cole, December 13th. Cole Collection, Nuffield College, University of Oxford. Document C/1/44/1-2.
Fletcher, R. (1957a). 'Letter to Cole, March, 27th. Cole Collection, Nuffield College, University of Oxford. Document C/1/60/1-2.
Fletcher, R. (1957b). Introduction. *British Journal of Sociology, 8*(2), 95–96.
Fletcher, R. (1971). *The Making of Sociology.* Nelson.
Foot, P. (1968). *The Politics of Harold Wilson.* Penguin.
Fordham, F. (2016). Utopia, Palestine, and Partition: Herbert Samuel's An Unknown Land (1942). *Journal of European Popular Culture, 7*(1), 59–71.
Gaitskell, H. (1960). At Oxford in the Twenties. In A. Briggs & J. Saville (Eds.), *Essays in Labour History: In Memory of G.D.H. Cole* (pp. 6–19). Macmillan and Co. Ltd.
Galton, F. (1904). Eugenics: Its Definition, Scope and Aims. In *Sociological Society, Sociological Papers 1904* (pp. 43–50). Macmillan.
Galton, F. (1905). Eugenics. In *Sociological Society, Sociological Papers 1905* (pp. 1–17). Macmillan.
Geddes, P. (1904). Civics as Applied Sociology. In *Sociological Society, Sociological Papers 1904* (pp. 103–118). Macmillan.

Geddes, P. (1905). Civics as Applied Sociology, Part II. In *Sociological Society, Sociological Papers 1905* (pp. 55–110). Macmillan.
Geddes, P. (1906). A Suggested Plan for a Civic Museum (or Civic Exhibition) and Its Associated Studies. In *Sociological Society, Sociological Papers 1906* (pp. 197–240). Macmillan.
Geddes, P., & Slater, G. (1917). *Ideas at War*. Williams and Norgate.
Ghamari-Tabrizi, B. (2005). Can Burawoy Make Everyone Happy? Comments on Public Sociology. *Critical Sociology, 31*(3), 361–369.
Giddens, A. (1973). *The Class Structure of the Advanced Societies*. Hutchinson & Co.
Giddens, A. (1981). *A Contemporary Critique of Historical Materialism: Power, Property and the State*. Macmillan.
Giddens, A. (1982). Class Division, Class Conflict and Citizenship Rights. In A. Giddens (Ed.), *Profiles and Critique in Social Theory* (pp. 164–180). Macmillan.
Giddens, A. (1984). *The Constitution of Society: Outline of the Theory of Structuration*. Polity Press.
Ginsberg, M. (1950). Sociology. In *Chambers Encyclopaedia New Edition* (Volume XII Róskilde-Spahi) (pp. 617–675). George Newnes Limited.
Ginsberg, M. (1953). *The Idea of Progress: A Revaluation*. Metheun & Co.
Ginsberg, M. (1961). *Evolution and Progress*. Heinemann.
Ginsberg, M. (1963). *Reason and Unreason in Society*. Heinemann.
Go, J. (2016). *Postcolonial Thought and Social Theory*. Oxford University Press.
Goldman, L. (1987). A Peculiarity of the English? The Social Science Association and the Absence of Sociology in Nineteenth-Century Britain. *Past & Present, 114*, 133–171.
Goldman, L. (2019). Victorians and Numbers: Statistics and Social Science in Nineteenth-Century Britain. In P. Panayotova (Ed.), *The History of Sociology in Britain: New Research and Revaluation* (pp. 71–100). Palgrave Macmillan.
Goldthorpe, J. (2016). *Sociology as a Population Science*. Cambridge University Press.
Goldthorpe, J. H. (1987). *Social Mobility and Class Structure in Modern Britain* (2nd ed.). Clarence Press.
Goldthorpe, J. H. (2019). Sociology and Statistics in Britain: The Strange History of Social Mobility Research and its Latter-Day Consequences. In P. Panayotova (Ed.), *The History of Sociology in Britain: New Research and Revaluation* (pp. 338–387). Palgrave Macmillan.
Goldthorpe, J. H. (2021). *Pioneers of Sociological Science: Statistical Foundations and the Theory of Action*. Cambridge University Press.
Goldthorpe, J. H., & Marshall, G. (1992). The Promising Future of Class Analysis: A Response to Recent Critiques. *Sociology, 26*(3), 381–400.
Goodway, D. (2021). G.D.H. Cole: A Libertarian Trapped in the Labour Party. In G. D. H. Cole (Ed.), *Towards a Libertarian Socialism*. AK Press.

Gotzler, S. (2019). Years in Cultural Studies: 1956- The British New Left and the "Big Bang" Theory of Cultural Studies. *Lateral, 8*(2). https://csalateral.org/section/years-in-cultural-studies/1956-british-new-left-gotzler/

Gouldner, A. (1962). Anti-Minotaur: The Myth of a Value-Free Sociology. *Social Problems, 9*(3), 199–213.

Gouldner, A. (1968). The Sociologist as Partisan. *The American Sociologist, 3*(2), 103–116.

Gross, N., & Fleming, C. (2011). Academic Conferences and the Making of Philosophical Knowledge. In C. Camic, N. Gross, & M. Lamont (Eds.), *Social Knowledge in the Making* (pp. 151–179). University of Chicago Press.

Gupta, P. S. (1975). *Imperialism and the British Labour Movement, 1914-1964.* Holmes and Meier Publishers.

Hall, S. (1960). Introducing NLR. *New Left Review, 1*(1), 1–3.

Hall, S. (2010). Life and Times of the First New Left. *New Left Review, 61*, 177–196.

Halliday, R. J. (1968). The Sociological Movement, the Sociological Society and the Genesis of Academic Sociology in Britain. *The Sociological Review, 16*(3), 377–398.

Halsey, A. H. (1982). Provincials and Professionals: The British Post-war Sociologists. *European Journal of Sociology, 23*(1), 150–175.

Halsey, A. H. (1996). *No Discouragement: An Autobiography.* Macmillan.

Halsey, A. H. (2004). *A History of Sociology in Britain: Science, Literature and Society.* Oxford University Press.

Hammersley, M. (1999). Sociology, What's it For? A Critique of Gouldner. *Sociological Research Online, 4*(3), 113–121.

Hammersley, M. (2016). An Ideological Dispute: Accusations of Marxist Bias in the Sociology of Education During the 1970s. *Contemporary British History, 30*(2), 242–259.

Hammersley, M. (2024). Should Sociology be Normative? *The American Sociologist, 55*(1), 24–37.

Harley, K. (2012). Sociology's Objects, Objectivity and Objectives Successes and Failures in Establishing the Discipline in America, England and Australia Before 1945. *Journal of Sociology, 48*(4), 410–426.

Harris, J. (1983). Did British Workers want the Welfare State? G.D.H. Cole's Survey of 1942. In J. Winter (Ed.), *The Working Class in Modern British History: Essays in Honour of Henry Pelling* (pp. 200–214). Cambridge University Press.

Hirst, P. (Ed.). (1989). *The Pluralist Theory of the State: Selected Writings of G.D.H. Cole, J.N. Figgis and H.J. Laski.* Routledge.

Hirst, P. (1990). *Representative Democracy and its Limits.* Polity Press.

Hirst, P. (1994). *Associative Democracy: New Forms of Economic and Social Governance.* Polity Press.

Hirst, P. (1997). *From Statism to Pluralism: Democracy, Civil Society and Global Politics*. Routledge.
Hirst, P., & Thompson, G. (1996). *Globalization in Question*. Polity Press.
Hobhouse, L. T. (1904). Eugenics: Its Definition, Scope and Aims (Discussion). In *Sociological Society, Sociological Papers 1904* (pp. 62–63). Macmillan.
Hobhouse, L. T. (1905). On the Relation Between Sociology and Ethics (Discussion). In *Sociological Society, Sociological Papers 1905* (pp. 187–191). Macmillan.
Hobhouse, L. T. (1906). *Morals in Evolution*. Chapman and Hall.
Hobhouse, L. T. (1908). Editorial. *The Sociological Review, 1*(1), 1–11.
Hobhouse, L. T. (1966). *Sociology and Philosophy: A Centenary Collection of Essays and Articles*. G. Bell and Sons.
Hobhouse, L. T. (1994). *Liberalism and Other Writings*. Cambridge University Press.
Hoecker-Drysdale, S. (1992). *Harriett Martineau: First Woman Sociologist*. Berg.
Holmwood, J. (2007). Sociology as Public Discourse and Professional Practice: A Critique of Michael Burawoy. *Sociological Theory, 25*(1), 46–66.
Holmwood, J., & Scott, J. (Eds.). (2014). *Palgrave Handbook of Sociology in Britain*. Palgrave Macmillan.
Holthaus, L. (2014). G.D.H. Cole's International Thought: The Dilemma of Justifying Socialism in the Twentieth Century. *The International History Review, 36*(5), 858–875.
Houseman, G. (1979). *G.D.H. Cole*. Twayne Publishers.
Husbands, C. T. (2019). *Sound and Fury: Sociology at the London School of Economics and Political Science, 1904-2015*. Palgrave Macmillan.
Kaspersen, L. B., & Mulvad, A. M. (2017). Towards a Figurational History of Leicester Sociology, 1954–1982. *Sociology, 51*(6), 1186–1204.
Katz-Fishman, W., & Scott, J. (2005). Comments on Burawoy: A View from the Bottom-Up. *Critical Sociology, 31*(3), 371–374.
King, A. (2010). The Odd Couple: Margaret Archer, Anthony Giddens and British Social Theory. *British Journal of Sociology, 61*(s1), 253–260.
Kumar, K. (2015). *The Idea of Englishness: English Culture, National Identity and Social Thought*. Ashgate.
Kuper, A. (2015). *Anthropology and Anthropologists: The British School in the Twentieth Century* (4th ed.). Routledge.
Lamb, P. (2005). G.D.H. Cole on the General Will: A Socialist Reflects on Rousseau. *European Journal of Political Theory, 4*(3), 283–300.
Lamont, M. (1987). How to Become a Dominant French Philosopher: The Case of Jacques Derrida. *American Journal of Sociology, 93*(3), 584–622.
Latouche, S. (2009). *Farewell to Growth*. Polity Press.
Law, A. (2005). The Ghost of Patrick Geddes: Civics as Applied Sociology. *Sociological Research Online, 10*(2), 21–34.

Leiss, W. (1972). *The Domination of Nature*. George Braziller.

Lengermann, P. M., & Niebrugge, J. (2002). The Meaning of "Things": Theory and Method in Harriet Martineau's How to Observe Morals and Manners (1838) and Émile Durkheim's The Rules of Sociological Method (1895). In M. Hill & S. Hoecker-Drysdale (Eds.), *Harriett Martineau: Theoretical and Methodological Perspectives* (pp. 75–98). Routledge.

Lepenies, W. (1992). *Between Literature and Science: The Rise of Sociology*. Cambridge University Press.

LeRoux, R., Martin, T., & Turner, S. (Eds.). (2023). *The Future of Sociology: Ideology or Objective Social Science?* Routledge.

Levitas, R. (2005a). *Morris, Hammersmith and Utopia*. William Morris Society.

Levitas, R. (2005b). *The Imaginary Reconstruction of Society: Or, Why Sociologists and Others Should Take Utopia More Seriously*. Inaugural Lecture Delivered at the University of Bristol, 24 October 2005. http://www.bris.ac.uk/spais/files/inaugural.pdf

Levitas, R. (2010). Back to the Future: Wells, Sociology, Utopia and Method. *Sociological Review, 58*(4), 530–547.

Levitas, R. (2013). *Utopia as Method: The Imaginary Reconstruction of Society*. Palgrave Macmillan.

Lockwood, D. (1958). *The Blackcoated Worker: A Study in Class Consciousness*. Unwin University Books.

MacDonald, K. (2019). Did British Sociology Begin with the Scottish Enlightenment? In P. Panayotova (Ed.), *The History of Sociology in Britain: New Research and Revaluation* (pp. 37–69). Palgrave Macmillan.

MacKenzie, N., & MacKenzie, J. (1977). *The First Fabians*. Weidenfeld and Nicholson.

Marshall, T. H. (1992). *Citizenship and Social Class*. Pluto Press.

Martell, L. (2023). *Alternative Societies: For a Pluralist Socialism*. Bristol University Press.

Martin, K. (1959). G.D.H. Cole. *New Statesman*, 17 January, 63.

Martineau, H. (1837/2009). *Society in America*. Cambridge University Press.

Martineau, H. (1838/2009). *How to Observe: Morals and Manners*. Bibliolife.

Marx, K. (1988). *Economic and Philosophical Manuscripts of 1844*. Prometheus Books.

Marx, K., & Landor, R. (1962). The Curtain Raised: Interview with Karl Marx, the Head of L'Internationale. *New Politics, 2*(3), 128–133.

Masquelier, C. (2023). *Intersectional Socialism: A Utopia for Radical Interdependence*. Bristol University Press.

Masquelier, C., & Dawson, M. (2016). Beyond Capitalism & Liberal Democracy: On the Relevance of GDH Cole's Sociological Critique & Alternative. *Current Sociology, 64*(1), 3–21.

Mass-Observation. (1939). *Britain*. Penguin.

McDonald, L. (1994). Classical Social Theory with the Women Founders Included. In C. Camic (Ed.), *Reclaiming the Sociological Classics: The State of Scholarship* (pp. 112–141). Blackwell.
McLaughlin, N. (1999). Origin Myths in the Social Sciences: Fromm, the Frankfurt School and the Emergence of Critical Theory. *The Canadian Journal of Sociology, 24*(1), 109–139.
McLaughlin, N. (2000). Optimal Marginality: Innovation and Orthodoxy in Fromm's Revision of Psychoanalysis. *The Sociological Quarterly, 42*(2), 271–288.
McLennan, G. (1989). *Marxism, Pluralism and Beyond: Classic Debates and New Departures*. Polity Press.
Meghji, A. (2021). *Decolonizing Sociology: An Introduction*. Polity Press.
Milani, T. (2020). Retreat from the Global? European Unity and British Progressive Intellectuals, 1930-1945. *The International History Review, 42*(1), 99–116.
Mills, C. (2019). Social Status, Social Position and Social Class in Post-War British Society. In P. Panayotova (Ed.), *The History of Sociology in Britain: New Research and Revaluation* (pp. 161–190). Palgrave Macmillan.
Mills, C. W. (1959). *The Sociological Imagination*. Oxford University Press.
Misztal, B. (2007). *Intellectuals and the Public Good: Creativity and Civil Courage*. Cambridge University Press.
Mogey, J. (1947). *Rural Life in Northern Ireland*. Oxford University Press.
Mogey, J. (1956). *Family and Neighbourhood: Two Studies in Oxford*. Greenwood Press.
Morgan, M., & Baert, P. (2015). *Conflict in the Academy: A Study in the Sociology of Intellectuals*. Palgrave Macmillan.
Morris, A. (2015). *The Scholar Denied: W.E.B. Du Bois and the Birth of Modern Sociology*. University of California Press.
Morris, W. (1993). *News from Nowhere and Other Writings*. Penguin.
Mumford, L. (1948). Patrick Geddes, Victor Branford and Applied Sociology in England: The Social Survey, Regionalism and Urban Planning. In H. E. Barnes (Ed.), *An Introduction to the History of Sociology* (pp. 677–695). University of Chicago Press.
Nielsen, F. (2004). The Vacant "We": Remarks on Public Sociology. *Social Forces, 82*(4), 1619–1627.
Oakley, A. (2011). *A Critical Woman: Barbara Wootton, Social Science and Public Policy in the Twentieth Century*. Bloomsbury.
Offer, J. (2010). *Herbert Spencer and Social Theory*. Palgrave Macmillan.
Orwell, G. (1937). *Road to Wigan Pier*. Victor Gollancz.
Owen, G. (1966). G.D.H. Cole's Historical Writings. *International Review of Social History, 11*(2), 169–196.
Owen, J. (1974). *L.T. Hobhouse, Sociologist*. Thomas Nelson and Sons.

Panayotova, P. (2019a). Introduction. In P. Panayotova (Ed.), *The History of Sociology in Britain: New Research and Revaluation* (pp. 1–33). Palgrave Macmillan.

Panayotova, P. (Ed.). (2019b). *The History of Sociology in Britain: New Research and Revaluation*. Palgrave Macmillan.

Panayotova, P. (2019c). Beyond Drink, Drainage and Divorce: What the Sociological Society Did for British Sociology. *The Sociological Review, 67*, 1212–1227.

Panayotova, P. (2019d). The Teaching of Research Methods in British Sociology in the Twentieth Century. In P. Panayotova (Ed.), *The History of Sociology in Britain: New Research and Revaluation* (pp. 301–335). Palgrave Macmillan.

Panayotova, P. (2020). *Sociology and Statistics in Britain, 1833-1979*. Palgrave Macmillan.

Pardo-Guerra, J. B. (2022). *The Quantified Scholar: How Research Evaluations Transformed the British Social Sciences*. Columbia University Press.

Payne, G. (2019). "Poor Cousins": The Lost History of Sociology in the Polytechnics. In P. Panayotova (Ed.), *The History of Sociology in Britain: New Research and Revaluation* (pp. 191–220). Palgrave Macmillan.

Perrin, E. (1904). On the Contingency Between Occupations in the Case of Fathers and Sons. *Biometrika, 3*, 467–469.

Piven, F. F. (2007). From Public Sociology to Politicized Sociologist. In D. Clawson et al. (Eds.), *Public Sociology* (pp. 158–166). University of California Press.

Platt, J. (1996). *A History of Sociological Methods in America, 1920-1960*. Cambridge University Press.

Platt, J. (2003). *The British Sociological Association: A Sociological History*. Sociology Press.

Platt, J. (2014). The International Library of Sociology and Social Reconstruction and British Sociology. In J. Holmwood & J. Scott (Eds.), *Palgrave Handbook of Sociology in Britain* (pp. 236–259). Palgrave Macmillan.

Platt, L. (2014). Poverty Studies and Social Research. In J. Holmwood & J. Scott (Eds.), *Palgrave Handbook of Sociology in Britain* (pp. 30–54). Palgrave Macmillan.

Postage, O. (2010). *Seeing Things: A Memoir*. Canongate Books.

Pūras, A. (2014). Robert Owen in the History of the Social Sciences: Three Presentist Views. *Journal of the History of Behavioral Sciences, 50*(1), 58–78.

Ranulf, S. (1939). Scholarly Forerunners of Fascism. *Ethics, 50*(1), 16–36.

Reay, D. (2004). "It's all Becoming a Habitus" Beyond the Habitual Use of Habitus in Educational Research. *British Journal of the Sociology of Education, 25*(4), 431–444.

Renwick, C. (2012). *British Sociology's Lost Biological Roots: A History of Futures Past*. Palgrave Macmillan.

Renwick, C. (2017). *Bread for All: The Origins of the Welfare State*. Penguin.
Renwick, C. (2019). Richard Titmuss, Eugenics, and Social Science in Mid-twentieth-Century Britain. In P. Panayotova (Ed.), *The History of Sociology in Britain: New Research and Revaluation* (pp. 137–160). Palgrave Macmillan.
Riddell, N. (1995). "The Age of Cole"? G.D.H. Cole and the British Labour Movement 1929-1933. *Historical Journal, 38*(4), 933–957.
Rocquin, B. (2006). *'The Floating Discipline': British Sociology and the Failure of Instutitional Attachment (1911-1938)*. MA Thesis. Oxford University.
Rocquin, B. (2014). British Sociology in the Inter-War Years. In J. Holmwood & J. Scott (Eds.), *Palgrave Handbook of Sociology in Britain* (pp. 189–210). Palgrave Macmillan.
Rocquin, B. (2019). *British Sociologists and French Sociologues in the Interwar Years: The Battle for Society*. Palgrave Macmillan.
Rose, J. (2021). *The Intellectual Life of the British Working Classes*. Yale University Press.
Runciman, D. (1997). *Pluralism and the Personality of the State*. Cambridge University Press.
Runciman, W. G. (2004). W.G. Runciman. In A. H. Halsey (Ed.), *A History of Sociology in Britain: Science, Literature and Society* (pp. 219–222). Oxford University Press.
Said, E. (1994). *Representations of the Intellectual*. Vintage Books.
Samelson, F. (1974). History, Origin Myth and Ideology: "Discovery" of Social Psychology. *Journal for the Theory of Social Behaviour, 4*(2), 217–231.
Samuels, S. (1969). English Intellectuals and Politics in the 1930s. In P. Rieff (Ed.), *On Intellectuals: Theorical Studies, Case Studies* (pp. 196–247). Doubleday.
Sassoon, D. (2010). *One Hundred Years of Socialism: The West European Left in the Twentieth Century*. I.B. Tauris and Co.
Savage, M. (2010). *Identities and Social Change in Britain Since 1940: The Politics of Method*. Oxford University Press.
Savage, M. (2016). End Class Wars. *Nature, 537*, 475–479.
Savransky, M. (2017). A Decolonial Imagination: Sociology, Anthropology and the Politics of Reality. *Sociology, 51*(1), 11–26.
Sayer, A. (2009). Who's Afraid of Critical Social Science? *Current Sociology, 57*(6), 767–786.
Schellenberg, W. (2006). *The Memoirs of Hitler's Spymaster*. Andre Deutsch.
Scott, J. (2005). Who Will Speak and Who Will Listen? Comments on Burawoy and Public Sociology. *British Journal of Sociology, 56*(3), 405–409.
Scott, J. (2007). The Edinburgh School of Sociology. *Journal of Scottish Thought, 1*(1), 89–102.
Scott, J. (2014). Building a Textbook Tradition: Sociology in Britain, 1900-68. In J. Holmwood & J. Scott (Eds.), *Palgrave Handbook of Sociology in Britain* (pp. 211–235). Palgrave Macmillan.

Scott, J. (2016a). The Social Theory of Patrick Geddes. *Journal of Classical Sociology, 16*(3), 237–260.
Scott, J. (2016b). Leonard Hobhouse as a Social Theorist. *Journal of Classical Sociology, 16*(4), 349–368.
Scott, J. (2018). *British Social Theory: Recovering Lost Traditions Before 1950.* Sage.
Scott, J. (2020). *British Sociology: A History.* Palgrave Macmillan.
Scott, J., & Bromley, R. (2013). *Envisioning Sociology: Victor Branford, Patrick Geddes, and the Quest for Social Reconstruction.* State University of New York Press.
Shils, E. (1985). On the Eve: A Prospect in Retrospect. In M. Bulmer (Ed.), *Essays on the History of British Sociological Research* (pp. 165–178). Cambridge University Press.
Shils, E. (1997). Karl Mannheim. In E. Shils (Ed.), *Portraits: A Gallery of Intellectuals* (pp. 202–218). University of Chicago Press.
Small, A. (1920). *Social Theory* by G.D.H. Cole. *American Journal of Sociology, 26*(2), 147–148.
Small, H. (2002). Introduction. In H. Small (Ed.), *The Public Intellectual* (pp. 1–18). Blackwell.
Smith, D. (1991). *The Rise of Historical Sociology.* Polity Press.
Smith, P. (2020). *Durkheim and After: The Durkheimian Tradition, 1893-2020.* Polity Press.
Sprott, W. J. H. (1949). *Sociology.* Hutchinson's University Library.
Stacey, J. (2007). If I Were the Goddess of Sociological Things. In D. Clawson et al. (Eds.), *Public Sociology* (pp. 91–100). University of California Press.
Steinmetz, G. (2014). British Sociology in the Metropole and the Colonies, 1940s-60s. In J. Holmwood & J. Scott (Eds.), *Palgrave Handbook of Sociology in Britain* (pp. 302–337). Palgrave Macmillan.
Steinmetz, G. (2023). *The Colonial Origins of Modern Social Thought: French Sociology and the Overseas Empire.* Princeton University Press.
Stones, R. (2005). *Structuration Theory.* Palgrave Macmillan.
Studholme, M. (1995). Durkheim and the Institutionalization of British Sociology. *Durkheimian Studies, 1*, 24–34.
Studholme, M. (2007). Patrick Geddes: Founder of Environmental Sociology. *The Sociological Review, 55*(3), 441–459.
Swingewood, A. (1970). Origins of Sociology: The Case of the Scottish Enlightenment. *British Journal of Sociology, 21*(2), 164–180.
Sydie, R. A. (1987). *Natural Women, Cultured Men: A Feminist Perspective on Sociological Theory.* Open University Press.
Tan, B. R. Y. (2024). Dissolving the Colour Line: L.T. Hobhouse on Race and Liberal Empire. *European Journal of Political Theory, 23*(1), 85–106.
Taylor, A. J. P. (1979). A Bolshevik Soul in a Fabian Muzzle. *New Statesman*, 1 October, 441–442.

Taylor, G. (2002). *G.D.H. Cole and the National Guilds League*. Sheffield Hallam University Press.
Tittle, C. (2004). The Arrogance of Public Sociology. *Social Forces, 82*(4), 1639–1643.
Tonn, J. (2008). *Mary P. Follett: Creating Democracy, Transforming Management*. Yale University Press.
Turner, B. S. (2006). British Sociology and Public Intellectuals: Consumer Society and Imperial Decline. *British Journal of Sociology, 57*(2), 169–188.
Turner, C. (2014). Exiles in British Sociology. In J. Holmwood & J. Scott (Eds.), *Palgrave Handbook of Sociology in Britain* (pp. 282–301). Palgrave Macmillan.
Turner, S., & Turner, J. (1990). *The Impossible Science: An Institutional Analysis of American Sociology*. Sage.
Urry, J. (2005). The Good News and the Bad News. *Critical Sociology, 31*(3), 375–378.
Valluvan, S., & Kapoor, N. (2023). Sociology After the Postcolonial: Response to Julian Go's "Thinking against Empire". *The British Journal of Sociology, 74*(3), 310–323.
Virdee, S. (2014). *Racism, Class and the Racialized Outsider*. Palgrave Macmillan.
Weber, M. (1922/1991). Science as a Vocation. In H. H. Gerth & C. W. Mills (Eds.), *From Max Weber: Essays in Sociology* (pp. 129–156). Routledge.
Weber, M. (1930). *The Protestant Ethic and the Spirit of Capitalism*. Routledge.
Weber, M. (1949a). The Meaning of 'Ethical Neutrality' in Economics and Sociology. In E. Shils & H. Finch (Eds.), *The Methodology of the Social Sciences* (pp. 1–47). Transactions Publishers.
Weber, M. (1949b). "Objectivity" in Social Science and Social Policy. In E. Shils & H. Finch (Eds.), *The Methodology of the Social Sciences* (pp. 49–112). Transactions Publishers.
Wells, H. G. (1906). The So-Called Science of Sociology. In *Sociological Society, Sociological Papers 1906* (pp. 357–369). Macmillan.
Williams, M., Sloan, L., & Brookfield, C. (2013). A Tale of Two Sociologies: Analysing versus Critique in UK Sociology. *Sociological Research Online, 22*(4), 132–151.
Wilson, M. (2018). A New Civic Spirit for Garden City-States: On the Lifework of Sybella Gurney. *Journal of Planning History, 17*(4), 320–344.
Witz, A., & Marshall, B. L. (2004). The Masculinity of the Social: Towards a Politics of Interrogation. In B. L. Marshall & A. Witz (Eds.), *Engendering the Social: Feminist Encounters with Sociological Theory* (pp. 19–35). Open University Press.
Worswick, G. D. N. (1960). Cole and Oxford, 1938-1958. In A. Briggs & J. Saville (Eds.), *Essays in Labour History: In Memory of G.D.H. Cole* (pp. 25–40). Macmillan and Co. Ltd.

Wright, A. W. (1979). *G.D.H. Cole and Socialist Democracy*. Clarendon Press.
Wright, E. O. (1985). *Classes*. Verso.
Wrong, D. (1961). The Oversocialised Conception of Man in Modern Sociology. *American Sociological Review, 26*(2), 183–193.
Ziff, M. L. (1978). *From Mill to Hobhouse: The Radical, Progressive Origins of British Sociology*. University of Leeds Occasional Papers in Sociology No. 7.
Zueblin, C. (1899). The World's First Sociological Laboratory. *American Journal of Sociology, 4*(5), 577–592.

Index[1]

[1] Note: Page numbers followed by 'n' refer to notes.

M. Dawson, *G.D.H. Cole and British Sociology*, https://doi.org/10.1007/978-3-031-75484-5

The manufacturer's authorised representative in the EU is Springer Nature Customer Service Centre GmbH, Europaplatz 3, 69115 Heidelberg, Germany. If you have any concerns regarding our products, please contact ProductSafety@springernature.com

Printed and bound by CPI Group (UK) Ltd, Croydon, CR0 4YY
01/10/2026
02225854-0001